Communism, Conformity, and Civil Liberties

Communism, Conformity, and Civil Liberties

A Cross-Section of the Nation Speaks Its Mind

Samuel A. Stouffer

With a New Introduction by James A. Davis

Transaction Publishers
New Brunswick (U.S.A.) and London (U.K.)

Library of Congress Catalog Number: 91-42668
ISBN: 1-56000-613-7
Printed in the United States of America

Library of Congress Cataloging-in-Publication Data

Stouffer, Samuel Andrews, 1900—
    Communism, conformity, and civil liberties: a cross-section of the nation speaks its mind/Samuel A. Stouffer with a new introduction by James A. Davis.
    p.   cm.
    ISBN 1-56000-613-7
    1. Civil   rights—United   States.   2.   Communism—United
States—1917- 3. Public Opinion—United States. I. Title.
JC599.U5S82   1992
320.5′32′097309045—dc20   91-42668
                                                              CIP

CONTENTS

INTRODUCTION TO THE TRANSACTION EDITION

Samuel A. ("Sam") Stouffer was born in Sac City Iowa in 1900, earned his Ph.D. in sociology at the University of Chicago in 1930, was a professor of sociology at Harvard 1946 to 1960, was elected president of both The American Sociological Association and The American Association for Public Opinion Research, and succumbed to an appallingly swift cancer at age sixty.

Sam didn't look charismatic. He looked a bit like the men who played fussy bookkeepers in 1930s screwball comedies. This effect was mitigated by his cigarette habit. He lit them off the butts and didn't believe in ashtrays. We students watched, hypnotized, as the cigarette ash slowly grew and grew and then, after a nod of his head, was deposited all over his suit jacket. His usual appearance, then, was of a fussy bookkeeper who had narrowly escaped a volcano eruption.

Stouffer was not charismatic, personally. He had no groupies among the Harvard graduate students. He was not disliked. Indeed, he was a kindly person. Rather, he simply lacked the combination of paternalism and narcissism that motivates the Great Man. Sam simply wanted to get on with the job, and if students wanted to listen in, fine. He left little behind him at Harvard, save for a belated plaque in a lounge. Gaining a foothold for empirical sociology in Ivy League sociology cannot be done by one person in one lifetime.

But Sam was a great sociologist, with at least two landmarks to his credit.

The first was *The American Soldier* research, possibly the most successful venture in applied sociology. From 1941 to 1946 Stouffer was "Director of the Professional Staff of the Research Branch, Information and Education Division of the War Department," heading a stellar team of researchers whose surveys of army personnel reshaped thinking about morale, mental health, and team performance. Their work contributed importantly to

3

making the World War II military responsive to the needs of ten million citizen soldiers. *Communism, Conformity and Civil Liberties* is his second landmark.

As I write this, there are hardly any "communists in high places" in the USSR, much less in the United States. In 1954, things seemed different. Sane people, spurred on by shameless demagogues, were seriously worried that "subversion" was rife. Sam's own data showed 43 percent of United States adults saying *American* communists were a "great" or "very great" danger to the country. But other sane people were worried that a national climate of hysteria was developing and basic civil liberties were in danger. The latter concern motivated the then courageous Ford Foundation to fund a national inquiry, whose final report is *Communism, Conformity, and Civil Liberties*. Stouffer, an Iowa-reared, War Department vetted Republican, as well as an outstanding scientist, was the inevitable and perfect choice to lead the project.

Two leading survey agencies, AIPO (the Gallup poll) and NORC (National Opinion Research Center), collected the 6,000 personal interviews but the analysis and writing were Sam's. He did all the work himself, with an undergraduate assistant. He hovered over the old fashioned IBM card sorter like an anxious chef with a tricky souffle to be seasoned with cigarette ash.

His report was published in 1955, less than a year after the field work. It remains a great classic of empirical sociology.

For the professional, *Communism* is a model of craftsmanship from sampling to write up. I believe this was the first national probability sample devoted to nonpolitical academic research and it had an excellent completion rate, 84 percent, plus a neat Stoufferian twist. The assignments were split between Gallup and NORC so their results could be compared. The agreement was near perfect, documenting what might be called the fundamental theorem of survey research: independent investigators with identical questionnaires and identical probability samples get identical results. Obvious? Perhaps, but it is seldom documented and were it untrue, survey research would be pointless.

The statistical work may seem elementary. There are no fancy statistics, just percentage tables. But the argumentation is exemplary. The key findings are buttressed with appropriate and ingenious controls. The sex difference in tolerance, for example, is tested with no less than eleven control variables: interest in the topic, education, age, region, size of place, worries, labor force participation, occupation, religion, church attendance, and authoritarianism.

The presentation has never been surpassed, perhaps never equaled. Despite a master's degree in English literature from Harvard, Sam had the gift of simple writing. The item wordings in the *American Soldier* question-naires are famous for their clarity and simplicity. My guess is the book would come in at about the eighth or ninth grade level on a readability index, while this prose is at about the eleventh grade level. The tables are as elegant as the words. The layouts are crisp, the graphics are appropriate, and, bless his memory, he reports his "Ns" even for subgroups! He even includes footnotes on how to read the more complex tables (See table 2, chapter 5 or table 1, chapter 8.) If you wish to present statistics to the "educated layman" without compromising the science, copy Stouffer.

Despite what you see in the leading professional journals, technique isn't everything in sociology. What about the content?

The main conclusion is in chapter Three, "Is there a national anxiety neurosis?" His answer is no. Despite wide concern about domestic com-munism, few respondents had it at the top or even near the top of their worry lists. His key evidence is that hardly anybody mentioned communism in response to the open-ended question, "What kinds of things do you worry about most?" To be honest, I don't think this is the best part of the study. Stouffer did unearth a fundamental point here — how distant the world of political issues is from the lives of most Americans. (See Richard F. Hamilton and James D. Wright, *The State of The Masses*, Aldine, 1986). But it could be that political concerns were *relatively* salient in the early 1950s. (See John Mueller, "Trends in Political Tolerance," *Public Opinion Quarterly*, Spring 1988, 1-25.) In methodological terms, his design was flawed by the absence of comparative data from other periods.

More impressive is his finding that a special sample of community leaders (mayors, Chamber of Commerce presidents, newspaper publishers, D.A.R. and American Legion officers, and so on) was more supportive of civil liberties than the national cross section. We are now familiar with the proposition that elite groups tend to be relatively "liberal" on social issues, and relatively "conservative" on economic ones. At the time, the finding reassured us a reactionary power elite was not oppressing a freedom loving grass roots.

Where he really shines is in uncovering social differences in tolerance. His measure was a scale based on questions of the general form "Would you allow an X to do Y?" (allow a communist to give a speech, allow an atheist to teach in a college, allow a socialist's book to remain in the library, and so on). They are now known as "the standard Stouffer questions." He uses the index to illuminate a wide array of tolerance differences — by age, education, sex, region, city size, leadership position, authoritarianism, and so on.

But *Communism* doesn't belong on the ancient history shelf.

"Paradigm" is now a buzz word for academic subspecialty. Actually, it denotes a scientific approach that creates research opportunities for the young and tenure seeking. (See Thomas S. Kuhn, *The Structure of Scientific Revolutions*, University of Chicago Press, 1970, 10.) *Communism* launched many a career and still generates research.

First, there is the problem of tolerance, itself. Common sense and Sam's critics say you can not tolerate something you like ("Should Mother Theresa be allowed to give a speech in your community?"). If so, it could be the classic tolerance scale is really an indirect measure of, pardon the expression, softness on communism. Perhaps young people, the better educated, urbanites, nonreligionists and the like are not really more tolerant, just more to the left in their politics. Since Sam's targets (communists, atheists, socialists) were all on the "left," the original study could not settle the problem. Professors John L. Sullivan, James Piereson, and George E. Marcus have worked at length on the matter. (See their *Political Tolerance and American Democracy*, University of Chicago Press, 1982.) Sam himself wrestles with it in chapter Eight. In 1972 we included some original Stouffer questions in the NORC General Social Survey, an annual sampling of the United States adult population, with dozens of questions repeated from year to year to monitor trends. Beginning in 1976 we added "Stouffer items" with right-wing targets such as racists and militarists. The ensuing analysis suggests that Sam's key tolerance predictors work the same way for both left- and right-wing targets. (See Lawrence Bobo and Frederick C. Licari, "Education and Political Tolerance," *Public Opinion Quarterly*, 1989, 285-308 and Robert L. Hall, Mark Rodeghier, and Bert Useem, "Effects of Education on Attitude to Protest," *American Sociological Review*, 1986, 564-573.)

The famous chapter "How Tolerant is the New Generation?" is a similar career builder. His finding is clear cut: younger Americans were more tolerant regardless of their schooling, the better educated were more tolerant regardless of their ages. No previous national study had shown both findings simultaneously. Stouffer elaborated this into a theory of long-term social change. He argued that two contradictory processes are at work. First, he believed we all become less tolerant as we age because of the frustrations and deprivations of what is now called "later maturity." Second, however, he believed the increasing educational levels of oncoming generations (birth cohorts) would raise tolerance. He doesn't flatly predict which effect will be stronger, but the last sentence of the chapter implies the race would go to the tolerance enhancing effects of cohort succession. It did.

Clyde Z. Nunn, Harry J. Crockett, Jr. and J. Allen William, Jr. confirmed the optimistic prediction in a 1973 national sample (*Tolerance For Noncon-*

formity, Jossey-Bass, 1978*)* and analyses of GSS data have tracked similar, though smaller increases in tolerance through the 1970s and 1980s.

These relationships are not immutable laws by any means. Current data cast doubt on the proposition that aging lowers tolerance. The GSS samples suggest the very youngest birth cohorts—the baby boomers and their successors who entered adulthood in the late 1970s and after—are not more tolerant than their immediate predecessors. Nevertheless, the Stouffer framework remains central for studying tolerance and its trends.

In both traditions — "what is tolerance" and "does tolerance evolve?" — the Stouffer approach is still generating research questions. The 1990 edition of *The Annotated Bibliography of Papers Using the General Social Surveys* (Tom W. Smith and Bradley J. Arnold, NORC, 1990) lists 2036 articles, books, and theses using data from the General Social Survey. Its index tells us 197 references, almost ten percent of the total, make use of the Stouffer item on Free Speech for Communists!

The book is not flawless. I think the overall organization is poor and many chapters trail off at the end, suggesting hasty writing. I also wish he has not limited so many of his analyses to "interested" people. But perfection is not required in a classic. If a classic is a model of craftsmanship, this book is a classic. If a classic is a study that continues to illuminate an important problem, this book is a classic.

Samuel A. Stouffer may not have been charismatic, but he certainly was and remains paradigmatic. No scientific craftsman could hope for a better-posterity.

We hope this reprinting of *Communism, Conformity, and Civil Liberties* will stimulate a new generation to continue the task of delineating the social roots of tolerance and intolerance and to track their evolution as its generations flow into the twenty-first century.

James A. Davis

INTRODUCTION TO THE ORIGINAL EDITION

This study was authorized by the Board of Directors of the Fund for the Republic during the period I served as President of the Fund. It is an honor to be asked to write these few introductory words, for I regard this study as a significant and valuable undertaking.

Some Americans will be surprised by what they find in these pages. Most readers, I think, will be helped to a better understanding of the disturbing situations that have marked the last few years in this country. Educators and others especially responsible for keeping our fellow citizens informed and alert will discern in *Communism, Conformity, and Civil Liberties* how much they have left to do.

To Professor Stouffer, his eminent committee, and my former colleagues on the Board of the Fund for the Republic belongs by far the major share of credit for conceiving and carrying through this important piece of work. The Fund is concerned with preserving and strengthening the fundamental liberties of all Americans. This book reminds us that this is a continuing and much-needed job.

CLIFFORD P. CASE

COMMUNISM, CONFORMITY, AND CIVIL LIBERTIES

Chapter One

WHAT THIS BOOK IS ABOUT

This is a report to the American people on the findings of a survey which was unique in its scope and in some of its methods.

More than 6000 men and women, in all parts of the country and in all walks of life, confided their thoughts in an interview which was as impartial as fallible ingenuity was able to devise. Over 500 skilled interviewers from two national research agencies did the field work.

The survey examines in some depth the reactions of Americans to two dangers.

One, from the Communist conspiracy outside and inside the country. Two, from those who in thwarting the conspiracy would sacrifice some of the very liberties which the enemy would destroy.

This inquiry, made in the summer of 1954, was concerned not with transient opinions but with deeper latent attitudes or dispositions. Some types of reactions to the Communist threat are not new and will be encountered in years to come. To think otherwise is to ignore what has happened throughout the long perspective of American history. Our Constitution was scarcely ten years old when national tempers were expressed in the Alien and Sedition Acts, under which editors went to jail for criticizing the government, and even bystanders at political meetings who made contemptuous remarks were hurried off to court. Eventually the "sober second thought of the people" prevailed. The Know-Nothing Party before the Civil War and the Ku Klux Klan in the Reconstruction period and again after World War I are other manifestations of intolerance. In the light of this record, will future historians find that the intolerance which thus far has marked the 1950s has been so extraordinary, considering the imagined provocation? There are people who see the danger from Communists as justifying drastic measures of repression, including the forfeiture of rights which were centuries in the making. Just as in the Civil War the North felt obliged to suspend the right of habeas corpus to cope

13

with the Copperhead conspiracy, so today do some alarmed citizens feel that the country cannot risk the luxury of full civil liberties for nonconformists. But there are others who disagree. They are convinced that our protection from Communist espionage and sabotage can be safely entrusted to the F.B.I. and other branches of an alert government, and that the diminishing risks of conversion of other Americans to Communism can be met by an enlightened public opinion.

The stark fact remains that for unknown years the free Western world must live under a menacing shadow. Vigilance cannot be relaxed against either the peril from without or varieties of perils from within. The question is: *How can the sober second thought of the people be maintained in a state of readiness to resist external and internal threats to our heritage of liberties?*

To contribute toward answers to this question, this book offers a body of data. Some of the specific findings may seem obvious. Some may not. A few may be so unexpected as to put a strain on acceptance. We hope that these findings, along with knowledge from other sources, can aid responsible citizens—in our government; in our newspaper offices and broadcasting studios; in our schools, churches, and other organizations within the local community—as they plan better for the task ahead. Following are some of the questions considered:

Who are the people most likely to have given the sober second thought to the problems with which we are concerned?

What about the attitudes of responsible civic leaders as compared with the rank and file within a community?

Is the American public in a state of pathological fear?

Are we raising a new generation which will be more sensitive or less sensitive than its elders to threats to freedom? What is the impact of our educational system, which provides more schooling to more youth than in any other nation in history?

Do attitudes differ in different regions of the country? In cities as compared with rural areas? Among men as compared with women? What role does religion play?

How are the images about Communists which people carry in their heads related to willingness to deprive other nonconformists, who are not necessarily Communists, of civil rights?

How important are agencies of mass communication likely to be in evoking more thoughtful reflection on the issues of Communism and civil liberties? How well do the people know the views of leaders they respect? What can be accomplished by responsible citizens in their local communities?

These are some of the topics which this study has investigated. Not with an eye on the opinions about any particular public figure or on issues which may be ephemeral. Rather on basic underlying sentiments which do not change abruptly or fluctuate with the day's headlines. No one study can provide all the answers we need. Further inquiries must follow. Here and there new studies should record new trends as time goes on, but the main patterns of basic attitudes reported in this book will not undergo a metamorphosis overnight.

Who Were Interviewed in This Survey

The survey, made in May, June, and July 1954, sought to combine the best features of several techniques of inquiry.

It is basically a public opinion poll and was conducted in the field not by just one but by two of the foremost public opinion research organizations. One was the American Institute of Public Opinion—the Gallup Poll. The other was the National Opinion Research Center, a non-profit organization with headquarters at the University of Chicago. Each agency used its own staff of sampling experts to draw independently what was intended to constitute a representative cross-section of the American population. The result is that, for the first time in the history of public opinion polling, the work of two different agencies can be compared on an entire questionnaire. Each of the two national cross-sections contains more than 2400 cases. The greatest advantage of utilizing two agencies was that each was able to carry out a very large assignment within a reasonable time without adding inexperienced interviewers to its staff. Quality was the first consideration. The total number of interviewers was 537.

The type of sampling method used was costly and time-consuming. Technically it is known as the "probability method," in contrast to the quota method more commonly used. In simplest outline, the probability method, as employed in the present survey, consists of the following steps:

1. From a list of all the counties and metropolitan areas in the United States, a sample is drawn at random. These selected counties and metropolitan areas are called "primary sampling units."

2. Within each primary sampling unit, urban blocks and rural segments are selected, also strictly at random.

15

3. Within each selected block or segment, interviewers list systematically every dwelling unit. Among these dwelling units a sample of X is selected, also strictly at random.

4. Within each of the selected dwelling units all adults are enumerated, and *one* in each dwelling is selected for the interview. This one is selected according to a fixed rule which leaves the interviewer no flexibility in making substitutions.

5. Once the individual adult within the household is designated as the sample person, the interviewer is required to make repeated calls until he finds him or her at home and available for interview. This is the most time-consuming and costly part of the procedure.

6. No substitutions are permitted, and every effort is made to track down absentees, even assigning them to interviewers in other parts of the country if away on vacation. Some refusals are inevitable but are kept to a minimum by the resourcefulness of the trained interviewers. If that resourcefulness is unavailing, letters and even telegrams from the home office of the agency often overcome the remaining resistance. A careful analysis of the "fish that got away" appears in Appendix A, with the conclusion that bias thus occasioned could not be appreciably large.

The probability method of sampling has important advantages over the method more often used; namely, the quota method. In using the quota method, communities, or even street segments, are selected at random as described above, but the interviewer is left free to choose respondents, provided he or she ends up with a prescribed proportion of people with various attributes, such as a given sex, age, etc. The probability method eliminates any possible bias of the interviewer in the selection of respondents. For example, those who respond readily without urging, or who live in more accessible places, or who are at home at the time of call may be so different in some respects relevant to the study that a bias is introduced. The probability method also has important advantages from the mathematical standpoint of calculating margins of error attributable to chance alone.

The probability method has disadvantages also. One is its cost, which can be two to five times as high as the quota method. An interviewer may have to spend the aggregate of a day's time on a succession of efforts to make contact with a single respondent. The other is its slowness. If a study must be completed in a few days, the quota method, or some modification of it, seems to be the only answer. But to stretch out the field work on a survey over a period of several weeks, as is necessary with a large probability sample, is to run the risk that some important happening in the news may change opinions in the middle of the survey. As will be noted in Chapter Two, there is no evidence of changes in basic attitudes during the course of the survey.

For further details on sampling, the reader is referred to Appendix A of this volume.

The aggregate number of cases obtained on the national cross-sections by the two agencies was 4933. In most of the tables and charts shown in the main body of this book, the two cross-sections are combined and treated as one. The agreement between the two cross-sections was quite close and most gratifying. Examples are shown in Chapter Two and subsequently.

But this combined cross-section of 4933 cases is only a part of the study. A unique feature of the survey lay in obtaining an additional special sample of 1500 selected local community leaders, entirely independent of the national cross-section. In this book the special sample of community leaders is always tabulated separately, never pooled with the cross-section.

Unlike the respondents in the cross-section, the community leaders were of necessity arbitrarily selected. But extreme care was taken to preclude interviewer bias in their selection. The steps in the sampling process were as follows:

1. From each of the cities of 10,000 to 150,000 in the sample, an arbitrary list of 14 occupational roles was drawn up. The same list was used in each city. It included the mayor, the president of the Chamber of Commerce, the chairman of the Community Chest, the president of a predesignated large labor-union local in the city, the chairmen of the Republican and Democratic county central committees, the commander of the largest American Legion post in the city, the regent of the D.A.R., the president of the local women's club, the chairmen of the school board and the library board, the president of the local council of the Parent-Teachers' Association (or if there was no such council, of the largest P.T.A. in the city), the president of the bar association, the publisher of the locally owned newspaper of largest circulation.

2. The list, it will be seen, was so drawn up that interviewer bias in selection was precluded, since one person only could fit a given description in a given community. Each interviewer prepared a list of the names and addresses of the 14 in his city, and to each of the

14 a letter was sent, signed by the head of the polling agency responsible for that city. (For this operation, each of the two polling organizations took full responsibility for half of the cities.) The letter, which spoke of the national importance of the survey without indicating the subject matter, was designed to pave the way for personal appointments at the least inconvenience to the respondents, many of whom are very busy people.

3. The selected community leaders were interviewed with questionnaires identical with those used in the national cross-section.

While the national cross-section can be defended as representative of all classes of the population, it must be stated here emphatically that the sample of leaders is not intended to be and is not a representative sample of community leaders in America. There is no objective definition of what constitutes a community leader and, even if there were, the cost of procuring a large and exhaustive sample would be prohibitive.

What, then, does the sample of leaders represent?

First, it represents only people in the cities of 10,000 to 150,000; people in rural communities, smaller cities, and larger metropolitan centers are by definition excluded.

Second, it represents only arbitrarily selected leaders. Strictly speaking, an average based on all such leaders combined is not susceptible of clear interpretation. What we can say, however, is the following: The mayors, for example, are a representative sample of all mayors in cities of 10,000 to 150,000. By "representative" we mean that if we had been able to interview all such mayors in all American cities of this size the result would differ from those in our sample only by a relatively small chance error, which is mathematically calculable. Similarly with each of the other incumbents of positions as defined. And this can provide very important, interpretable knowledge.

But why 14? This is not a magic number but is simply the maximum which the budget of time and money permitted in a given city. And why these particular 14? There is no right or wrong answer to this question. Each leadership role was chosen either because, as in the case of the president of the Community Chest, for example, he was likely to be a generally respected figure; or because, as in the case of the president of the Chamber of Commerce or the bar association or the largest labor-union local, he was likely, on the average, to be influential among certain segments of the population; or because, as in the case of heads of patriotic organizations or in the case of various

18

elected or appointed officials, the specific nature of their responsibility made their views especially relevant.

It would be easy to construct a list twice as long or longer. Women's groups, for example, are inadequately represented—missing are such organizations oriented to public affairs as the League of Women Voters. The clergy are unrepresented—it proved to be too difficult to settle on a satisfactory objective definition of a single clergyman to represent each city. Fraternal groups are omitted. So are leaders of ethnic minority organizations.

On the whole, in so far as the sample of leaders is biased, there are fewer rather than more leaders who would automatically be expected to have liberal attitudes.

For purposes of comparison with the views of each of the 14 selected types of leaders, a special sub-sample of the national cross-section has been segregated for exactly the same cities as those used for the sample of leaders. This sub-sample should be representative of the total population of all such cities, in the same sense as the mayors are representative of all mayors in cities of 10,000 to 150,000.

So much for the samples. We see that they introduce features some of which are rare and some of which are new in national surveys of this type.

What Kinds of Questions Were Asked?

The questionnaire used is reproduced in full in Appendix B. It is somewhat unconventional, by customary opinion-survey practice, in two main respects.

First, *it relied more heavily than many surveys on what are called free-answer or open-ended questions.* Much care was taken not to introduce specific check-list questions until the respondent had had a chance to talk generally about a subject. For example, the first twenty minutes or so of the interview were devoted to a general discussion of whatever things the respondent had most on his or her mind, without any hint as to the ultimate purpose of the survey. This was facilitated only by such leading questions by the interviewer as the following:

Everybody of course has some things he worries about, more or less. Would you say you worry more now than you used to, or not as much?

19

What kinds of things do you worry most about?

Are there other problems you worry or are concerned about, especially political or world problems?

We are interested in what kind of things people talk about. Offhand, **what problems do you remembering discussing with your friends in the last week or so?**

(Unless volunteered above) **Were there other things? For example, did you talk about any dangers facing people in the United States?**

The questionnaire then led into a series of check-list questions on war and civil liberties, with no direct question on attitudes toward the internal Communist threat until nearly half of the interview was completed. Here, again, open-ended questions were introduced to get the flavor of opinions in the respondent's own language, which the interviewer was instructed to take down as nearly as possible verbatim. For example, if the respondent said that the Communists within the United States were dangerous or were not dangerous, he was asked:

Why do you think this?

What kind of people in America are most likely to be Communists?

(Unless volunteered) **What racial and religious groups are they most likely to be in?**

(Unless volunteered) **What kind of jobs are they most likely to be in?**

What kinds of things do Communists believe in? (Probe) **Anything else?**

Have you ever known a person who you thought might be a Communist?

(If yes) **How could you tell? What made you think this?**

A number of open-ended questions also were used in later portions of the questionnaire, dealing with methods of handling the internal Communist threat.

The approach is not too dissimilar to what would be used by an expert newspaper reporter. It provides invaluable data on the depth and intensity of opinions which may be later ascertained systematically by more conventional check-list questions. It evokes a given

20

opinion within a larger context of the general attitudes of the individual. And it does not put into a person's head ideas that may not have been there before.

There are disadvantages as well. One is the sheer time it takes to conduct such an interview. Another is dependency on the objectivity and accuracy of the interviewer in recording the salient remarks when, as is often the case, he or she cannot set down every word. A third is the monumental task of summarizing systematically such qualitative data from thousands of interviews, and the further dangers of bias or subjectivity in preparing such summaries.

Therefore, there is an important place for simple check-list questions to which there is a prescribed set of answer categories. Such questions were used in considerable numbers.

The second respect in which the questionnaire used on this survey represented some departures from current practice was in the planned use of *a series of questions to summarize a given opinion rather than in reliance upon a single question.* One would not think of offering a single word to a person to spell as a test of his spelling ability, nor a single little problem in arithmetic as a test of his ability to multiply or divide. Often one can come closer to ascertaining an opinion by a single question than to measuring ability by a single test item. But experience has shown that a test or a scale of opinions based on a series of related questions is usually much more stable than a single item and also makes possible an internal test for validity. Do the various answers a person gives hang together in some systematic, consistent way? If they do, and if they satisfy certain fairly rigorous technical requirements, we can say they constitute *a scale of measurement.*

Two subjects of central importance to this study were studied by means of such scales. These were:

> Degree of willingness to tolerate nonconformists, such as Socialists, atheists, or Communists, or suspected nonconformists such as people whose loyalty has been criticized.

> Degree to which the internal Communist threat is regarded as a serious danger.

The first of these scales, based on 15 questions, will be introduced in Chapter Two. The second scale, based on 9 questions, will be introduced in Chapter Eight. For the technical reader, a description of the scales appears in Appendix C.

One of the important reasons for scales like these is to provide a standard against which to compare a particular question. There are some items, especially those agreed to by very few people, which will be answered "Yes" by some who do not understand the meaning— even by some who say "Yes" when their real opinion is "No." By trying to fit such questions into a scale we can learn about their limitations and discount their reliability.

It is never easy to construct check-list questions so simple and clear that they can be readily grasped by people with only a limited education. Question wording is something of an art in itself, but the most ingenious deviser of questions seldom can be sure of their clarity until they have been field-tested. For the present survey, five successive drafts of questionnaires were prepared under the auspices of the special committee appointed by the president of the Fund for the Republic to plan this study. Each form was tried out in the field and brought back for revision. The semi-final pre-test involved interviews with 250 people at all educational levels in different parts of the United States, and the final dress rehearsal was done on 50 persons also at different levels. Perhaps twice as many questions were tried out and discarded as appeared in the final questionnaire. Yet, as always seems to happen, there were a few disappointments on the main survey— and these will be duly noted in the text of this volume.

How This Study Relates to Previous Studies

The central purpose of this book is to tell the story of what Americans were thinking in the early summer of 1954, as learned by this particular study. This book is not intended to be an exhaustive compendium of previous research. Nevertheless, the reader is entitled to some intimations as to how findings of a given chapter relate to earlier findings, from public opinion polls or from other research in the literature of psychology and sociology. Just before the summary of each chapter, therefore, the findings are very briefly placed within the setting of past research. To reduce textual details, each specific reference to the literature is keyed simply by number to a bibliography which appears as Appendix E.

A Note to Enthusiasts and Skeptics

The limitations of studies like the present one are not always properly appreciated. There are some people who are disposed to seize a little too uncritically upon a reported number, like the percentage of people reported as giving a particular response to a question. There are others, perhaps reacting against too zealous enthusiasts, who retreat into agnosticism about all such figures.

It is a fact that no number reported in this study is exact. This is also the case with numbers reported in official statistics like the United States Census. No one really knows the actual population of New York City within plus or minus 100,000 or more. But this does not mean that Census figures are useless. One learns to take them for what they are—approximations. And normally they are closer approximations than somebody's guess.

Numbers in the present study are, of course, even less adequate approximations to unknown and unknowable "true national figures" than are most Census data. For they are based on a sample which, though larger than is customary and obtained with meticulous care, is still only a sample.

Even if the people whose opinions we report constitute a truly random sample of the population, we would expect the percentages in several such random samples to differ. The laws by which they would differ are well known—in fact, they constitute the basis of the science of mathematical statistics. Some of our percentages, calculated on the entire national cross-section, would fluctuate by chance only slightly. Others, based on sub-samples with much fewer cases, could have a theoretical variation of as much as 15 or 20 percentage points 5% of the time. In Appendix D we have sought to provide a compact rule-of-thumb guide. The reader may not want to bother often with such a guide. Therefore, we have sought to be careful not to stress the importance or implications of findings which theoretically could have occurred fairly often by chance alone.

In addition to instability attributable to chance, there are other sources of error which could happen even in a total enumeration of a population, as in the Census. For example, even slight variations in the wording of a question can produce variations in response, just as is the case with questions used by the Census to ascertain whether a person is in the labor market and seeking work. In this book we have tried to pin a finding not upon one question alone but upon a variety of questions.

When we report that one class of persons has different attitudes from another class of persons—say, women as compared with men— our best test is the *consistency* with which we find this result in differ-

23

ent parts of the country, or in different ages, or in different educational groups. The reader will encounter again and again in this book a sentence in effect like this: "Individual percentages wobble around for various reasons, but note how consistent the *pattern* is." Consistency of a repeated finding is not a sure guarantee, because of some possible systematic error, but it adds considerably to our confidence.

A book like this should be read with just as critical an eye as a book based solely on impressions garnered here and there unsystematically. In the present study, impressions can be checked by actual counts based on scientifically selected samples, and therein lies much of its significance. But there will be times when the author necessarily offers his interpretation of what these counts mean, and this interpretation may be wrong. The author has tried earnestly to be objective —to keep his own convictions about the danger of assaults by both Communists and anti-Communists upon the dignity and freedom of the human spirit from coloring his judgment as an analyst and reporter. Yet unconscious bias can occur. Readers will and should watch for it and supply their own correction factors in interpretation.

There are some people who have a humanist's dislike of tables and charts, even though they may be daily readers of a sports page or the financial sections of a newspaper. They recoil against statistical findings, even when thoroughly documented, especially if these should fly in the face of preconceived impressions as to what Americans think.

One could only wish that such a skeptic would sit down for a day with his own random selection from among the original questionnaires and read them through. When he sees the detail with which the data are recorded, when he sees the frank outpouring of personal problems in this confidential relationship with a skilled interviewer, he can have little doubt as to the integrity of almost all the documents —whether from the storekeeper in Nebraska, the semi-literate grandmother in a mountain cabin, or a leader of the American bar. There are human foibles of overstatement which may have crept into the responses, but there was little holding back and, in view of the sensitive character of the questions, surprisingly little evidence of suspicion once the interview got under way. (See Appendix A.)

Because of the importance of satisfying oneself on what has just been said, the following invitation is issued to bona fide scholars or journalists. Any who wish to read at their leisure some or all of the original questionnaires are invited to do so. (Data, such as name of the city and state, which might identify respondents have, of course, been removed.) The documents are on file at the offices of the Fund for the Republic in New York City.

If the skeptic who reads this book cannot avail himself of this offer, we have only one further suggestion. That is to beg of him the boon of at least a suspended judgment until he sees what the next two or three chapters have to offer.

We believe that they open a window into the mind of America.

Chapter Two

ARE CIVIC LEADERS MORE TOLERANT THAN OTHER PEOPLE?

This chapter compares our special sample of 14 kinds of community leaders with a cross-section of the population in the cities of 10,000 to 150,000 from whom these leaders are drawn, and also with a cross-section of the entire United States, with respect to the following question:

Are various types of community leaders more likely, or less likely, than people in the cross-section to respect the civil rights of radicals and other nonconformists, even though they may suspect or disapprove their opinions?

To illustrate: Most business leaders can scarcely be expected to endorse the views of a man who advocates government ownership of the railways or all big business. Neither, presumably, does the rank and file of the population in an American community. But should the views of a Socialist be suppressed? Should he be allowed to make a speech in one's community? Should a book he wrote be eliminated from the public library? Should he be allowed to teach in a college or university?

The findings to be presented here will show that community leaders of all types—including businessmen—are *more likely* than the cross-section to accord a Socialist the right to express his views freely.

Again, consider a man who is against churches and religion. Few Americans would share his views, and even more of them would suspect the atheist of being a Communist than would suspect the Socialist. But our findings will show that community leaders are *more likely* than the rank and file of the public to accord an atheist the right to express his views freely.

Or take quite a different category of person. Consider a man whose loyalty has been criticized by a Congressional investigating committee but who swears under oath he is not a Communist. We find that the community leaders are almost unanimous in granting him the right to speak or teach or the right to have his book read—or the right to hold a job. The majority of the rank and file hold likewise, but there is a large minority in the rank and file who would withdraw such privileges from him.

Finally, a much more drastic case; namely, the man who admits he is a Communist. Many of the community leaders draw a line here. They split about 50–50 on the subject of letting him make a speech in their community or letting a book he writes remain in the public library, and they differ widely in their willingness to let him hold a job. They are overwhelmingly against his holding jobs in government or defense plants and against his teaching in schools or universities, but they tend to be willing to tolerate him in non-sensitive employment. The rank and file, however, is more sweeping and undiscriminating. Only a small minority, for example, would let an admitted Communist make a speech in their community or would let his book remain in the public library.

Attitudes toward curtailing the civil liberties of the four kinds of nonconformists or suspected nonconformists can be combined in a single summary measure. This is a general scale of willingness to tolerate nonconformity, described in detail in Appendix C. On this scale, all categories of community leaders, including commanders of the American Legion and regents of the D.A.R., tend on the average to be *more respectful of the civil rights of those of whom they disapprove* than the average person in the general population, either of the same cities from which the leaders come or of the nation as a whole.

What does this mean?

It *does not mean* that the community leaders approve of the nonconformists or suspected nonconformists whose rights they would uphold.

It *does mean* that the community leaders, being especially responsible and thoughtful citizens, are more likely than the rank and file to give a sober second thought to the dangers involved in denying civil liberties to those whose views they dislike.

Tolerance is not absolute. It may be presumed that almost nobody would support the right to cry "Fire!" in a crowded theater; to engage, if a teacher, in sexual relations with students; to conspire, if a government official, with agents of the Soviet Union. The issues before America are not and never have been the preservation of absolute

27

rights of freedom, but rather of *how and where to set the limits*. If the limits are set too high, orderly activity, and even life itself, of the nation might become impossible. If the limits are set too low, all of the Anglo-Saxon heritage of relative freedom may be endangered.

That different Americans would set different limits is to be expected. It is the purpose of the present study to show where different kinds of Americans, as of the summer of 1954, thought those limits should be set.

CIVIL RIGHTS FOR SOCIALISTS

If a person wanted to make a speech in your community favoring government ownership of all the railroads and big industries, should he be allowed to speak, or not?

Chart I compares the answers to this question by our sample of community leaders, by a cross-section of people in those cities, and by a national cross-section, rural and urban.

To give the reader some feeling for error on such a survey as this, the results are also shown separately from each of the two survey agencies, which collected their data independently. Chart I makes it clear that the community leaders, on the average, would be more tolerant than the cross-sections. Looking at the data from both agencies pooled, we see that 84% of the leaders would let the Socialist speak, 61% of the cross-section in the same cities, and 58% of the national cross-section, rural and urban. The absolute figures differ somewhat, but the *pattern* is the same, whichever survey organization's samples are considered.

As we indicated in Chapter One, the "community leaders" are arbitrarily selected. Hence, only in a restricted sense does a figure based on all such leaders have meaning. If, however, we look at individual categories, such as "Mayors" or "Presidents of the Parent-Teachers' Association," we can be more specific. We have two samples, for example, of mayors of cities of 10,000 to 150,000 populations. True, we have only about 50 cases in each sample and therefore, by chance alone, the two samples of mayors will be expected to differ somewhat. In fact, about a third of such samples, according to probability theory, should differ by about 10 percentage points, and about one in 20 should differ by more than 20 percentage points. (For more technical details, see Appendix D.)

CHART I

COMMUNITY LEADERS ARE MORE WILLING THAN THE RANK AND FILE TO GIVE A SOCIALIST A RIGHT TO SPEAK

QUESTION: If a person wanted to make a speech in your community favoring government ownership of all the railroads and big industries, should he be allowed to speak, or not?

PERCENTAGE ANSWERING

ALL CASES

	NO ANSWER	NO	YES	
SELECTED COMMUNITY LEADERS		14	84	1500
CROSS-SECTION IN SAME CITIES AS LEADERS	29	10	61	897
NATIONAL CROSS-SECTION, RURAL AND URBAN	31	11	58	4953

BY EACH SURVEY AGENCY

		NO ANSWER	NO	YES	
SELECTED COMMUNITY LEADERS	AIPO SAMPLE		14	84	742
	NORC SAMPLE		14	84	758
CROSS-SECTION IN SAME CITIES AS LEADERS	AIPO SAMPLE	27	13	60	409
	NORC SAMPLE	31	8	61	488
NATIONAL CROSS-SECTION, RURAL AND URBAN	AIPO SAMPLE	32	11	57	2483
	NORC SAMPLE	30	10	60	2450

Numbers inside the bars show percentages; numbers at the ends of the bars show the size of sample. AIPO is the American Institute of Public Opinion (the Gallup Poll); NORC is the National Opinion Research Center.

The data are shown in Table 1. The important fact in this table is *not any one particular percentage*—comparison of the findings of the two agencies shows how such percentages differ, as would be expected, for any given occupational category. The important fact, rather, is that *without a single exception,* no matter which agency's data we use, each type of community leader was on the average more likely to be willing to let a Socialist make a speech than was the cross-section of the population.

Community leaders differed by types. At the extremes, the leaders of the women's clubs, the American Legion, and the D.A.R. were less willing to tolerate a Socialist speech than, say, the chairmen of the school board or the presidents of the bar association. If the difference between two types of leaders, based on the combined samples, is about 14% or more, we can be reasonably sure that it is big enough not to be attributable to sampling error.

But, to repeat, the most important finding in Table 1 is the fact that every type of leader, without exception, was more willing to permit a Socialist speech than were the cross-sections of population.

Similar patterns are found on other specific questions. About the same proportions, and in most instances the same people as were willing to let a Socialist speak, said "No" to the following question:

If some people in your community suggested that a book he wrote favoring government ownership should be taken out of your public library, would you favor removing the book, or not? Responses were as follows:

	Favor	No Opinion	Not Favor	Total
Community Leaders	18%	3%	79%	100%
Cross-Section in Same Cities	35	13	52	100
National Cross-Section	35	13	52	100

A good many people who would let a Socialist speak or would retain his book in the library balked at saying "Yes" to the question: **Should such a person be allowed to teach in a college or university, or not?** Percentages were:

	No	No Opinion	Yes	Total
Community Leaders	47%	5%	48%	100%
Cross-Section in Same Cities	54	13	33	100
National Cross-Section	54	13	33	100

TABLE 1

WILLINGNESS TO GIVE A SOCIALIST THE RIGHT TO SPEAK

(Types of Community Leaders Compared with Cross-Sections)

	NUMBER OF CASES		PERCENTAGE WILLING TO LET SOCIALIST SPEAK IN THEIR COMMUNITY		
	AIPO Sample	NORC Sample	AIPO Sample	NORC Sample	Combined Sample
Public Officials					
Mayors	56	56	79%	80%	80%
Presidents, School Board	53	58	90	85	88
Presidents, Library Board	56	53	93	91	92
Political Party Chairmen					
Republican County Central Committee	55	55	86	88	87
Democratic County Central Committee	53	50	96	87	91
Industrial Leaders					
Presidents, Chamber of Commerce	57	56	82	88	85
Presidents, Labor Union	51	55	77	82	80
Heads of Special Patriotic Groups					
Commanders, American Legion	55	59	81	70	76
Regents, D.A.R.	50	50	76	74	75
Others					
Chmn., Community Chest	52	48	89	98	93
Presidents, Bar Assoc.	53	46	94	96	95
Newspaper Publishers	44	48	97	98	97
Pres., Women's Club	54	55	62	75	68
Presidents, Parent-Teachers' Assoc.	53	59	83	75	79
Average of Community Leaders	742	758	84%	84%	84%
Cross-Section of Same Cities as Leaders	409	488	60	61	61
National Cross-Section, Rural and Urban	2483	2450	57	60	58

31

CIVIL RIGHTS FOR ATHEISTS

For many people, protection of the rights of atheists is a tougher problem than protection of the rights of Socialists. In Chart II and Table 2, answers are tabulated to the question: **If a person wanted to make a speech in your community against churches and religion, should he be allowed to speak, or not?**

In all groups the percentages saying "Yes" are less than for the corresponding question about a Socialist, but the *pattern* is the same as before. The community leaders, on the average and in every individual category, are more likely than the cross-sections to say "Yes." These findings hold for every type of leader, irrespective of which of the two agencies reported, in spite of some substantial differences between the two agencies.

Two other questions about atheists are of interest:

If some people in your community suggested that a book he wrote against churches and religion should be taken out of your public library, would you favor removing the book or not? Percentages answering:

	Favor	No Opinion	Not Favor	Total
Community Leaders	34%	2%	64%	100%
Cross-Section in Same Cities	60	5	35	100
National Cross-Section	60	5	35	100

Should such a person be allowed to teach in a college or university, or not? The vote, even among leaders, tends to be "No."

	No	No Opinion	Yes	Total
Community Leaders	71%	4%	25%	100%
Cross-Section in Same Cities	85	3	12	100
National Cross-Section	84	4	12	100

CHART II

COMMUNITY LEADERS ARE MORE WILLING THAN THE RANK AND FILE TO GIVE AN ATHEIST A RIGHT TO SPEAK

QUESTION: If a person wanted to make a speech in your community against churches and religion, should he be allowed to speak, or not?

PERCENTAGE ANSWERING

ALL CASES

	NO	NO OPINION	YES
SELECTED COMMUNITY LEADERS	34		64
CROSS-SECTION IN SAME CITIES AS LEADERS	58		39
NATIONAL CROSS-SECTION, RURAL AND URBAN	60		37

BY EACH SURVEY AGENCY

		NO	YES
SELECTED COMMUNITY LEADERS	AIPO SAMPLE	33	66
	NORC SAMPLE	35	63
CROSS-SECTION IN SAME CITIES AS LEADERS	AIPO SAMPLE	58	39
	NORC SAMPLE	57	40
NATIONAL CROSS-SECTION, RURAL AND URBAN	AIPO SAMPLE	60	37
	NORC SAMPLE	61	37

Based on same samples as Chart I.

TABLE 2

WILLINGNESS TO GIVE AN ATHEIST THE RIGHT TO SPEAK

(Types of Community Leaders Compared with Cross-Sections)

	PERCENTAGE WILLING TO LET ATHEIST SPEAK IN THEIR COMMUNITY		
	AIPO Sample	*NORC Sample*	*Combined Samples*
Public Officials			
Mayors	61%	62%	62%
Presidents, School Board	68	50	59
Presidents, Library Board	84	66	75
Political Party Chairmen			
Republican County Central Com.	70	75	72
Democratic County Central Com.	72	58	66
Industrial Leaders			
Presidents, Chamber of Commerce	69	66	68
Presidents, Labor Union	59	60	59
Heads of Special Patriotic Groups			
Commanders, American Legion	49	44	47
Regents, D.A.R.	56	52	54
Others			
Chairmen, Community Chest	65	85	75
Presidents, Bar Association	80	86	83
Newspaper Publishers	82	83	82
Presidents, Women's Club	43	51	46
Presidents, Parent-Teachers' Assoc.	67	52	59
Average of Community Leaders	66%	63%	64%
Cross-Section of Same Cities as Leaders	39	40	39
National Cross-Section, Rural and Urban	37	37	37

Number of cases in each sample same as in Table 1.

CIVIL RIGHTS FOR A MAN WHOSE LOYALTY HAS BEEN QUESTIONED BUT WHO SWEARS HE IS NOT A COMMUNIST

Consider a man whose loyalty has been questioned before a Congressional committee, but who swears under oath he has never been a Communist. Should he be allowed to make a speech in your community, or not?

Relatively few Americans—community leaders and rank and file alike—were willing to put roadblocks in the way of such a man. But, as in all other cases, the leaders were more tolerant than the rank and file.

Chart III shows the reactions toward letting such a man make a speech in their community. Among the leaders, 87% would accord him the right; in the cross-section of people in the same cities, 71%; in the national cross-section, 70%. The agreement between the findings from the two survey agencies is, again, strikingly close.

Moreover, we see from Table 3 that whichever survey agency's results we look at, each of the 14 types of community leaders is, on the average, more tolerant on this issue than the average of the cross-sections.

Although all of the percentages tend to go up and down together, depending on the particular topic, the *pattern* observed in Chart III holds for a variety of other questions asked about this person whose loyalty has been questioned before a Congressional committee but who swears under oath that he has never been a Communist. For example:

Suppose he wrote a book which is in your public library. Somebody in your community suggests the book should be removed from the library. Would you favor removing the book, or not?

	Favor	*No Opinion*	*Not Favor*	*Total*
Community Leaders	7%	5%	88%	100%
Cross-Section in Same Cities	18	10	72	100
National Cross-Section	17	12	71	100

35

CHART III

COMMUNITY LEADERS ARE MORE WILLING THAN THE RANK AND FILE TO GIVE RIGHT TO SPEAK TO A MAN WHOSE LOYALTY HAS BEEN CRITICIZED BUT WHO SWEARS HE IS NOT A COMMUNIST

QUESTION: Consider a man whose loyalty has been questioned before a Congressional committee, but who swears under oath he has never been a Communist. Should he be allowed to make a speech in your community, or not?

PERCENTAGE ANSWERING

ALL CASES

	NO	NO OPINION	YES
SELECTED COMMUNITY LEADERS		11	87
CROSS-SECTION IN SAME CITIES AS LEADERS	21	8	71
NATIONAL CROSS-SECTION, RURAL AND URBAN	21	9	70

BY EACH SURVEY AGENCY

		NO	NO OPINION	YES
SELECTED COMMUNITY LEADERS	AIPO SAMPLE		12	86
	NORC SAMPLE		10	87
CROSS-SECTION IN SAME CITIES AS LEADERS	AIPO SAMPLE	20	10	70
	NORC SAMPLE	21	7	72
NATIONAL CROSS-SECTION, RURAL AND URBAN	AIPO SAMPLE	21	9	70
	NORC SAMPLE	21	8	71

Based on same samples as Chart I.

TABLE 3

WILLINGNESS TO GIVE RIGHT TO SPEAK TO A MAN WHOSE LOYALTY HAS BEEN QUESTIONED BUT WHO SWEARS HE IS NOT A COMMUNIST

(Types of Community Leaders Compared with Cross-Sections)

	PERCENTAGE WILLING TO LET HIM SPEAK IN THEIR COMMUNITY		
	AIPO Sample	*NORC Sample*	*Combined Samples*
Public Officials			
Mayors	88%	88%	88%
Presidents, School Board	85	88	87
Presidents, Library Board	95	83	89
Political Party Chairmen			
Republican County Central Com.	82	90	86
Democratic County Central Com.	87	92	89
Industrial Leaders			
Presidents, Chamber of Commerce	83	93	88
Presidents, Labor Union	92	82	87
Heads of Special Patriotic Groups			
Commanders, American Legion	89	83	86
Regents, D.A.R.	76	92	84
Others			
Chairmen, Community Chest	88	88	88
Presidents, Bar Association	85	89	87
Newspaper Publishers	93	93	93
Presidents, Women's Club	80	82	81
Presidents, Parent-Teachers' Assoc.	92	80	86
Average of Community Leaders	86%	87%	87%
Cross-Section of Same Cities as Leaders	70	72	71
National Cross-Section, Rural and Urban	70	71	70

Number of cases in each sample same as in Table 1.

Respondents were asked to consider whether such a person should be fired from various jobs. The large majority said "No," but those who would not let him teach in a college or high school or would not let him work in a defense plant were somewhat more numerous, as might be expected, than those who would fire him if he were a clerk in a store or a radio singer:

Suppose this man is a high school teacher. Should he be fired, or not?

	Yes	No Opinion	No	Total
Community Leaders	16%	4%	80%	100%
Cross-Section in Same Cities	21	8	71	100
National Cross-Section	22	9	69	100

Suppose he is teaching in a college or university. Should he be fired, or not?

	Yes	No Opinion	No	Total
Community Leaders	15%	4%	81%	100%
Cross-Section in Same Cities	20	8	72	100
National Cross-Section	22	9	69	100

Suppose he has been working in a defense plant. Should he be fired, or not?

	Yes	No Opinion	No	Total
Community Leaders	13%	5%	82%	100%
Cross-Section in Same Cities	16	9	75	100
National Cross-Section	18	10	72	100

Suppose he is a clerk in a store. Should he be fired, or not?

	Yes	No Opinion	No	Total
Community Leaders	4%	3%	93%	100%
Cross-Section in Same Cities	12	7	81	100
National Cross-Section	11	8	81	100

Suppose he is a radio singer. Should he be fired, or not?

	Yes	No Opinion	No	Total
Community Leaders	6%	3%	91%	100%
Cross-Section in Same Cities	12	9	79	100
National Cross-Section	12	8	80	100

The subject of boycott was also brought up. The question was asked about the radio singer: **Now suppose the radio program he is on advertises a brand of soap. Somebody in your community suggests you stop buying that soap. Would you stop, or not?** The percentages endorsing such a boycott are very small:

	Yes	No Opinion	No	Total
Community Leaders	5%	3%	92%	100%
Cross-Section in Same Cities	10	7	83	100
National Cross-Section	9	8	83	100

CIVIL RIGHTS FOR ADMITTED COMMUNISTS

Everybody has a line which he draws somewhere. We shall see in later chapters that there are wide differences in opinion as to the danger of the internal Communist threat but that there was almost nobody in any of the samples who expressed sympathy with Communist doctrines. For example, only 5% in the national cross-section thought it possible for a man to believe in Communism and still be a loyal American. And even among this 5% the overwhelming majority supported a firm stand against Russia, most of them saying, for example, that we should fight Russia if necessary to prevent the Communists from taking over the rest of Europe or Asia.

But the lines marking the limits of tolerance of American Communists vary, depending on how clear the risk to society seems in a specific situation.

For example, community leaders and the rank and file alike are generally agreed that Communists have forfeited the right to hold certain kinds of jobs—as teachers in high schools or colleges or as workers in defense plants.

But the community leaders are more likely than others to take the calculated risk of letting Communists speak in their communities or letting their books remain in the public library. And the leaders are more likely than others to support the right of Communists to hold non-sensitive jobs.

39

Consider first the question: **Suppose an admitted Communist wants to make a speech in your community. Should he be allowed to speak, or not?** We see in Chart IV that 51% of the community leaders would let him speak, as compared with 29% of the cross-section in the same cities and 27% of the national sample. Moreover, Table 4 shows that each of the 14 selected types of leaders was more willing, on the average, to let a Communist speak than were the cross-sections. This is true, whichever survey agency's findings we look at.

We get much the same picture from the question: **Suppose he wrote a book which is in your public library. Somebody in your community suggests the book should be removed from the library. Would you favor removing it, or not?**

	Favor	No Opinion	Not Favor	Total
Community Leaders	54%	4%	42%	100%
Cross-Section in Same Cities	66	6	28	100
National Cross-Section	66	7	27	100

Community leaders are just as much in favor as the cross-section, if not more so, of getting Communists out of defense plants: Question: **Suppose he is working in a defense plant. Should he be fired, or not?**

	Yes	No Opinion	No	Total
Community Leaders	93%	2%	5%	100%
Cross-Section in Same Cities	91	4	5	100
National Cross-Section	90	4	6	100

And community leaders are only slightly less likely than the general population to think that a Communist has forfeited his right to teach in schools or colleges.

Suppose he is a high school teacher. Should he be fired, or not?

	Yes	No Opinion	No	Total
Community Leaders	89%	2%	9%	100%
Cross-Section in Same Cities	93	3	4	100
National Cross-Section	91	4	5	100

CHART IV

COMMUNITY LEADERS ARE MORE WILLING THAN THE RANK AND FILE TO GIVE A COMMUNIST THE RIGHT TO SPEAK

QUESTION: Suppose an admitted Communist wants to make a speech in your community. Should he be allowed to speak, or not?

PERCENTAGE ANSWERING

ALL CASES

	NO	NO OPINION	YES
SELECTED COMMUNITY LEADERS	47		51
CROSS-SECTION IN SAME CITIES AS LEADERS	66		29
NATIONAL CROSS-SECTION, RURAL AND URBAN	68		27

BY EACH SURVEY AGENCY

		NO	NO OPINION	YES
SELECTED COMMUNITY LEADERS	AIPO SAMPLE	46		51
	NORC SAMPLE	47		51
CROSS-SECTION IN SAME CITIES AS LEADERS	AIPO SAMPLE	64		30
	NORC SAMPLE	69		28
NATIONAL CROSS-SECTION RURAL AND URBAN	AIPO SAMPLE	67		27
	NORC SAMPLE	69		27

Based on same samples as Chart I.

41

TABLE 4

WILLINGNESS TO GIVE A COMMUNIST THE RIGHT TO SPEAK

(Types of Community Leaders Compared with Cross-Sections)

	PERCENTAGE WILLING TO LET COMMUNIST SPEAK IN THEIR COMMUNITY		
	AIPO Sample	*NORC Sample*	*Combined Samples*
Public Officials			
Mayors	44%	34%	39%
Presidents, School Board	43	36	40
Presidents, Library Board	74	60	67
Political Party Chairmen			
Republican County Central Com.	54	63	59
Democratic County Central Com.	62	50	56
Industrial Leaders			
Presidents, Chamber of Commerce	42	49	46
Presidents, Labor Union	47	44	45
Heads of Special Patriotic Groups			
Commanders, American Legion	47	47	47
Regents, D.A.R.	36	42	39
Others			
Chairmen, Community Chest	56	68	62
Presidents, Bar Association	60	66	63
Newspaper Publishers	72	73	73
Presidents, Women's Club	42	35	39
Presidents, Parent-Teachers' Assoc.	41	44	43
Average of Community Leaders	51%	51%	51%
Cross-Section of Same Cities as Leaders	28	30	29
National Cross-Section, Rural and Urban	27	27	27

Number of cases in each sample same as in Table 1.

Suppose he is teaching in a college. Should he be fired, or not?

	Yes	No Opinion	No	Total
Community Leaders	86%	3%	11%	100%
Cross-Section in Same Cities	91	5	4	100
National Cross-Section	89	5	6	100

On the other hand, community leaders are strikingly more willing to grant Communists the right to hold relatively non-sensitive jobs:
Suppose he is a clerk in a store. Should he be fired, or not?

	Yes	No Opinion	No	Total
Community Leaders	51%	4%	45%	100%
Cross-Section in Same Cities	68	7	25	100
National Cross-Section	68	6	26	100

Suppose this admitted Communist is a radio singer. Should he be fired, or not?

	Yes	No Opinion	No	Total
Community Leaders	48%	4%	48%	100%
Cross-Section in Same Cities	64	8	28	100
National Cross-Section	63	8	29	100

A majority both of the leaders and of the cross-section would not boycott his sponsor. Question: **Now, suppose the radio program he is on advertises a brand of soap. Somebody in your community suggests that you stop buying that soap. Would you stop, or not?**

	Yes	No Opinion	No	Total
Community Leaders	27%	4%	69%	100%
Cross-Section in Same Cities	37	8	55	100
National Cross-Section	36	8	56	100

Two questions, pertaining to penalties which the public would impose on Communists, are worth noting:
Should an admitted Communist have his American citizenship taken away from him, or not?

	Yes	No Opinion	No	Total
Community Leaders	66%	7%	27%	100%
Cross-Section in Same Cities	80	8	12	100
National Cross-Section	77	10	13	100

Should an admitted Communist be put in jail, or not?

	Yes	No Opinion	No	Total
Community Leaders	27%	10%	63%	100%
Cross-Section in Same Cities	52	13	35	100
National Cross-Section	51	15	34	100

Do you or don't you think the government should have the right to listen in on people's private telephone conversations, in order to get evidence against Communists?

	Yes	No Opinion	No	Total
Community Leaders	62%	5%	33%	100%
Cross-Section in Same Cities	66	7	27	100
National Cross-Section	64	9	27	100

It is interesting and perhaps surprising to note that the majority of people, most of whom would be very tough on Communists, say that they would not break their friendship with a man who they discovered had been a Communist *but who is not one now.*

Suppose you discovered that one of your friends today had been a Communist ten years ago, although you are sure he is not now. Would you break your friendship with him, or not?

	Yes	No Opinion	No	Total
Community Leaders	7%	4%	89%	100%
Cross-Section in Same Cities	15	8	77	100
National Cross-Section	14	8	78	100

Suppose you discovered that one of your good friends today had been a Communist until recently, although he says he is not now. Would you break your friendship with him, or not?

	Yes	No Opinion	No	Total
Community Leaders	28%	11%	61%	100%
Cross-Section in Same Cities	35	14	51	100
National Cross-Section	34	14	52	100

Almost half of the cross-section also would be relatively lenient with a man who invoked the Fifth Amendment because he does not want to be forced into testimony against his former friends. The leaders were slightly *less* likely than others to be lenient in this case.

44

Sometimes a man says he refuses to answer certain questions about Communism because he does not want to be forced to testify against his former friends. Should he be punished very severely, severely, not too severely, or not at all?

	Very Severely	Severely	No Opinion	Not too Severely	Not at all	Total
Community Leaders	6%	33%	11%	32%	18%	100%
Cross-Section in Same Cities	6	24	16	32	22	100
National Cross-Section	6	23	15	34	22	100

On another question dealing with possible personal action against suspected Communists, the picture is somewhat different:

On the whole, do you think it is a good idea or a bad idea for people to report to the F.B.I. any neighbors or acquaintances whom they suspect of being Communists?

	Good Idea	No Opinion	Bad Idea	Total
Community Leaders	65%	3%	32%	100%
Cross-Section in Same Cities	72	8	20	100
National Cross-Section	73	8	19	100

Although most of the leaders, like the cross-section, tended to feel it their duty to report to the F.B.I., the leaders were more likely than the cross-section to see dangers of damage to innocent people. Among leaders who would report to the F.B.I., 27% volunteered in a free-answer question that this might hurt innocent people, and 14% suggested dangers of creating an atmosphere of fear and suspicion. In the national cross-section, the corresponding figures were only 13% and 4%. It might also be noted that a danger mentioned by 5% of the leaders who would report to the F.B.I. and by as many as 25% of the corresponding people in the cross-section was the possibility of personal reprisal by Communists.

A quite general question also differentiates local community leaders from the cross-section. Respondents were handed a card and were asked which, in their opinion, of the two statements printed on the card is more important:

To find out all the Communists even if some innocent people should be hurt.

To protect the rights of innocent people even if some Communists are not found out.

Answers were as follows:

	Find out Communists	Don't Know	Protect Rights	Total
Community Leaders	42%	6%	52%	100%
Cross-Section in Same Cities	60	9	31	100
National Cross-Section	58	10	32	100

HOW MUCH CAN WE TRUST QUESTIONS LIKE THESE?

The problem needs discussion at two levels. First, do people understand the questions and do they answer honestly? Second, even if they do, how seriously should we take a given question as a predictor of action in a concrete future situation?

How Reliable Are the Responses?

There are two kinds of tests as to the first level of problems. If the respondents have difficulty in understanding certain questions or are evasive, the skilled interviewers are likely to notice it (or suspect it). Each interviewer was required to submit a report of such difficulties —and there appears to have been relatively little trouble with most of the questions in this chapter. There were some misunderstandings but practically no signs of lack of candor. Probably the reason for the candor was the nature of the *rapport* established in the early part of the interview. The full questionnaire appears in Appendix B, and the reader will note that none of the direct questions examined in this chapter was asked until the interview was quite far along. Furthermore, when one reads questionnaires as a whole he gets no impression of evasiveness, even where he encounters evident errors of understanding.

A second test which can be applied is a systematic statistical check on what we call *internal consistency*. Suppose a respondent says he

46

would let an admitted Communist work in a defense plant, but would fire a store clerk whose loyalty is suspected but who swears he has never been a Communist. He *could* mean both of these things. But it is a good bet that one or the other response is wrong. He probably misunderstood one of the questions. No matter how skilled we are in question wording, people will misunderstand a question here and there and give answers exactly the opposite of what they mean. This can happen through a lack of attention alone. Inconsistencies become especially serious with respect to questions about which opinion is overwhelmingly on one side. For example, only 298 people of the entire national cross-section of 4933 said they would not fire an admitted Communist in a defense plant. But analysis shows that as many as 100 of the 298 who said they would be lenient in this situation said they would *not* be lenient in *a variety* of situations which most people think are far less dangerous. These 100 people constitute only 2% of our entire sample, but they constitute a *third* of all who say they would not fire a worker in a defense plant. Another example: The American people overwhelmingly rejected the idea of boycotting the product of the sponsor of a radio singer who was accused of being disloyal but denied under oath he was a Communist. Indeed, the very suggestion of such an idea was regarded by some as silly enough to laugh at. Yet 433 people were found who said they agreed with the idea. Let us examine these 433 further. Did they mean it? As many as 150 of them—and possibly many more—evidently did not, because they were very lenient on answers to a *considerable variety of questions* which most people thought required serious sanctions. These 150 people constitute only 3% of the entire sample, but their errors are sufficient to damage the reliability of the question, since they constitute over a third of all who said "Yes" to it.

On the other hand, if we have a question to which 60% said "Yes" and 40% said "No," we can permit a considerable margin of error on both sides. The procedure of *scaling,* introduced in the next section, provides an objective statistical test which enables us to reject questions which are misunderstood by too many people.

How Well Can We Predict Action?

The second level of problems with respect to questions like those used in this chapter has to do with specific predictions which one might wish to make. Obviously one cannot predict the behavior of any small segment of people if a substantial fraction of them misunderstood a question. But let us assume that we are dealing with a question which was quite clearly understood. It still does not follow that most people who say, for example, that they would favor throwing a Socialist's book out of a library would be *active* proponents of such an idea if it were proposed in their town. For many people this is an idea which may never have occurred before. Chapter Three, based on the free, unguided responses to the first part of the questionnaire, will show that most people are not thinking very seriously about such matters, let alone worrying about them. All that the answer to such a question describes is what we call a *latent tendency*. If some friends came around to stir such people up it is quite likely that it would be easier to arouse them in favor of throwing out the book than it would be to arouse them against it. But whether they would be stirred at all in an actual life situation would depend on *who did the arousing*. This is why our data on the local community leaders are so crucial. Some of these leaders may have had to face actual problems of this kind, and even more of them may have imagined themselves as involved in such problems. The fact that, on the average, the leaders are more likely than the rank and file to give tolerant answers is highly important, because their own *latent tendencies* are more likely to be activated than those of the rank and file, and indeed it is some of these leaders in turn who would activate responses in others.

In other words, we must not take the answers to any specific question as explicit predictions of action. Rather, we must regard them as indexes of *latent tendencies*. The best such index is one based not on a single question but on a composite of many questions. This composite, which we shall call a scale, tends to cancel out many of the accidental errors of reporting which are bound to attach to the answers to any one particular question. The scale ranks people according to their latent tendencies—leaders as well as others—and this ordering is extremely important. But, as will be discussed further at various points in the book and especially in Chapter Eight, rank on the scale alone must not be expected to *guarantee* specific future actions.

INTRODUCING A SCALE OF WILLINGNESS TO TOLERATE NONCONFORMISTS

Even if each question were reliable, it would be tediously repetitive to examine it in a variety of contexts. We will want to ask: In the cross-sections of the population, who are relatively the most tolerant toward nonconformists and who are least tolerant? City people or rural people? Easterners, Midwesterners, or Southerners? Older or younger? Men or women? Educated or the less educated? Etc. For sheer economy of presentation as well as for question reliability, we need a single index or scale which will summarize an individual's relative degree of tolerance.

Fortunately, we have such a scale. One of the most important findings in the charts and tables presented is the remarkable consistency in *patterns* of response. The community leaders, on almost all questions, are more willing to respect the rights of the nonconformist than are the rank and file. This is true on questions which 75% favor, or on which people split 50–50, or on questions which only 25% favor. It is true with respect to the rights of Socialists, atheists, suspected Communists who swear to their innocence, or admitted Communists. Further cross-tabulations show that, if a man or woman is one of only 25% who would be tolerant on a given item, he tends to be tolerant on most other items to which a still larger proportion give "tolerant" answers. And vice versa. If a person is one of a minority who would be severe on a Socialist, he tends to be one of a still larger group who would be tough on an atheist or admitted Communist. Not all questions are consistent, in this sense, with other questions, but most of them are.

These facts make a scale possible. Out of the questions here reported, 15 were selected to constitute that scale. Questions on which there was near unanimity were omitted, as were a few others which showed more than average inconsistency. Details of the scale appear in Appendix C.

The scale as originally constructed ranked respondents in one of six ranks. For simplicity of presentation, the scale scores have been recombined into three still broader rank groups with the following labels:

Relatively more tolerant. Constituting about a third of the national cross-section, these people give *tolerant* types of answers on more of the 15 questions than other people.

Relatively less tolerant. Constituting about a fifth of the national cross-section, these people give *intolerant* types of answers on more of the 15 questions than other people.

In-between. Between these two groupings are the rest of the population.

Chart V uses this scale to make a summary comparison just like the comparisons which have already been made for selected individual items.

Now, a word as how *not* to read this chart. It does *not* say that 66% of the community leaders are tolerant as compared with 31% of the national cross-section. Or that only 5% are intolerant as compared with 19% of the cross-section. The scale does not measure tolerance in any absolute sense.

What does Chart V say? It says (1) that we decided on a score on our tolerance scale high enough so that 31% of the national cross-section got that score or a higher one. We call these people our "more tolerant" group. Having set that score, we found that 66% of the community leaders got that score or a higher one. Similarly, (2) that we decided on a score that was low enough so that 19% of the national cross-section got that score or a lower one. We call that group our "less tolerant" group. Having set that score, we found that only 5% of the community leaders got that score or a lower one. For still more explicit details, see Appendix C.

It is so important to see clearly the distinction made here between an unjustifiable *absolute* statement and a justifiable *relative* statement that we venture to illustrate further what we mean by an analogy from baseball. Suppose we found that two thirds of the players on one team batted above .250, as compared with only half the players on another team. We might arbitrarily call anybody who hits above .250 a "good hitter," but another person might apply this term only to people who hit above .300. He might think that a mere .250 batter is terrible. Hence he can properly object if we say two thirds of the players on a team are good hitters—just as readers can properly object if we say 66% of the community leaders are tolerant. Many such leaders, by his standards, may be intolerant. But he cannot object if we say that a .250 hitter is usually a *better* hitter than one with a lower batting

50

CHART V

COMMUNITY LEADERS ARE RELATIVELY MORE TOLERANT THAN THE RANK AND FILE ON SCALE OF TOLERANCE OF NONCONFORMISTS

PERCENTAGE DISTRIBUTION OF SCALE SCORES

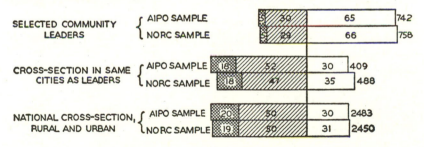

ALL CASES

	LESS TOLERANT	IN-BETWEEN	MORE TOLERANT	
SELECTED COMMUNITY LEADERS	5	29	66	1500
CROSS-SECTION IN SAME CITIES AS LEADERS	18	50	32	897
NATIONAL CROSS-SECTION, RURAL AND URBAN	19	50	31	4933

BY EACH SURVEY AGENCY

		LESS TOLERANT	IN-BETWEEN	MORE TOLERANT	
SELECTED COMMUNITY LEADERS	AIPO SAMPLE	5	30	65	742
	NORC SAMPLE	5	29	66	758
CROSS-SECTION IN SAME CITIES AS LEADERS	AIPO SAMPLE	18	52	30	409
	NORC SAMPLE	18	47	35	488
NATIONAL CROSS-SECTION, RURAL AND URBAN	AIPO SAMPLE	20	50	30	2483
	NORC SAMPLE	19	50	31	2450

Based on same samples as Chart I.

TABLE 5

SCALE OF WILLINGNESS TO TOLERATE NONCONFORMISTS

(Types of Community Leaders Compared with Cross-Sections)

	PERCENTAGE "RELATIVELY MORE TOLERANT" ON SCALE		
	AIPO Sample	NORC Sample	Combined Samples
Public Officials			
Mayors	59%	62%	60%
Presidents, School Board	66	59	62
Presidents, Library Board	82	75	79
Political Party Chairmen			
Republican County Central Com.	60	80	70
Democratic County Central Com.	70	58	64
Industrial Leaders			
Presidents, Chamber of Commerce	77	54	65
Presidents, Labor Union	61	63	62
Heads of Special Patriotic Groups			
Commanders, American Legion	45	47	46
Regents, D.A.R.	38	56	48
Others			
Chairmen, Community Chest	77	87	82
Presidents, Bar Association	75	79	77
Newspaper Publishers	85	83	84
Presidents, Women's Club	46	53	49
Presidents, Parent-Teachers' Assoc.	68	68	68
Average of Community Leaders	65%	66%	66%
Cross-Section of Same Cities as Leaders	30	35	32
National Cross-Section, Rural and Urban	30	31	31

Number of cases in each sample same as in Table 1.

average. Hence he can agree that one team has a larger proportion of "better hitters" than the other team. Likewise, even if some of the community leaders ranked as "relatively more tolerant" by us are intolerant by a given reader's absolute standards, he still can accept the statement that the community leaders contain a larger proportion of "relatively more tolerant people" than does the cross-section.

As the reader would expect from the previous data in this chapter, the two survey agencies agree quite closely in their findings when translated into the summary scale in Chart V.

Table 5, like previous tables, shows that each of the 14 selected categories of community leaders contains a larger proportion of individuals who are classed as "more tolerant" on the scale than are contained in the cross-section in the same cities or in the national cross-section. This result holds without exception even if we base our findings on the samples from each survey agency taken separately.

There is considerable range among the different types of leaders. But a further caution must be exercised in making such comparisons. Even the combined sample for any particular category of leader is small and therefore subject to considerable chance variation. For example, the comparative percentages in Table 5 for presidents of the Chamber of Commerce and for labor unions are 65 and 62, respectively. But in the AIPO sample the difference is in one direction; in the NORC sample the difference is reversed. Moreover, by the rule suggested earlier in this chapter, on page 30, we require differences between two categories of leaders to be at least 14% to be significant. We do see in Table 5 that the commanders of the American Legion are significantly less likely to be at the tolerant end of the scale than most of the other community leaders. Similarly, the regents of the D.A.R. and the presidents of the women's clubs. On the other hand, the presidents of the library board, the chairmen of the Community Chest, the presidents of the bar associations, and the newspaper publishers are significantly more tolerant on this scale than several others on the list.

A final comment may be needed. From one point of view the word "tolerance" as used in the present context may be an unhappy choice. To a careless reader it may imply "approval," which again let us say it does not. If I am tolerant of a kidnaper, it is only in the sense that I want him to have every right to which the laws of the land entitle him. If I am tolerant of a totalitarian, Fascist or Communist, I do not have to approve his views. I can be as implacably against his views as Jefferson was against those of repressive authoritarians a century and a half ago: "I have sworn upon the altar of God eternal hostility against every form of tyranny over the mind of man." But if I am tolerant, there are rights which I will grant, within the law, even to those whom I most condemn. The scale of willingness to tolerate nonconformity is measuring tolerance in this sense. But again let it be pointed out, this scale does not measure such tolerance *in general*. It deals only with attitudes toward certain types of nonconformists or deviants. It does not deal with attitudes toward extreme right-wing agitators, toward people who attack minority groups, toward faddists or cultists, in general, nor, of course, toward a wide variety of criminals. For purposes of this study, the tolerance of nonconformity or suspected nonconformity is *solely* within the broad context of the Communist threat.

We shall find this scale, purposely limited as it is, quite illuminating as we explore further aspects of American society in the pages to come.

A NOTE ON THE TIME SPAN OF THE STUDY AS RELATED TO THESE ATTITUDES

It was pointed out in Chapter One that this study went into the field in mid-May 1954, while the Army-McCarthy hearings were still in progress. About a third of the respondents were interviewed in May, about half in the first two weeks of June, and the remainder during the rest of June and July.

There were not many unusually dramatic events during this period. But, in any case, one would not expect the kind of latent tendencies reported here to shift markedly with ups and downs in the news over a period of a few weeks or even of several months.

There is evidence consistent with the probability of little change. The date of all but 51 of the interviews in the cross-section was reported on the questionnaires. The following table compares the tolerance scores of the national cross-section by time of interview:

Time of Interview	Relatively Less Tolerant	In-Between	Relatively More Tolerant	Total	Number of Cases
May 15–31	18%	51%	31%	100%	1476
June 1–15	19	51	30	100	2391
June 16–30	22	47	31	100	533
July 1–31	19	52	29	100	482

The differences in scores by time periods are clearly not significant. In general, the characteristics by education, etc., of those interviewed late were about the same as the characteristics of those interviewed early. We cannot, of course, say that some people's attitudes did not change during this period. But if there were changes, those in the direction of more tolerance were almost exactly balanced by other changes in the direction of less tolerance.

HOW THESE FINDINGS RELATE TO PREVIOUS KNOWLEDGE*

No previous studies have compared civic leaders with the general public, as to their attitudes toward nonconformity, in the same kind of systematic detail which the present chapter provides. But there is a wide variety of evidence about the public as a whole, as summarized by Hyman and Sheatsley (references 8 and 9 in the bibliography in Appendix E).

The readiness of most of the American public to limit the civil rights of Communists and the readiness of substantial minorities to restrict the liberties of Socialists, atheists, and other deviant or radical groups find ample support in past survey findings.

As far back as 1937, Gallup found the majority of voters in favor of banning Communist literature and of denying Communists the right to hold public office, to hold public meetings, and to express their views. (8). In 1940 a Roper survey found a majority of the people urging some kind of restriction or punitive action against American Communists (5). During the war years, when Russia was allied with the United States in the fight against Hitler, tolerance of the rights of

*Numbers in parentheses refer to sources listed in bibliography in Appendix E.

Communists in America rose slightly, but even in 1943, after the battle of Stalingrad, two Americans out of five would have prohibited any Communist Party member from speaking on the radio. By 1948 this proportion was up to 57%; by 1952 it had risen to 77%; and in a survey conducted by the NORC in January 1954, the figure was 81% (9). If it is true that speaking to a potentially nation-wide radio audience is regarded as more dangerous than "making a speech in your community" to a more limited audience (as the question was put in the present survey), our figure of 68% who would deny this right to Communists is not out of line with past findings.

The willingness of minorities (and sometimes majorities) of the public to abridge the civil liberties of groups other than Communists is also documented by earlier research. Even before World War II, for example, Roper found 44% taking the view that freedom of speech should be restricted with respect to certain times, subjects, and groups, while Gallup reported 34% of the opinion that newspapers should not be allowed to take sides during an election campaign and 41% who felt that teachers should not be free to express their views on government and religion in college classrooms. An NORC survey before the war found 25% who would deny Socialists the right to publish newspapers (8).

By 1953, those who would deny Socialists the right to publish increased from 25% to 45%, and the proportion who opposed unlimited free speech went up from 32% to 45%. Those who would forbid newspapers to criticize our form of government rose from 30% to 42%. The present findings, therefore, showing a considerable intolerance of Socialists, atheists, and other radicals, are strongly supported by all past research (8, 9).

The reader may have noticed that, while many in the present survey would allow nonconformists to make speeches and to circulate their writings, many fewer would permit them to teach in colleges and universities. This view of the college classroom as an especially sensitive area is also documented by earlier surveys. Back in the thirties Gallup found that two thirds of the public would not allow Communists to speak to student groups, and almost two out of five felt that schools should not teach the facts about Fascism and Communism. Since the war there has been general public support for teacher loyalty oaths, and there has been more opposition to Communist teachers than to permitting Communists to hold "a government job." In general, as also shown in the present study, past research has found that the degree of tolerance of Communists depends upon the perceived risk to the country or the community; and teaching, government jobs, and sensitive jobs in industry have long been barred to Communists by public opinion (8).

SUMMARY

This chapter has shown, on a large variety of individual questions and on a scale of tolerance of nonconformity, the following facts:

1. Without exception, each of the 14 types of community leaders tends to be more willing to respect the civil rights of Socialists, atheists, those suspected of disloyalty who deny they are Communists, and self-avowed Communists than either the rank and file in the same cities as the leaders or the national cross-section. A considerable variety of rights was considered—rights to speak, to hold jobs, and many others.

2. The consistency of the main findings of two different survey agencies adds confidence to the conclusions. On large samples, differences between the two agencies are negligible. On small samples of individual types of leaders, the two agencies differ considerably in some instances—but the main conclusion is the same, whether based on the samples of each agency alone or whether based on the combined samples.

3. From various points of view, the detailed attitudes reported in this chapter—even the attitudes of civic leaders—may not be a pleasant picture. But the fact that responsible community leaders are more likely than the rank and file to give the sober second thought to the civil rights of the nonconformists or suspected nonconformists here studied can be of much significance to America's future. If the reverse had been found, the future might look dark indeed to those who view with anxiety current threats to historic liberties. Plans of public education which aim at building more respect for the American tradition should be able to count on strong support from influential civic leadership at the grass roots.

57

Chapter Three

IS THERE A NATIONAL ANXIETY NEUROSIS?

To help interpret the findings in Chapter Two and in the chapters to follow, we need what light we can get on the following question:

How deeply concerned are the American people, either about the Communist threat or about the threat to civil liberties?

As was indicated in Chapter One, this survey took some care to learn the context in which an individual's opinions are held. The entire first part of the interview was a quite free-flowing conversation between the interviewer and respondent. Its purpose was to find out what things were worrying people in the summer of 1954, and to find these out with a minimum of prompting. During the first part of this conversation the interviewer was not permitted to introduce on his own initiative the topic of Communism or civil liberties or any other specific issue, lest this bias the replies.

PERSONAL AND FAMILY PROBLEMS ARE OF FIRST CONCERN

After showing credentials and obtaining consent, the interviewer opened with the question:

On the whole, do you think life will be better for you or worse, in the next few years than it is now?

This was followed by:

Everybody of course has some things he worries about, more or less. Would you say you worry more now than you used to, or not as much?

And then:

What kinds of things do you worry about most?

The answers may not be surprising to the managing editor who has to know what kind of news people like to read, or to the television producer who has to know what kind of programs most closely relate to the personal concerns of viewers, or to the precinct captain who has to deliver a vote for his political party. But they possibly will be surprising to some persons whose major concern is with great issues of the day and whose occupations are somewhat remote from the rank and file—for example, to academic people, to executives in government or business, and to some professional writers concerned with analyzing public issues.

First we shall examine the national cross-section. The separate sample of leaders will come later.

The big, overwhelming response to the question, **What kind of things do you worry about most?** was in terms of personal and family problems. Eighty per cent of the men and women in the cross-section answered *solely* in these terms. And many of the remainder answered in the same terms but went on to express anxiety about other problems. Ten per cent professed no worries about any problems.

The number of people who said that they were worried either about the threat of Communists in the United States or about civil liberties was, even by the most generous interpretation of occasionally ambiguous responses, *less than 1%!*

Even world problems, including the shadow of war, did not evoke a spontaneous answer from more than 8%. It will be argued, of course, that some people tend to suppress or mask deep anxieties about which they can do little. Being unconscious, the anxieties cannot be reported. Even if we grant this possibility, it is still hard to argue that the American people, as of the summer of 1954, were consumed with anxieties about war, not to mention internal Communism or civil liberties. Otherwise we should have heard more frequent spontaneous comments, even if the respondent talked first of personal or domestic affairs. In the "door-opener" question, the most striking fact was the essential optimism in the American climate. Only 13% said they expected life to be worse for them in the next few years than it is now—an answer which is hardly compatible with an overwhelming concern with impending doom. This is especially significant when we note that a disproportionately large number among this 13% were people in their sixties, seventies, and older, whose answers often were couched in terms of failing health or loss of earning power.

59

Yet even the most optimistic tended to have some worries and talked quite freely about them to the interviewer under the pledge of anonymity. The largest single block of personal worries involved concern over personal business or family economic problems. A total of 43% volunteered anxieties in this general area. The date of the survey must be remembered—late May, June, and July 1954. As compared with previous high levels of employment, there was a mild recession involving some unemployment or limited employment, as well as reduction in overtime. How many people would make responses like this in a period of even higher or in even lower employment, we do not know. Some illustrations:

"How to make a living for my family is my biggest worry. We've got the new house now if we can ever get it paid for. I don't worry about things like politics, because we have people who are paid to do that kind of worrying."

—*Furnace maker*, Michigan.

"My children. They are too ambitious for our income; takes more money than we've got. And I work too, in an office, to help out the income."

—*Wife of fish-hatchery owner*, Georgia.

"Meeting payments of interest and some principal on the mortgage. But I don't really worry compared with how my folks did."

—*Farm wife*, Iowa.

"Business conditions at the store worry me some. Trade isn't as good as it was."

—*Grocer*, Texas.

"Mainly with my employment now. They're having a lot of shifting around and just where will I end up? They're reducing the force in my place of work. Who's going to go and who's going to stay? Wonder if I'll be one of them to go."

—*Carpenter*, New Jersey.

"How I'll manage to finance my way through college. I'm working nights as a switchboard operator and have a responsibility to keep my mother and my younger brother."

—*College student* (male), Pennsylvania.

"I work hard when I can. I don't see where I'm getting anywhere now. I can't get no work to do."

—*Timber cutter*, Georgia.

"Paying bills. My husband has been in the hospital and may have to go back again."

—Wife of shipping clerk, New Jersey.

"I've been laid off three months. I'm worried about making a living. Doesn't seem to be much work. I worry I may lose my job, also I might get sick."

—Employee in axle plant, Pennsylvania.

"I've served my time on Guadalcanal and now I'm home minding my own business. I work graveyard shift and put in a crop besides. The plant has cut down to a four-day week. That's what bothers me. I don't worry about world problems. When trouble gets here I can take it. I'm paying taxes for someone to do my worrying for me."

—Textile worker, North Carolina.

"Ever since I came home from the Army last year I have been having troubles getting a job."

—Factory worker, Illinois.

"My job. I'm just new at managing this chain store and I'm very concerned about it."

—Grocer, North Dakota.

"I worry about my pension. Might not have enough to eat. Hard times now and no work. I want fixings for my new house, but things cost a lot."

—Coal miner, Pennsylvania.

"Money goes too fast. Food, it is so expensive. High rent. We are moving to California to see if we can get a better living there."

—Finisher in suit factory (female), New York.

"It appears that I can't prosper at nothing I do."

—Farmer, Texas.

"Security, we do not own our place. We want to and hope to. And we want to educate our children."

—Farmer, North Carolina.

"Money to take care of children, health. I have seven children and I'm 51. I wouldn't worry if I had enough money and the kids were healthy. But one of them is sick and I am off in work now. I wish business be what it was in '50 and '51."

—Tool estimator, Michigan.

"The financial future. How am I going to send my children to college?"

—Wife of telephone supervisor, Indiana.

61

"Oh God, to find work. My man started to work four days a week. So I've tried to find work too, but it's poor—only a couple of hours a week at a dress factory."

—*Wife of steelworker*, Pennsylvania.

"Trying to pay my honest and just debts."

—*Truck driver*, Alabama.

"The weather and the crops. My income depends on that."

—*Farmer*, Nebraska.

"Whether I'll sell enough cars to keep going, business conditions being what they are."

—*Auto salesman*, Massachusetts.

"I've got to support two children. If I don't work I can't pay for them. My mother-in-law keeps them and she don't have no income. Down at my plant everybody's talking about who's going to work and who's going to be laid off—talking about borrowed money if you're laid off."

—*Mixer's helper, glass factory*, Pennsylvania.

"Husband hasn't worked since January, but I really don't worry like I did when my son was missing in Burma. I depend entirely on God."

—*Wife of glass blower*, Pennsylvania.

"Cattle and hogs is about the only thing I can think about right now. And the wind and the sand."

—*Farmer*, Idaho.

"Business problems. Whether business will hold up and how to get more business."

—*Salesman*, Virginia.

"The neighborhood worries me. We need a yard. The kids have to play on the porch. I can't let them out in this dirty neighborhood. But we can't move because we've got so many bills to pay. Doctor bills and hospital bills."

—*Wife of taxi driver*, New York.

It is particularly notable that few people in the cross-section made general remarks about business conditions in the abstract. It was almost always in terms of what the situation *means to me*.

Health of Self and Family

The second largest block of answers was in terms of health, either of oneself or of members of the family. A total of 24% in the cross-

62

section mentioned health problems (including some who *also* mentioned family finances or other problems). As might be expected, a larger proportion of women than of men were in this category. Men were somewhat more likely than women to respond in terms of finances; women somewhat more likely than men to respond in terms of the health of the family, especially of the children. Some illustrations:

"I worry about my husband because he has tuberculosis of the spine and eventually faces surgery."
> —*Wife of worker in aircraft factory,* California.

"I've got a mother that isn't well and a young sister that's been in bed six years with rheumatic heart, and I don't feel so well myself."
> —*Wife of textile worker,* New York.

"I worry most about my sister, Edith, than anything else. She is mentally ill."
> —*Proprietor of soft-drink parlor,* North Carolina.

"My health. I worry most about not being able to call on the people as much as I want to. My husband is a minister and I am supposed to do a good deal of calling."
> —*Wife of preacher,* Oklahoma.

"I worry most about my children getting hurt someday driving in the traffic we have on the highways."
> —*Salesman,* Illinois.

"My health—I've got three kinds of illnesses—diabetes, cardiac, and black lumps. I've got a granddaughter paralyzed for two years and that worries me too."
> —*Retired cigar maker,* New York.

"Someone said worry is like a rocking chair. It gives you something to do and doesn't get you anywhere. I am not really the worrying kind, but I do worry about my mother's health right now."
> —*Wife of hospital orderly,* Wisconsin.

"I'm going to have a baby and I worry about if it's going to turn out all right."
> —*Wife of bellhop,* Indiana.

"It's the polio season at the present time [June] and that has me worried."
> —*Wife of furniture dealer,* Texas.

"I worry about my health. Other worries I leave to Papa. He's got the brains in the house."

—*Wife of brewery bottler*, Missouri.

"Will I get sick? I worry for fear I'd have to go to the county home. I worry about other people, too."

—*Widow of factory worker*, Pennsylvania.

Other Personal Problems

Thirty per cent of the respondents mentioned personal problems not classifiable strictly under the categories of financial or health. Some of these were included in the former categories also. They cover a miscellany of personal problems. Illustrations:

"My marriage difficulties. I have just divorced my husband."

—*Schoolteacher*, California.

"I worry about having the ability to raise my children to be God-fearing children. I have two boys coming up and I wonder what will become of them."

—*Wife of electrician*, Georgia.

"It's the future of the children. I don't care for much in an economic way, as much as I concern myself with their contribution to society. What I'm trying to get at is that I want to provide them with a good perspective."

—*Insurance salesman*, North Dakota.

"I worry about my son in the Navy. Also keep worrying about my younger son. Hope he won't get in any trouble."

—*Wife of construction worker*, Indiana.

"I worry about my husband living in another city from mine."

—*Wife of oil driller*, Kentucky.

"I wish my wife was a better housekeeper. When I was married I found out she was dirty and I had to come home and clean."

—*Steelworker*, Pennsylvania.

"In-law troubles worry me most. Just trying to keep peace in the family and get along with my daughters-in-law. Otherwise I have no worries."

—*Wife of foundry worker*, Washington.

"The draft. My husband is subject to the draft and that's the only thing I worry about."

—*Wife of a college student*, New Jersey.

"My children's welfare. I work all day at an office and have two small children at home. That keeps me occupied. I am worried too about my father's health. Daddy is in the hospital now."
—*Wife of grocery clerk,* Georgia.

"My 17-year-old son wants to marry and that really is bothering me."
—*Wife of implement dealer,* Nevada.

"Well, you know we have a girl 13 and the way things are—my goodness, the things that happen—I'm afraid to let her out after dark."
—*Wife of restaurant owner,* California.

"I worry about the care I'll get when I get older. I'd probably have to go into a home eventually."
—*Widow, practical nurse,* New York.

"If things go wrong with the house I don't know how to go about repairs. Being a woman alone, employing mechanics and things I'm inclined to think they take advantage of you."
—*Widow,* Connecticut.

"I worry about getting pregnant again. My doctor tells me not to worry, but I do."
—*Wife of maintenance man, furniture factory,* Wisconsin.

"Living in town and I like the country but I married a town lady the second time. I need the country."
—*Retired farmer,* Georgia.

"I don't have any worries except about the baby we're having. When it arrives, there will be a big difference in ages between our boy, 11, and the baby."
—*Farmer's wife,* Kansas.

"I guess I worry about my people mostly. I ran away from home at 13. Never saw my family for years. Now I'm in the middle between my wife and family. They don't like each other."
—*Tavern proprietor,* New Jersey.

"I worry about my grandsons. Their mother and father are divorced. The mother works and the children are in the care of others. It would be better if the mother could make a home for them."
—*Wife of locomotive engineer,* Wisconsin.

"I worry about my children's future, especially about some of the playmates they have. And about their health."
—*Wife of lumber estimator,* Kentucky.

"I worry about our children. Will I be able to educate them and will they be able to grow up without getting into trouble?"

—*Farmer*, Texas.

Concerns about World Affairs, Including War

In interpreting the responses of those concerned about war, one must exercise two cautions, in addition to noting the possibility that some people may be suppressing or masking their anxiety.

On the one hand, the figure of 8%, which we have cited, includes everybody who mentioned the international situation or world affairs, even if he did not explicitly speak about war or Russia or atom bombs. In fact, less than half of this 8% directly used the word "war." Responses were quite commonly couched in such terms as: "I don't like what is happening in Asia," or "I worry about what Russia is up to," or "When will the international situation settle down?"

On the other hand, some people who responded in personal terms may have been anxious about war but resisted verbalizing their anxiety even though they were not suppressing it. If a mother says, "I am worried about the future for my children," she may be thinking explicitly about war, but we cannot tell unless she offers further information. Interviewers were carefully instructed not to put forth suggestions of their own but rather to probe by asking general questions like, "You say you worry about the future of your children. What things about their future do you worry about especially?"

Some interviewers were more skillful than others in this difficult art of non-directive interviewing. Some tended to accept the first answer and dispense with probing. Others, to an extent we do not know, may have been too explicit in further probing. In any event, further probing on such questions often made it quite clear that the respondent was thinking in terms of family finances or risks of accident or illness, or of possible juvenile delinquency.

Among the 8% who, by a generous interpretation of their responses, expressed anxiety about world affairs, about one in ten couched his or her worry explicitly in personal terms. Examples:

"The biggest worry is about our boy in R.O.T.C. We wonder if they take him in the Army, that will mean the end. Will he have any future? War would ruin his future."

—*Purchasing agent*, New York.

66

"I can get into an awful stew about the next war. Whether my son will go to war. Russia—why do they want to control so much and not let everyone live in peace?"

—*Wife of engraver*, Massachusetts.

"A son in the service. Things look bad. We can't go on forever feeding the youth of the world into wars and bloodshed."

—*Teacher*, California.

"I worry about this war business because one of my grandsons just returned and another soon will be called."

—*Farmer*, Indiana.

"Worry about my youngsters. One is in Korea, and I do worry about how the war will affect them all. I am afraid America is going to be drawn into another world war. We're living in fear."

—*Foreman*, North Carolina.

"With a boy 15, I'm concerned about the war."

—*Textile worker* (female), New Hampshire.

"I worry about war, as I'm still in the age. I don't know where I stand. I don't like wars and I wouldn't want to leave my family either."

—*Milk delivery man*, Pennsylvania.

"World War III. I am of draft age and I have a wife."

—*Machinist*, West Virginia.

"I am worried about my grandson going to war."

—*Master mariner*, Washington.

It must be remembered, however, that such responses are not typical. They come from less than 1% of the cross-section. The more frequent comments about war were of the order: "I worry quite a bit about the atom bomb"; "I hope Eisenhower won't let us get mixed up in Indo-China"; "Oh, why can't we live in peace like we used to?"; or, as a Louisiana farm wife put it, "I hate to think about carrying off our home boys and they being slaughtered up."

Other Local and National Problems

There was a miscellany of expressions of concern about other local and national problems, including the subject of Negro segregation, and including some comments about the political and economic scene, not couched in a personal reference. These are again somewhat difficult to classify, but at the most they do not aggregate more than about 6% of all responses.

Communists and Civil Liberties

We come now to the truly minuscule proportion of the national cross-section which was sufficiently worried about the internal Communist threat or the threat to civil liberties to mention it.

Actually, the figure of 1% is an overstatement. From the context of the remarks, it was not always possible to separate comments about Communist aggression abroad from those about Communist infiltration in the United States. For example, such a comment as the following: "I am worried about the Communists. They are more deadly than most people think." In such a case, the interviewer should have probed further, but this was not always done. The few explicit comments about Communist infiltration can be illustrated by the following:

"I am worried most about Communism and all activities sponsored by subversives in all branches of our government and in education."
—*Wife of physician*, California.

"American Communists. I am afraid we might be sold out."
—*Postal clerk*, New Hampshire.

"I am 100% American. Seventh generation in America. I worry most about Communists and their influx into America—subversives in our government."
—*Wife of attorney*, Indiana.

"Gradual selling out of our country to foreign ideologies following the Communist line and getting away from American individualism. The U.N. was a good idea but at present detrimental to our country. It is being run by Communists."
—*Insurance man*, Texas.

"So many honest decent Americans have swallowed sugar-coated Marxism."
—*Caterer*, Connecticut.

"I pray the Lord that the Communists won't get a hold of our government and our schools. I pray the Lord will strengthen our President."
—*Widow of farmer*, Arkansas.

68

If the expressed anxieties about Communist infiltration were few, those about the threat to civil liberties were even fewer. This, like the small response on the Communist threat, is particularly surprising in view of the timing of the study. The Army-McCarthy hearings were not over when the survey went into the field and were still fresh in the minds of most respondents. Only a mere handful—not over 20 out of nearly 5000 respondents in the cross-section—volunteered a worry about civil liberties, excluding a few where the context was clearly in terms of Negro-white segregation. These comments were almost invariably personalized in terms of Senator McCarthy as a symbol. Examples:

"I am concerned about McCarthy—a potential Hitler. It's bad to have a man who gets hold of people as he does. I believe in wiping out Communism. If we can keep him from getting too much power, we wouldn't have to worry. We have to be on the job against Communism, but I think that Eisenhower and the Army, Navy, and State Department are capable."
—*Wife of school superintendent*, Delaware.

"I am most worried about what McCarthy is doing to our American way of life."
—*Businessman*, Georgia.

"McCarthy being allowed to do as he does concerns me greatly."
—*Wife of owner of trucking business*, Iowa.

"I'm concerned about the fact that McCarthy can pull all the stuff he's pulled. All he develops is the froth on top of the glass and no beer underneath. For 14 years I said J. Parnell Thomas was a mental two-spot, not fit to be in Congress. Neither is McCarthy, though he has a little more brains."
—*Newspaper editor*, New Jersey.

We have seen, then, in response to the question, **What kinds of things do you worry about most?** most Americans answered in terms of personal, family, or business problems. Only a small minority expressed anxiety about problems outside the orbit of their immediate personal life—even the threat of war. And in spite of all the headlines and radio and television stimuli, very few mentioned either the internal Communist threat or the threat to civil liberties.

69

WHAT A SECOND PROBE REVEALED

So much for a question that sought responses without suggestion or coaching. This question was followed immediately in the interview by another: **Are there other problems you worry or are concerned about, especially political or world problems?**

This question was designed, on the basis of careful pre-testing, to accomplish two purposes: One, to encourage responses from people who might feel "worry" to be too strong a word but who would reply in terms of "concern." Two, by suggesting non-personal problems, but not specifying them, to find out what further matters were high on the list of concerns.

Half of the people in the cross-section, 52% to be exact, said they had nothing to add.

But the additional question did succeed in raising the number who expressed a concern about world affairs from an initial 8% to 30%. In a great many cases, the concern seemed somewhat perfunctory; such as, "Oh yes, I guess I would say I'm concerned about what's going on in world affairs." There is presumably a "prestige effect" in saying that one is concerned about world affairs, not unlike that which leads a person to say that he reads the editorial pages of a newspaper regularly, even when his usual diet is the comic strips. In view of this possible bias, it is surprising that the number is as low as 30%. Of these, about half spoke explicitly about their concern about war, and others voiced such a concern implicitly.

Stimulated by this second probe, the number speaking of the Communist threat rose from less than 1% to about 6%, including some of the same people who spoke about foreign affairs.

The number expressing concern with civil liberties (apart from the segregation question) rose from less than 1% to about 2%, certainly not a spectacular increase.

WHAT PEOPLE DISCUSS IN CONVERSATIONS

Next, a third question was introduced, to cast the net in a somewhat different way: **We are interested in what kind of things people talk about. Offhand, what problems do you remember discussing with your friends in the last week or so?**

This is a rather unsatisfactory question for a survey spread over several weeks in time. It is too dependent on events in the news of the day, local or national. Personal and familial problems again headed the list, this time mentioned by 50% of the respondents. World problems, including war, were mentioned by 28%; problems of the local community, by 21%; "McCarthyism" (mostly references to the Army-McCarthy hearings), by 17%; economic problems, not personal, by 15%; other national problems, including politics, by 15%; Negro-white problems, including segregation, by 9%; and the problem of Communists in the United States, by 6%. An attempt to derive a figure for the number talking about civil liberties is not possible—most who said they talked about the Army-McCarthy hearings, for example, did not elaborate and were not pressed to do so.

Figures on what people say they talked about must not be taken too seriously. They are important for the present purposes only in that they supply no decisive additional evidence of a burning preoccupation with either the internal Communist threat or with the threat to civil liberties.

Next in the interview, a *check list* was tried of things people might be talking about. The respondent was handed a card with a list of 12 topics, such as danger of World War III, possibilities of another depression, and various others. (The order of the items was varied in a systematic way to reduce bias from order of presentation alone.) The question was asked: **Which ones do you remember talking about with your friends in the last week or so?**

This approach is least defensible of all as a serious research inquiry. Poorly educated people have difficulty with such a check list, and it is very easy for a glib respondent at any educational level to say "Yes" to all or most of the items suggested. Nevertheless, there is some value in providing a probable upper boundary to the percentage of people who have some current interest in a problem. Most frequently mentioned were high prices of things one buys, 52%; Negro-white relationships, 46% (the Supreme Court decision on segregation was current news); crime and juvenile delinquency, 37%; danger of World War III, 35%; Communists in the United States, 34%; high taxes, 32%; possibilities of another depression, 29%; atom or hydrogen bombs, 25%; farm prices, 19%. At the bottom in frequency was the category, "threats to freedom in the United States," checked by 17%. This last category was an unhappy choice because of its ambiguity. To some people, as we can see from a reading of later answers to the questionnaires, it meant threats to civil liberties, especially from those seeking to rid the country of Communists; to others it meant threats to the American way of life from Communists themselves. The ambiguity showed the item to be a good example of the kind of item *not* to use on a survey of this type.

Without defending the validity of the responses to any of these items, we can note that whatever bias is present should tend to be in the direction of exaggeration. Hence when 34% checked that sometime during the past week they talked about Communists in the United States, we can take it as a very generous outside figure.

After checking off the subjects which they claimed they talked about in the past week, respondents were asked: **Which one on that whole list seems most important to you?** We find that in the cross-section 12% said "Communists in the United States" was the most important of these topics. Almost the same proportion called "threats to freedom" the most important—whatever that phrase may have meant to them.

The significance of these results, like those from the free-answer question on topics discussed, lies not in any exact figures but rather in the fact that, by providing upper bounds, they add some confirming evidence to the earlier intimations that for most people neither the internal Communist threat nor the threat to civil liberties was a matter of universal burning concern. Such findings are important. They should be of interest to a future historian who might otherwise be tempted, from isolated and dramatic events in the news, to portray too vividly the emotional climate of America in 1954.

HOW CONCERNED ARE THE COMMUNITY LEADERS?

The questionnaire that was given to the national cross-section also was given to the arbitrarily selected sample of community leaders whose attitudes we studied in Chapter Two. Thus far in the present chapter these leaders have not been mentioned, nor are they included in the data thus far reported.

Let us now look at these selected leaders. Going back to the question, **What kinds of things do you worry about most?** we find that among the leaders, as among the cross-section, personal and family problems are most frequently mentioned. The data are portrayed in Chart I. A smaller proportion of the leaders than of the cross-section

CHART I

WHAT PEOPLE SAY THEY WORRY ABOUT MOST— COMMUNITY LEADERS AND NATIONAL CROSS-SECTION COMPARED

QUESTION: *What kinds of things do you worry about most?*

PERCENTAGE OF PEOPLE WITH A GIVEN TYPE OF ANSWER

PERSONAL OR FAMILY ECONOMIC PROBLEMS	LEADERS	28%
	CROSS-SECTION	43%
PERSONAL AND FAMILY HEALTH PROBLEMS	LEADERS	16
	CROSS-SECTION	24
OTHER PERSONAL AND FAMILY PROBLEMS	LEADERS	38
	CROSS-SECTION	30
WORLD PROBLEMS, INCLUDING WAR	LEADERS	22
	CROSS-SECTION	8
COMMUNISTS OR CIVIL LIBERTIES	LEADERS	5
	CROSS-SECTION	
OTHER NATIONAL OR LOCAL PROBLEMS	LEADERS	25
	CROSS-SECTION	6
"NEVER WORRY"	LEADERS	11
	CROSS-SECTION	9

Community leaders, 1500 cases; national cross-section, 4933 cases. Percentages add to more than 100 per cent, since multiple answers are possible.

73

mentioned personal or family economic or health problems, but somewhat more mentioned other kinds of personal or family problems. As might be expected, more of the leaders than of the cross-section were likely to say they were worried about world problems, including war, or about other national and local issues. The proportion spontaneously mentioning Communists or civil liberties is very small—only 5%—although it is appreciably larger than the corresponding proportion in the cross-section.

Parenthetically, it may be reported that the pattern of responses shown in Chart I would be almost identical if the data were based solely on the American Institute of Public Opinion sample or the National Opinion Research Center sample, respectively. Responses in some categories differ by a few percentage points, but nowhere by enough to affect the interpretation. Hence the data are shown for the two surveys combined. The same observation applies to all other statistics cited in this chapter.

Our second free-answer question, **Are there other problems you worry or are concerned about, especially political or world problems?** raised the proportion of community leaders mentioning world problems to 50% as compared with 30% in the cross-section. The number mentioning Communism explicitly went up to 14% as compared with 6% among the rank and file. The number mentioning civil liberties rose to 3% as compared with 2% in the rank and file.

Further comparisons show, as might be expected, that the community leaders were more likely than the cross-section to *volunteer* that they talked about world affairs, 44% as compared with 28%; "McCarthyism," that is, in most cases, the Army-McCarthy hearings, 27% as compared with 17%; and Communism in the United States, 17% as compared with 6%. Likewise, on every check-list item, they were more likely to say they discussed a given topic in the past week.

Although 62% of the leaders, as compared with 35% of the cross-section, said on the check list that they had talked about Communism in the United States, the proportion who rated it the Number One problem in importance on the list was 15%, only slightly higher than the 12% among the rank and file.

For the purposes of the present study, the most significant finding is the *absence* of striking evidence of deep personal concern among the majority about either the Communist threat or the threat to civil liberties. Even among the community leaders, personal, family, and business problems clearly take high priority among their anxieties, along with other world, national, and local issues.

HOW ARE THE EXTERNAL AND INTERNAL COMMUNIST THREATS RELATED IN PEOPLE'S MINDS?

In spite of the fact that the threat of war is an anxiety spontaneously verbalized by few people and the internal Communist threat by still fewer, it is also a fact that most people have opinions on both subjects when asked direct, explicit questions.

We should expect that people who say that war with Russia is imminent or likely would also be more apt than others to tell us that the internal Communist threat is very dangerous, since both dangers are aspects of the same international conspiracy to conquer the free world.

Or *should* we expect this? The findings earlier in this chapter are at least not inconsistent with the theory that people tend to suppress such frightening possibilities as an atomic war which might exterminate mankind. Lurking only in the unconscious, these anxieties could become manifest as projections upon convenient targets of aggression provided for them in the news, such as internal Communists. Those who can realistically face the danger from the outside might not have to build up in their minds an exaggerated internal threat and might not even be sensitized to the threat at all. Those who cannot face the external danger realistically would see the internal threat as lethal. In terms of this hypothesis, we could expect that those who overtly appear to be least alarmed about the imminence of war might be the most concerned about the internal threat.

In the latter part of the interview on which this study is based, several direct check-list questions about the internal Communist threat were asked. They will be reviewed in later chapters, but it may be of interest to select one for brief consideration at this point. It is: **How great a danger do you feel American Communists are to this country at the present time—a very great danger, a great danger, some danger, hardly any danger, or no danger?**

75

The percentages giving each answer were:

	Community Leaders	National Cross-Section
A very great danger	15%	19%
A great danger	22	24
Some danger	45	38
Hardly any danger	15	9
No danger	2	2
Don't know	1	8
Total	100%	100%
Number of cases	1500	4933

Along with this question let us consider two questions about war with Russia:

In your opinion, how likely is it that World War III will break out in the next two years?

	Community Leaders	National Cross-Section
Very likely	10%	17%
Rather likely	16	25
Rather unlikely	45	25
Not likely at all	23	18
Don't know	6	15
Total	100%	100%

Cross-tabulating the answers to these questions, we find that people who are disposed to think that World War III is very likely or rather likely within two years are also more disposed than others to think that the Communist danger is "very great" or "great":

PERCENTAGE, AMONG THOSE WITH A GIVEN OPINION ABOUT WAR, WHO SAY AMERICAN COMMUNISTS ARE A GREAT OR VERY GREAT DANGER

	Community Leaders	National Cross-Section
Think war "very likely"	42% (144)	56% (749)
Think war "rather likely"	47 (208)	52 (1064)
Think war "rather unlikely"	33 (623)	42 (1143)
Think war "not likely at all"	32 (320)	38 (775)

Number of cases in parentheses.

76

Consider also the following question: **Of these three ways of dealing with Russia, which do you think is best for America now?**
(Alternatives printed on card handed to respondent.)

	Community Leaders	National Cross-Section
Fight Russia	13%	14%
Have nothing to do with Russia	17	17
Talk over problems with Russia	62	61
Don't know	8	8
Total	100%	100%

When we cross-tabulate the answers to this question with estimates of the severity of the internal Communist threat, we find that the activists who say that we ought to fight Russia now are the most likely to see the internal threat as a serious danger:

PERCENTAGES, AMONG THOSE WITH A GIVEN OPINION ON HOW TO DEAL WITH RUSSIA, WHO SAY AMERICAN COMMUNISTS ARE A GREAT OR VERY GREAT DANGER

	Community Leaders	National Cross-Section
Think we should fight Russia now	53% *(186)*	59% *(589)*
Think we should have nothing to do with Russia	41 *(236)*	47 *(667)*
Think we should talk things over with Russia	40 *(873)*	44 *(2475)*

These findings do not support the hypothesis that those who are overtly least alarmed about the *external* threat may be suppressing their anxieties and therefore may be most likely of all to view the *internal* threat with alarm. This tendency may be operating among some people, and the net used in this survey may have too coarse a mesh to catch the evidence. But the data lend main support to the idea that most people who anticipate peace are not suppressing deep anxiety. Most of them may be perceiving the situation calmly, even optimistically. Because the external and internal threats are seen as two aspects of the same problem, such persons tend also to be less bothered than others about the Communists within our gates.

DO PEOPLE THINK THEIR OWN FREEDOM
OF SPEECH IS ENDANGERED?

The fact that so few people list threats to civil liberties among either their primary worries or their secondary concerns does not mean, of course, that civil liberties are not valued highly. Like the air one breathes or the water one drinks, one may presume that American freedoms are taken for granted. Only if the air over a city is polluted by smog, or if drought cuts off the water supply, or if civil rights are put dramatically into jeopardy would one expect an arousal of anxiety or concern.

There are some people whose anxiety is aroused because they think the actions to repress the Communist threat have generated a climate that puts civil rights in jeopardy. From the spontaneous expressions we have been reviewing, it would appear that such people are very few in number in the total population.

However, it seemed wise to probe somewhat further in one area of civil liberties. Specifically, do people feel that their own right to speak their mind has been abridged? This subject was explored rather early in the interview, *before* any explicit questions on attitudes toward the Communist threat.

First, the respondent was handed a card and asked to choose that one of three responses which was closest to his own opinion. The results:

	Selected Community Leaders	National Cross-Section
All people in this country feel as free to say what they think as they used to	52%	56%
Some people do not feel as free to say what they think as they used to	41	31
Hardly anybody feels as free to say what he thinks as he used to	7	10
Don't know	—	3
	100%	100%

Those answering "some people" or "hardly anybody" were asked: **Which groups or kinds of people may feel less free now to speak their mind than they used to?** Multiple answers were recorded if given,

78

and at the same time there are many persons who had no opinion. It is interesting that 4% of leaders and cross-section alike said "Communists," or "subversives," or "traitors." Others mentioned by more than 1% were as follows:

	Selected Community Leaders	National Cross-Section
People in government, public life, public eye	16%	7%
Educators, intellectuals	11	3
"The average person"	9	10
Non-Communist liberals	5	2
Special minorities, like foreign-born, Negroes, etc.	2	4

As would be expected, almost unanimously they agreed that this abridgment of freedom of speech was a bad thing for the country, but some noted exceptions: for example, the government official entrusted with classified information whose freedom to speak is of necessity restricted.

All respondents were then asked: **Is this something you have thought about lately a great deal, some, a little, or hardly at all?** There is an intrinsic bias in favor of answering any such question in the affirmative; hence those who said "A great deal" constitute probably an inflated and almost certainly a maximum outside figure. The answers:

	Selected Community Leaders	National Cross-Section
Thought about it:		
A great deal	35%	16%
Some	24	19
A little	11	13
Hardly at all or don't know	30	52
	100%	100%

These questions were designed mainly to set the stage for three more crucial questions, probing for personal involvement.

79

The interviewer asked, **What about you personally? Do you or don't you feel as free to speak your mind as you used to?** The results:

	Selected Community Leaders	National Cross-Section
Yes, as free	85%	87%
No, less free	13	13
Don't know	2	—
	100%	100%

The 13% in turn were asked: **How do you feel about this? Does it bother you, or not?** Replies:

	Selected Community Leaders	National Cross-Section
Much	5%	2%
Some	5	6
None	3	5
	13%	13%

Those who said they felt less free to speak their minds also were asked, **In what ways? Why?** The free answers are classified as follows:

	Selected Community Leaders	National Cross-Section
In general, to keep out of trouble	4%	6%
Would hurt my job or business	4	2
Would be suspected of being too radical	2	1
Just because I am getting older	1	1
I might be talking to a subversive	—	1
Don't know	2	2
	13%	13%

Although, as we saw above, only a small minority—5% of the community leaders and 2% of the cross-section—said they were much bothered about the restriction of their freedom to speak, a few of them spoke with considerable indignation or anxiety. For example, some quotations from leaders:

"Being a labor leader, there are things I might say which could be misconstrued and used against myself and my organization. The radio, TV, and press have publicized subversive activities to the extent that people are beginning to mistrust life-long friends."

—*Labor leader*, West Virginia.

"Because of the McCarthy affair and the general witch hunt, people are suspicious of political beliefs. But we are putting a book on Communism into our library."

—*Chairman, library board*, Colorado.

"I am speaking perfectly freely to you. However, I give a lot of speeches; I wouldn't dare speak freely. I never know who will be in the audience. It's an awful situation."

—*President, local bar association*, Ohio.

"I feel freer now than I did three months ago and less free than I did three years ago. Because of the tendency to foster regimentation in public thinking, in part due to demagogues like McCarthy and pressure groups, there has been an atmosphere of hysteria and thought control."

—*President, local bar association*, California.

"If people feel very strongly about individual freedom, they run the risk of being called Communist because of the trend of the times. If I identified myself with groups with unpopular views, I too might be labeled Communist."

—*Newspaper publisher*, Michigan.

"Well, I have to be careful because of my position. I have to be careful not to express liberal views which run counter to ideas which have been built up for the public. Because of the unrest and the investigations, people look at neighbors and even close personal friends with hesitation."

—*Chairman, Republican County Central Committee*, New Jersey.

"Fear of being misunderstood or misquoted. It would and does reduce my effectiveness as a citizen. Too many experts are afraid to speak up for fear of being called disloyal."

—*Chairman, Community Chest*, Missouri.

While such comments could be multiplied from the questionnaires, it is extremely important to keep in mind their rarity as compared with the total number of respondents. Moreover, most of the comments actually made, as the last tabulation presented suggests, were less specific—like that of the New York State mayor who said, "I'm in politics, and there's no point in saying something that can be attacked unless you must." Or the Chamber of Commerce president in Texas who said, "In business we can't have adverse publicity. You hardly dare voice an opinion which might be misconstrued." Finally, it should be noted that threats to freedom of speech can cut in different directions. There was a scattering of mentions of fear of reprisal at the hands of liberals:

"You are accused of prejudice if you speak out about minority groups, accused of causing ill feeling among people. For instance, you can't say anything against Jews or Catholics, only against Protestants."

—*Lawyer,* New Jersey.

"People are afraid to talk about Negro-white problems lest they be accused of discrimination. You can't really discuss things frankly or you've insulted freedom. I think Negroes are wonderful people, but I wish some of them—especially the younger ones—would take the chip off their shoulders."

—*Labor-union president,* Connecticut.

How shall we interpret the finding that only 5% of the community leaders and only 2% of the national cross-section say, even on a check-list question, that they are personally "much" bothered about infringement of their right to speak their minds? It is a finding consistent with evidence offered earlier in this chapter that the vast majority do not experience a serious assault on their civil liberties. If they did, evidence almost certainly would have appeared in this survey, to which people trustingly confided highly personal problems, and in which they expressed freely their opinions with every appearance of frankness, on a variety of sensitive topics.

It should be noted once again that the general picture we get is the same, whether we pool the data from the two agencies making the survey, as has been done in this chapter in the interests of brevity, or whether we review each agency's sample separately.

These findings do not refute the possibility that in certain limited but important enclaves of the population there is a climate of anxiety far different from that reported here. What about the government? Even if in Washington the anxiety should be found mainly in certain sectors, as in the State Department, for instance, the situation giving rise to it could be of extreme importance for the nation. And what about scientists and university people generally? Consequences of unnecessary repression of such people, if it exists, could be of immediate significance in the defense program, which depends on our keeping ahead of Russia in the race to produce better weapons, both material and ideological. And the longer-range consequences of limitations on American intellectual creativity would not be pleasant to contemplate. Samples of opinion from government officials or from scientists are too small in the total cross-section to permit any conclusion about their attitudes to be drawn from the present study. But further research is needed, aimed specifically to assay experience and opinion among such strategic persons.

TWO BROAD CLASSES OF PEOPLE: THE MORE INTERESTED AND THE LESS INTERESTED

While this chapter has shown that few people have feelings of deep personal involvement either with respect to the internal Communist threat or with respect to the threat to civil liberties, we see also that most Americans do not hesitate to express opinions of the kind already reviewed in Chapter Two.

This evidence of lack of involvement should make us all the more cautious about accepting the responses in Chapter Two as other than *latent* tendencies. Few people, indeed, have been in a position where action in terms of these tendencies has been called forth. But some people are more likely than others to become involved in the future and to translate their latent tendencies into action.

Since we cannot usefully divide our population for further analysis into two large groups according to amount of present personal involvement, we seek another way of segregating those most likely to be interested in the problems and thinking about them. In one sense, we have done this already, for the community leaders clearly have given more thought to these problems than the rank and file. But we would like to subdivide the national cross-section itself into at least two broad groups, *by degree of interest.*

This can be done quite conveniently, it turns out, by utilizing a simple check-list question asked near the end of the interview. The question is: **Frequently there is something in the news about Communists in the United States and what is being done about them. On the whole, would you say you follow this news very closely, fairly closely, or hardly at all?**

83

The responses in the national cross-section were, for the two survey agencies separately and for the combined sample:

	AIPO Sample	NORC Sample	Combined Sample
Very closely	13%	10%	11%
Fairly closely	45	44	45
Hardly at all	42	46	44
	100%	100%	100%

Corresponding figures for the combined sample of community leaders are: very closely, 26%; fairly closely, 61%; hardly at all, 13%, with the two agencies differing by only one percentage point.

For convenience in later analysis, in order to have two large groups of the cross-section, we shall combine those who answer "very closely" and "fairly closely" and call them the "more interested" people.

In spite of the fact that any single item is rather untrustworthy and that an item like this one is usually inflated by people expressing more interest than they really have, we shall find the subdivision into two groups important for interpreting later tabulations.

A variety of cross-checks, which hardly need be reviewed in detail here, shows that this item relates closely to other items to which it should relate if it is to have validity.

For example, as would be expected, practically all of those who expressed in their free comments earlier in the interview a worry or concern with Communism or civil liberties or with world problems or foreign affairs are in our "more interested" group, as are those who said they discussed such topics in the past week.

Those in the "more interested" group are more likely than those in the "less interested" group to say they read daily newspapers or listen to radio or television:

	Among "Less Interested"	Among "More Interested"
Percentage who say they read a daily newspaper every day	23%	67%
Percentage who say they listen to news programs on the radio every day	19	45

84

	Among "Less Interested"	Among "More Interested"
Percentage who say they listen to news programs on television every day	11%	32%
Number of cases	2155	2778

Also, we find that the "more interested" group is better informed.

In the course of the interview, the question was asked: **Do you happen to remember how Alger Hiss was caught? How?** Among the "more interested," 34% showed some accurate knowledge of the case; among the "less interested," only 9%.

At another point in the interview, the following question was presented: **There is a good deal of discussion these days about Congressional committees investigating Communism. Do you happen to know the names of any of the Senators or Congressmen who have been taking a leading part in these investigations of Communism? Who are they?**

The findings on this question may seem incredible to one not familiar with the political apathy of a major fraction of the American public. But it is a fact that 30%, nearly one third of the total cross-section sample, could not come up with a single correct name—not even the name of Senator McCarthy! Among our "more interested," 16% failed to produce a correct name; but among our "less interested," a total of 50% failed.

There is also evidence that the "more interested" are somewhat more likely to vote than others. (The number of people who say they voted tends to be an exaggeration. This human foible is, as expected, illustrated in the present survey, in which the proportion who say they voted in the 1952 presidential election is 67% as compared with the actual figure from official election records of 62%.) Among our "more interested," 74% said they voted in 1952; among the "less interested," 58%.

In the next chapter we shall analyze further the national cross-section, keeping these two "interest" groups separate. It will be instructive to keep them separate. It is upon the attitudes of the "more interested" group that we shall focus our main attention. Such people are more likely than others to include among them those who are influential, or outspoken, or reflective, or active, and who are more likely to translate an opinion into action, whatever their station in life.

WHAT PREVIOUS STUDIES HAVE SHOWN

Past surveys support the finding that the internal threat of Communism has not been a matter of salient concern among the American people. Surveys have generally put the question in terms of the "biggest problem" or "biggest danger" facing the country, thus ruling out the many answers considered here in terms of personal health and financial worries. But even when the question is put in national terms, no past survey has found more than 10% of the public listing the threat from American Communists as the country's biggest problem or danger. It is of some interest, however, that the percentage who rate Communism as the Number One problem has been increasing fairly steadily—at least until 1953. Polls conducted in 1947 and 1948, for instance, reveal fewer than 1% in this group. In 1949 it was 2%, in 1951 it reached 4% of the public, and by mid-1953 the proportion who regarded American Communists as the biggest problem facing the country had more than doubled and was at the level of 9% **(9)**. But even when the question is put in terms of the "two or three biggest problems facing the country," as Roper did in 1952, no more than 13% of the public spontaneously mentioned the internal Communist threat **(19)**.

There is little past research which is comparable to our present questions concerning feelings of freedom to speak. A different kind of trend question which has been asked periodically by the NORC may conceivably bear on the issue. This question, which asks simply, "Do you think most people can be trusted?" may be a good index of the climate of freedom. It is significant that when this question was first asked simultaneously by polling organizations in the United States and in Germany in 1948, 66% of the Americans but only 7% of the Germans expressed the view that "people" were essentially trustworthy **(17)**.

When the question was repeated in the United States early in 1954, "trust" had dropped slightly to 62% of the public. It is noteworthy, however, that among particular minority groups the feeling that "most people can be trusted" declined at a much more rapid rate. The figure among Jews, for example, dropped from 71% to 57%. Negroes, only

86

39% of whom thought people could be trusted in 1948, shifted even farther down the scale by 1954, when only 31% voiced this opinion (16).

It was noted in this chapter that nearly one third of the population could not name a single Senator or Congressman who had taken a leading part in the investigation of Communism. This lack of information on the part of a large minority of the public has also been documented by prior surveys. In June of 1953, for example, the Gallup Poll found 35% who had no opinion at all on Senator McCarthy (1). Even at the height of presidential election campaigns, the same poll has consistently found that only about half the voters can name either vice-presidential nominee and that approximately one in ten do not even know who is running for President (11). A research study by Wiebe at the time of the Kefauver investigations illustrates what its author calls "social impotence" (22).

SUMMARY

This chapter has asked: *How much personal anxiety or involvement do Americans feel with respect to the internal Communist threat or with respect to the loss of civil liberties?* We get quite a clear-cut answer. Very few Americans are worried or even deeply concerned about either issue. These issues do not even compare with issues like personal or family economic problems, personal or family health, or other family crises. A "business recession" finds a path into almost every home—whether it is that of a factory worker or that of a butcher who finds his sales of meat declining. It becomes a threat that is immediate and personal. In the same way, the threat of future war can stir apprehension in the breasts of parents of children of any age —although surprisingly few parents or other adults in our sample put war high on their list of worries. The internal Communist threat, perhaps like the threat of organized crime, is not directly felt as personal. It is something one reads about and talks about and even sometimes gets angry about. But a picture of the average American as a person with the jitters, trembling lest he find a Red under the bed, is clearly nonsense. There may be such Americans, but they are very few in number. Moreover, very few have experienced any personal threat to their freedom of speech or are really worried about the threat to civil liberties in general. They take freedom for granted. Only if the threat should come home to them in dramatic and personal ways are they likely to experience a deep concern.

If very few are deeply worried about Communism or civil liberties, there are nevertheless many who are interested in the news about such matters. Somewhat more than half of the national cross-section put themselves in that class. Since such people tend to include the better informed and the more reflective or politically active, it is important to focus special attention on them in the analysis to follow.

Of course one must not draw the inference from this chapter that the internal Communist menace or the chipping away of civil liberties does not constitute a serious problem merely because the general public is not deeply anxious about either of these problems. Rather, the state of mind reported in this chapter suggests why the very remoteness of these matters from personal involvement makes them so difficult to discuss soberly and yet effectively before the bar of public opinion.

Chapter Four

HOW TOLERANT IS THE NEW GENERATION?

Actions designed to raise the level of understanding of threats to freedom in America would be of two types: (a) short-range actions, based mainly on the media of mass communication or on organized work within local communities; (b) long-range actions, based on the education of the youth who will be the leaders of tomorrow.

This chapter assembles some data of special relevance to the longer-range actions.

Here we ask whether the younger generation is more willing or less willing than its elders to be tolerant of nonconformity.

Having found the answer, we seek to trace out how it may be related to education in America—education as reflected in child-rearing practices in the family as well as formal training in schools and colleges.

In the present chapter we shall focus our attention primarily on attitudes of those in the national cross-section who, by the classification described in Chapter Three, are more interested than others in the issues of concern to this study. Evidence was presented in Chapter Three that the people we call "more interested" are much more likely than others to be better informed and to translate attitudes into action—for example, to vote.

First let us ask: *Are those who are classed as relatively "more tolerant" on our scale, introduced in Chapter Two, likelier to be the younger people or the older people?*

The answer is clear. It is the younger people:

AGE	PERCENTAGE DISTRIBUTION OF SCORES ON SCALE OF TOLERANCE				Number of Cases
	Less Tolerant	In-Between	More Tolerant	Total	
21 to 29	10%	43%	47%	100%	528
30 to 39	11	46	43	100	682
40 to 49	15	48	37	100	615
50 to 59	18	51	31	100	426
60 and over	21	61	18	100	517

89

This result may not be surprising to many readers, but the answers to the following questions are by no means obvious:

Does this mean that a young man of 30 is likely to be less tolerant when he becomes 60 than he is today? Or does it mean that a young man at 30 is likely to be more tolerant when he becomes 60 than his father is today?

In other words, do these figures reflect mere age change within a static culture, or do they reflect some basic trends in our culture which are working toward increasing tolerance?

From one standpoint, such questions are unanswerable. Nobody knows what the external incentives for intolerance, such as the Communist threat, will be like, even a decade hence. If the threat were to increase over the years, the younger generation of today might become more intolerant as it grows older, merely because of the increase in the threat; if the threat were to decrease or disappear, the opposite might happen.

But if we are willing to imagine that the external incentives for intolerance remain constant, we may get some insight which will show us in what direction the *underlying tendencies* with respect to tolerance are headed.

Before undertaking our analysis let us seek one additional tabulation from our data. This is with respect to schooling:

PERCENTAGE DISTRIBUTION OF SCORES
ON SCALE OF TOLERANCE

	Less Tolerant	*In-Between*	*More Tolerant*	*Total*	*Number of Cases*
College Graduates	5%	29%	66%	100%	*308*
Some College	9	38	53	100	*319*
High School Graduates	12	46	42	100	*768*
Some High School	17	54	29	100	*576*
Grade School	22	62	16	100	*792*

These data, like the previous data by age, are for those in our national cross-section who are more interested in the Communist threat and how it is being combated. They show decisively that the more the schooling, the more the tolerance.

Few findings of this study are more important. It will now be placed in juxtaposition with the earlier finding—the younger the person, the more tolerant.

THE YOUNGER GENERATION HAS MORE SCHOOL-ING—WHAT DOES THIS FACT PORTEND?

There is one very crucial fact which could support the prediction that as the younger generation ages it will still be more tolerant than its elders—given more or less the same external conditions. This fact is *the greater schooling which the younger generation has received.*

In thirty years, America has seen an almost revolutionary uplift in the schooling of its population at both the high school and college levels. Consequently, if education, *independent of age,* makes for tolerance, the present younger generation, when it reaches later years, should be more tolerant than its elders are today.

In all surveys, including the Census, there is a tendency for people to report more schooling than they have actually had. Thus, some people who tell us they finished high school probably did not. And there is some inflation in the college group, although trained interviewers will keep on questioning in order to screen out trade schools which the interviewee may call college. For our present purpose it is not necessary to take the educational levels with precise literalness. It is quite safe to assume that most people who reported some high school education had more schooling than most of the people who reported grammar school only.

Chart I shows how sharply education differs by age. In the complete cross-section shown at the top of the chart, 64% of the people over 60 reported only a grade school education, as compared with only 14% of the younger people in their twenties. Among the more interested people shown in the lower half of the chart, the *pattern* is the same, but the educational level in each age group is higher.

The question that we now ask of our data is important: *Among older people, as well as among younger people, by separate age groups, are the better educated more tolerant toward nonconformists?* If so, then one cannot say that aging alone will account for a difference between generations.

Chart II shows that in *all* age groups the better educated tend to be more tolerant than the less educated. The picture is quite decisive until we reach age 60. Even among those 60 and over, those who have attended or graduated from college are more likely to be tolerant of nonconformists than those who have not completed high school, though the differences are smaller. Some bars in Chart II are based on too few cases to be decisive, but the over-all pattern is unmistakable.

CHART I

THE OLDER GENERATION HAS MUCH LESS EDUCATION THAN THE YOUNGER GENERATION

NATIONAL CROSS-SECTION
(COMPLETE)

	21 TO 29	30 TO 39	40 TO 49	50 TO 59	60 AND OVER
COLLEGE GRADUATES	8				
SOME COLLEGE	14	10			
		10	9		
HIGH SCHOOL GRADUATES	40	33	9	7	4
			20	9	6
				14	13
SOME HIGH SCHOOL	24	23	24	20	13
GRADE SCHOOL	14	24	38	50	64

NATIONAL CROSS-SECTION
(MORE INTERESTED IN ISSUES)

	21 TO 29	30 TO 39	40 TO 49	50 TO 59	60 AND OVER
COLLEGE GRADUATES	11	14			
SOME COLLEGE	15	13	14		
			10	9	5
HIGH SCHOOL GRADUATES	44	35	22	11	8
				15	19
SOME HIGH SCHOOL	21	23	24	23	13
GRADE SCHOOL	9	15	30	44	55

Numbers inside the bars show percentages; when numbers occur at the ends of the bars, they show the size of the samples.

CHART II

THE OLDER GENERATION AND THE LESS EDUCATED ARE LESS TOLERANT OF NONCONFORMISTS

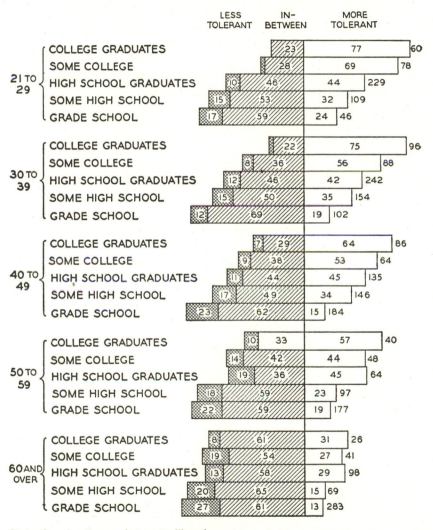

PERCENTAGE DISTRIBUTION ON SCALE OF
WILLINGNESS TO TOLERATE NONCONFORMISTS

	LESS TOLERANT	IN-BETWEEN	MORE TOLERANT

21 TO 29

COLLEGE GRADUATES	23	77	60
SOME COLLEGE	28	69	78
HIGH SCHOOL GRADUATES	10	46	44	229
SOME HIGH SCHOOL	15	53	32	109
GRADE SCHOOL	17	59	24	46

30 TO 39

COLLEGE GRADUATES	22	75	96
SOME COLLEGE	8	36	56	88
HIGH SCHOOL GRADUATES	12	46	42	242
SOME HIGH SCHOOL	15	50	35	154
GRADE SCHOOL	12	69	19	102

40 TO 49

COLLEGE GRADUATES	7	29	64	86
SOME COLLEGE	9	38	53	64
HIGH SCHOOL GRADUATES	11	44	45	135
SOME HIGH SCHOOL	17	49	34	146
GRADE SCHOOL	23	62	15	184

50 TO 59

COLLEGE GRADUATES	10	33	57	40
SOME COLLEGE	14	42	44	48
HIGH SCHOOL GRADUATES	19	36	45	64
SOME HIGH SCHOOL	18	59	23	97
GRADE SCHOOL	22	59	19	177

60 AND OVER

COLLEGE GRADUATES	8	61	31	26
SOME COLLEGE	19	54	27	41
HIGH SCHOOL GRADUATES	13	58	29	98
SOME HIGH SCHOOL	20	65	15	69
GRADE SCHOOL	27	61	13	283

Data for the "more interested" only.

93

We can say with some confidence, then, that older people are less tolerant not merely because they are older. As the educational level of those entering the older generation goes up decade after decade, we should expect our oldsters to be *increasingly tolerant*—unless external conditions change drastically.

At the same time, if we examine Chart II carefully, we observe that there is *also* a consistent tendency for the upper educational groups to become less tolerant as they get older. The percentages classed as "more tolerant" among college graduates goes down progressively on Chart II as age increases—77, 75, 64, 57, 31. A similar pattern, in spite of lower percentages throughout, exists for the "some college" group. The two high school groups and the grade school people show no very consistent tendency to become less tolerant with age, though all drop off somewhat in this respect by age 60. This does not in the least invalidate the conclusion in the preceding paragraph. We may still, in effect, predict that a person, on the average, is likely to be more tolerant than his own parents. To this we must add: Although he is likely to be more tolerant when he reaches 60 than were his own parents at 60, he may at the same time be less tolerant than he was in his own younger days.

In its implications for the future of the American scene, Chart II may have very considerable significance. Whatever may happen externally to stimulate greater or less tolerance, we now have a glimpse at the tendencies inherent in the changing structure of our population.

And we can improve that glimpse with the aid of further information from the survey.

SOME INTERESTING PSYCHOLOGICAL VARIABLES

Rigidity of Categorization

One of the aims of all education is to teach the importance of qualifying statements: for example, the concepts of true and false. In matters not immediately concerned with his daily life, the uneducated person sometimes has difficulty with statements such as, "This is likely to be true under such and such conditions; it is not so likely to be true under such and such conditions." Possibly, that is why education has somewhere been rather cynically defined as "a weakening of certainties." Moreover, one of the necessary conditions of tolerance of nonconformists would seem to be the ability to make distinctions— between the menace of a Communist in a key defense plant, let us say, and the risk to the community of a Socialist making a speech in a local hall. Rigidity of categorization—to use a rather clumsy though accurate phrase—would be expected among intolerant people in our sample.

How measure rigidity of categorization? We do not pretend to have a very good measure. Preferably we need a scale based on several internally consistent items. But one question was asked which sought, however imperfectly, to get at this factor. The interviewer read the following statement: **People can be divided into two classes—the weak and the strong,** and asked the respondent whether he agreed or disagreed with it.

Among "more interested" people, about a third disagreed and two thirds agreed. Omitting 3% who did not answer, we can cross-check the answers with the responses on the scale of tolerance toward nonconformists. Here is what we find:

PERCENTAGE DISTRIBUTION

	Less Tolerant	In-Between	More Tolerant	Total	Number of Cases
"Disagreed"	9%	42%	49%	100%	940
"Agreed" (Categorizers)	17	53	30	100	1745

The "rigid categorizers," even though defined by a single, rather crude statement, are likely to be less tolerant of nonconformists than those who disagreed with the statement.

Now let us look at Chart III. It shows that in each age group the better educated are more likely than others to disagree with the statement about two classes, the weak and the strong. The lower the educational level, the more numerous the rigid categorizers.

This finding must be regarded as suggestive rather than as proved. But the general pattern of relationships in Chart III, which says nothing whatever about Communism or radicalism, is strikingly similar to the pattern in Chart II, which was based on our scale of tolerance of selected types of nonconformists.

95

CHART III

THE OLDER GENERATION AND THE LESS EDUCATED ARE MORE LIKELY TO BE "RIGID CATEGORIZERS"

QUESTION: People can be divided into two classes—the weak and the strong. Do you agree or disagree?

PERCENTAGE "DISAGREEING" AMONG THOSE ANSWERING

21 TO 29
COLLEGE GRADUATES	73	60
SOME COLLEGE	64	76
HIGH SCHOOL GRADUATES	48	223
SOME HIGH SCHOOL	42	106
GRADE SCHOOL	33	45

30 TO 39
COLLEGE GRADUATES	60	95
SOME COLLEGE	49	88
HIGH SCHOOL GRADUATES	40	238
SOME HIGH SCHOOL	34	149
GRADE SCHOOL	28	97

40 TO 49
COLLEGE GRADUATES	55	82
SOME COLLEGE	43	63
HIGH SCHOOL GRADUATES	33	128
SOME HIGH SCHOOL	27	142
GRADE SCHOOL	23	174

50 TO 59
COLLEGE GRADUATES	44	39
SOME COLLEGE	52	48
HIGH SCHOOL GRADUATES	33	63
SOME HIGH SCHOOL	18	94
GRADE SCHOOL	24	170

60 AND OVER
COLLEGE GRADUATES	40	25
SOME COLLEGE	20	40
HIGH SCHOOL GRADUATES	23	95
SOME HIGH SCHOOL	15	67
GRADE SCHOOL	17	268

Data for the "more interested" only. Also excludes about 3% who did not express an opinion on this particular question.

96

Now let us try two more statements to tap psychological dispositions. Both have to do with ideas about child-rearing. They are:

A child should never be allowed to talk back to his parents, or else he will lose respect for them.

If a child is unusual in any way, his parents should get him to be more like other children.

People who agree with the first statement are expressing what we might call an *authoritarian* attitude; those who agree with the second, a *conformist* attitude. In their extreme forms, both tendencies, like the previous one on categorization, contain a strong element of rigidity. (The wording of each question might be improved. In particular, there may be a legitimate objection to using the words "talk back" rather than "differ." But these are old questions used in previous research, and, as will be observed, they seem to be discriminating.) We see that those who would be very strict in not letting children talk back to parents are less likely to be tolerant on our scale of tolerance toward selected types of nonconformists:

PERCENTAGE DISTRIBUTION OF SCORES ON
SCALE OF TOLERANCE

	Less Tolerant	In-Between	More Tolerant	Total	Number of Cases
"Disagreed"	7%	38%	55%	100%	979
"Agreed" (authoritarian answer)	19	56	25	100	1717

(Excluding 3% who did not answer.) Likewise, we get a relationship between strict conformity in child-training and intolerance toward the kind of adult nonconformity we are studying:

PERCENTAGE DISTRIBUTION OF SCORES ON
SCALE OF TOLERANCE*

	Less Tolerant	In-Between	More Tolerant	Total	Number of Cases
"Disagreed"	8%	41%	51%	100%	1142
"Agreed" (conformist answer)	19	55	26	100	1484

*Excluding 5% who had no opinion.

97

CHART IV

OLDER GENERATION AND LESS EDUCATED ARE LESS LIKELY TO OPPOSE AUTHORITARIAN AND CONFORMIST CHILD-REARING PRACTICES

QUESTION: A child should never be allowed to talk back to his parents, or else he will lose respect for them. Do you agree or disagree?

QUESTION: If a child is unusual in any way, his parents should get him to be more like other children. Do you agree or disagree?

PERCENTAGE DISAGREEING AMONG THOSE ANSWERING

PERCENTAGE DISAGREEING AMONG THOSE ANSWERING

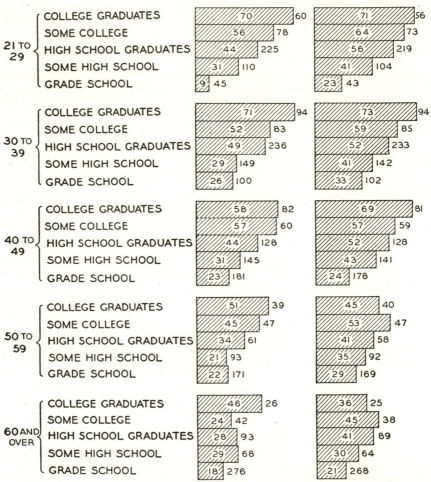

		Authoritarian	N	Conformist	N
21 TO 29	COLLEGE GRADUATES	70	60	71	56
	SOME COLLEGE	56	78	64	73
	HIGH SCHOOL GRADUATES	44	225	56	219
	SOME HIGH SCHOOL	31	110	41	104
	GRADE SCHOOL	9	45	23	43
30 TO 39	COLLEGE GRADUATES	71	94	73	94
	SOME COLLEGE	52	83	59	85
	HIGH SCHOOL GRADUATES	49	236	52	233
	SOME HIGH SCHOOL	29	149	41	142
	GRADE SCHOOL	26	100	33	102
40 TO 49	COLLEGE GRADUATES	58	82	69	81
	SOME COLLEGE	57	60	57	59
	HIGH SCHOOL GRADUATES	44	128	52	128
	SOME HIGH SCHOOL	31	145	43	141
	GRADE SCHOOL	23	181	24	178
50 TO 59	COLLEGE GRADUATES	51	39	45	40
	SOME COLLEGE	45	47	53	47
	HIGH SCHOOL GRADUATES	34	61	41	58
	SOME HIGH SCHOOL	21	93	35	92
	GRADE SCHOOL	22	171	29	169
60 AND OVER	COLLEGE GRADUATES	46	26	36	25
	SOME COLLEGE	24	42	45	38
	HIGH SCHOOL GRADUATES	28	93	41	89
	SOME HIGH SCHOOL	29	68	30	64
	GRADE SCHOOL	18	276	21	268

Data for the "more interested" only. Also excludes those who did not express an opinion on these particular questions, 3% on the authoritarian question and 5% on the conformity question.

Clearly, there are psychological elements in common between these attitudes toward child-training and our scale of tolerance.

Now, as before, let us see how age and education are related to these attitudes toward child-training. Chart IV tells the story. In the case of both authoritarian and conformist attitudes, the pattern of response by age and education is remarkably similar to Chart II. Within every age group the tendency exists, though somewhat less consistent among the oldest than among the youngest, for the less educated to approve authoritarian and more conformist child-rearing practices. Also within educational groups, particularly among the better educated, the older tend more to be authoritarian and conformist than the younger.

Just as education tends to introduce shadings of categorization between true and false, strong and weak, etc., so, presumably, it tends to encourage respect for dissenting points of view. In school, people are taught about great dissenters of history, including the founding fathers of this nation. The farther pupils go up the educational ladder, the more likely they are to learn to respect the right of people to be different from themselves, *even if* and *especially when* they disapprove of such people. This ought to be reflected in attitudes toward child-rearing. To allow a child to differ with his parents and to develop his own individuality—as long as this does not lead to anti-social behavior or delinquency—is apparently much more common in better-educated families than in others, in spite of the fact that the words "talk back" used in our question may to some people imply defiance rather than mere difference of opinion.

But let us not overlook another fact shown in Charts III and IV. That is the tendency for older people, especially among the better educated, to have more rigidly authoritarian or conformist attitudes toward child-training than younger people *at the same educational level.* Is this a mere function of aging, of hardening of the arteries? It could be, but it seems highly unlikely in the light of what we know about *changing cultural patterns* in the last thirty years. The people of 50 and over, at any educational level, were more likely themselves to have grown up in authoritarian families than the people in their twenties and thirties. "Life with Father" is as antique as the gaslight. Moreover, the climate of formal education is different today from what it was a generation ago. Corporal punishment has almost disappeared from the schools. Progressive education, even though its more extreme forms of permissiveness may be rare, has penetrated to some

99

degree into every little red schoolhouse. The older forms of drill and discipline have been replaced by efforts to motivate the child to develop his own enthusiasms and incentives to learn, and some people, including some educators, think the pendulum may have swung too far. Be that as it may, what we see in Charts III and IV—especially the latter—may be the effect, above all others, of a changing *climate* of education in both school and family.

If this is true, we need to be very cautious about guessing that when the man or woman, at a given educational level, who is 30 today becomes 60 he or she may be less tolerant than now.

Optimism as a Psychological Variable

What we have just said may lead some to conclude that *mere aging by itself* is not an important consideration at all. Before leaping to that conclusion, we need to look closely at another variable. In Chapter Three we noted that the very first question asked in the interview was: **On the whole, do you think life will be better for you or worse, in the next few years than it is now?** We observed that, in spite of many anxieties, the largest proportion of which had to do with financial, health, and other matters that were personal or familial, the majority of the cross-section seemed to be optimistic about their personal future.

Now there is substantial psychological theory which would predict a relationship between optimism about personal affairs and tolerance toward nonconformists. Optimism is not a perfect index of lack of anxiety. Some optimists may be very anxious people who are whistling in the dark. But the idea is that the individual who is very troubled, for whatever reason, needs to blame someone aside from himself for his troubles. (We discussed this same mechanism in Chapter Three, but in the much more specific context of anxieties about war.) It may be a quite unconscious process. The dark forces of Communism, some of whose followers can be suspected of operating in disguise as loyal Americans, are one of the obvious targets for blame, directly for the world's troubles and indirectly, if sometimes unconsciously, for one's personal troubles. It is consistent with such a theory, though not necessarily proof of it, that we find optimists more likely to be tolerant of nonconformists on our scale than are other people. (Those who predicted that life for themselves would be better in the next few years than it is now constituted 63% of the interested cross-section with whom we are dealing. We call them "optimists." Those who said life would be worse constituted 11%; those who said the same, 21%; and those who said "don't know," 5%. We lump all these together, not as pessimists, but as less hopeful, on the whole, than the "optimists.") Findings:

PERCENTAGE DISTRIBUTION OF SCORES
ON SCALE OF TOLERANCE

	Less Tolerant	In- Between	More Tolerant	Total	Number of Cases
"My life will be better" (optimists)	9%	42%	49%	100%	1717
All Others	18	53	29	100	1046

The relationship is significant, in spite of the imperfections of optimism as an index, and also in spite of a further psychological expectation; namely, that some people will be both optimists and relatively free of anxiety primarily because they have found a comfortable scapegoat to blame for their troubles. Such a sequential relationship, if it occurs, could be delineated only by a much more penetrating examination than the interview on which this study is based.

Now optimism is a variable which we should expect to have some relation both to education and age, as it does indeed, according to Chart V, and with a pattern on the whole very much like the patterns of the preceding charts.

The education variable could have some direct relationship to optimism-pessimism because, presumably, education should equip a person to handle better the fear of the uncertain and unknown. But, with even more plausibility and less subtlety, we can simply point out that the more educated a person is, *on the average,* the more income he is likely to have and the better and probably more secure is his future. He therefore has greater cause for personal optimism on economic grounds alone.

But what about optimism and age within a given educational group? First, let it be noted again that Chart V shows a quite regularly declining proportion of optimism with age at each educational level, with the exception of the grade school people, who are relatively low at all age groups. For example, for college graduates the figures

CHART V

THE OLDER GENERATION AND THE LESS EDUCATED ARE LESS LIKELY TO BE OPTIMISTS

QUESTION: On the whole, do you think life will be better for you or worse, in the next few years than it is now?

PERCENTAGE ANSWERING "BETTER"
AMONG ALL RESPONDENTS

		%	n
21 TO 29	COLLEGE GRADUATES	87	60
	SOME COLLEGE	85	78
	HIGH SCHOOL GRADUATES	83	229
	SOME HIGH SCHOOL	71	110
	GRADE SCHOOL	46	46
30 TO 39	COLLEGE GRADUATES	90	96
	SOME COLLEGE	78	88
	HIGH SCHOOL GRADUATES	74	242
	SOME HIGH SCHOOL	69	154
	GRADE SCHOOL	49	102
40 TO 49	COLLEGE GRADUATES	74	86
	SOME COLLEGE	73	64
	HIGH SCHOOL GRADUATES	62	135
	SOME HIGH SCHOOL	67	146
	GRADE SCHOOL	53	184
50 TO 59	COLLEGE GRADUATES	64	40
	SOME COLLEGE	56	48
	HIGH SCHOOL GRADUATES	64	64
	SOME HIGH SCHOOL	53	97
	GRADE SCHOOL	51	177
60 AND OVER	COLLEGE GRADUATES	35	26
	SOME COLLEGE	34	41
	HIGH SCHOOL GRADUATES	38	98
	SOME HIGH SCHOOL	40	69
	GRADE SCHOOL	35	283

Data for the "more interested" only.

102

by age are 87%, 90%, 74%, 64%, and 35%. One can plumb some psychological depths on the subject of age and optimism, but there are also plausible explanations on the surface. Obviously, a person of 80 can hardly be as hopeful about his future in the next few years as a man of 30. The older one gets, the more physical infirmities he or she acquires and the more worries about security. Physical and social factors which are inevitable accompaniments of aging would tend to combine in the production of increased personal anxiety, would tend to produce increased pessimism, which in turn would tend to produce increased intolerance, at least in some people. Here, then, we have a factor which should operate to make the person of 60, say, somewhat less likely to be tolerant than he himself was at 30.

This analysis has been based solely on the three fifths of the national cross-section which we have labeled as "more interested" in the internal Communist threat and the methods of dealing with it. This sub-group is a strategic one to study because it includes most, though not all, of the people who can be expected to translate opinions into action. A separate analysis has been made of the "less interested" segment of our cross-section, duplicating in most respects what we have presented in this chapter for the "more interested." The data hardly need be reported here, because without any important exceptions they show the same patterns as have been exhibited in this chapter. The only exceptions are occasionally among the better-educated people who happen to be among the "less interested." They are so few in number, however, that no conclusions about them can be safely drawn. Most of the above analysis also has been run in duplicate for the American Institute of Public Opinion and National Opinion Research Center surveys separately. The number of cases in some of the boxes gets too small for confident analysis, but it can be reported that the broad conclusions reached in this chapter, especially as based on Charts I–V, would be identical if either survey had been used alone.

Throughout this chapter, attention has been focused on the "more interested" block of the national cross-section, but not on our special sample of arbitrarily selected community leaders. These leaders, it must be remembered, are not part of the national cross-section. We shall conclude the chapter with a brief analysis of the community leaders when differentiated by age and education.

THE YOUNGER AND BETTER-EDUCATED COMMUNITY LEADERS ARE THE MOST LIKELY TO TOLERATE NONCONFORMITY

Study of the community leaders adds confirmation to what was reported above. As we learned in Chapter Two, the leaders, on the average, were much more likely than others to be tolerant toward nonconformists.

We now can report that among the community leaders the most tolerant were found among the relatively younger and better educated. Since the leaders tend to be well educated and middle-aged, we shall analyze them by two age groups, under 50 and 50 and over, and by two educational groups, college graduates and others. Findings for all leaders combined:

	Percentage Scoring "More Tolerant" on Scale	Number of Cases
College Graduates	79%	673
All Others	51	827
Under 50	70%	864
50 and Over	59	634

It will be remembered from Chapter Two that 14 types of community leaders appear in this special sample. Among these 14, there were enough cases in each of the two educational categories—college and non-college—to permit 12 comparisons by education. (Presidents of bar associations were all college graduates except one; only five of the presidents of labor-union locals were college graduates.) In all 12 comparisons, without exception, the college graduates were more tolerant than the non-college graduates. Enough cases were available to make 13 comparisons by age (only four of the presidents of the Parent-Teachers' Association were 50 years old or over). In 12 of the comparisons, those under 50 were more likely to be tolerant on our scale than those 50 and over. In one case (chairmen of the school board), the younger and older chairmen were tied in percentage among the more tolerant.

As might be expected, the community leaders were less likely than the cross-section to fall into the classes which we called "rigid categorizers" or "endorsers of authoritarian or conformist attitudes toward child-rearing." Nevertheless, many of the leaders did fall into each of these classes, and those who did tended to be less tolerant of nonconformists on our scale than those who did not. The one exception to the picture which we have seen in the cross-section was with respect to the "optimism" variable. Four out of five of the leaders said that they thought life would be better for them in the next few years than it is now, as compared with three out of five in our cross-section of "interested" people. But so few of the remainder of the leaders said life would be worse (most saying it would be "about the same") that there is no difference on our tolerance scale between those who said "better" and all others.

All in all, we may find in the special sample of leaders the same general patterns, with minor exceptions, which we found in the cross-section. Clearly, the younger generation of leadership tends to be more tolerant than the older generation which it will gradually be replacing.

RELATIONSHIP TO OTHER STUDIES

While an analysis of age and education jointly as related to tolerance of the kind of nonconformity which we are studying has not been reported before on a nation-wide basis, there is ample confirmation from past polls of the greater tolerance among the better educated. Younger adults have consistently shown greater tolerance than older adults in public opinion polls on issues such as freedom of the press or free speech (9). On the other hand, questionnaires mailed to high school students by the Purdue Panel of Young People showed a sample of high school students to be no more tolerant than adults (17).

Polling data show that while the better educated are more tolerant than the less educated, *both* classes of the population have tended to become less tolerant in recent years. For example, the proportion of college-educated people who would deny freedom of speech to a Communist increased from 31% to 71% between 1945 and 1953, while the corresponding proportions among less educated people increased from 42% to 78% (8).

With respect to the psychological factors discussed in this chapter, there is a large literature, much too detailed for systematic review here. Several national polls have shown the inverse relationship between "authoritarianism" and tolerance of nonconformity. See especially Star, et al. (20). A basic source with respect to the analysis of such variables is Adorno, et al., *The Authoritarian Personality* **(23)**.

The findings in this chapter gain in significance when seen in the context of research on tolerance or intolerance of Americans toward ethnic groups. Much of this literature is summarized in G. W. Allport, *The Nature of Prejudice* **(24)**. Studies of the educational variable indicate that it plays a larger part in questions having to do with *knowledge* of out-groups and a lesser part when *emotional attitudes* toward out-groups are in question. We cannot yet say whether the educational variable plays a larger part in attitudes toward political and social nonconformity (as in the present study) than in prejudice toward minority ethnic and religious groups. It seems reasonable to suppose, however, that well-educated people may tolerate ideological nonconformity more easily than they can ethnic and cultural differences, for the latter often arouse subtle emotions of repugnance, class distinction, and hostility. However that may be, it is clear that higher education, by and large, makes for greater tolerance of human differences, whether ideological, racial, or cultural. The question used in this chapter to measure *rigid categorization* has also proved diagnostic of ethnic prejudice **(23)**. "It is characteristic of the prejudiced mentality," says Allport, "that it forms, in all areas of experience, categories that are monopolistic, two-valued, and rigid" **(24)**. That *authoritarianism and conformist attitudes toward child-rearing* lead to intolerance is a basic argument of *The Authoritarian Personality*. It has been shown that mothers with such attitudes are more likely to have children who themselves are markedly prejudiced. Harris, et al. **(30)**. See also Frenkel-Brunswik **(28)**. Relation of *lack of optimism* to prejudice has been widely explored. While frustration, fear of the future, and personal anxiety are related to suspicion and hostility toward out-groups, the "scapegoat" theory as a single explanation is now considered too simple. Among numerous studies may be cited M. Brewster Smith **(36)**, Bettelheim and Janowitz **(26)**, Miller and Bugelski **(34)**, Morse and F. H. Allport **(35)**, G. W. Allport and Kramer **(25)**, and Zawadski **(37)**. Recent evidence suggests that American youth, as a whole, have a more optimistic outlook on the future than do youth of other nations and possibly more tolerance. Gillespie and G. W. Allport **(29)**.

Ethnic prejudice may have much the same psychological mechanisms as the intolerance of the kind of nonconformity with which this volume deals. The psychological literature has tended to treat intol-

106

erance toward nonconformity as nothing more than a special case of a disposition to prejudice in general. "Reds" and intellectuals tend to be scapegoats as well as Jews or Negroes. Lowenthal and Gutterman (31) and Luthin (32). Intolerance may be a systemic factor in personality, whatever its object, and distrust of political deviants may be only one phase of a larger social and psychological problem—distrust of one's fellow man. Yet even the man who has many targets of prejudice is not likely to be prejudiced against all possible targets. The survey reported in the present volume should be followed up by other studies specifically designed to learn what other kinds of groups are also the objects of hostility for people who are intolerant of the kind of nonconformity with which this book deals.

SUMMARY

This chapter centered its attention on education and age as related to tolerance of nonconformists, measured by our scale. The principal analysis was based on those people in the national cross-section who evinced interest (though not necessarily anxiety or concern) in the internal Communist threat and in methods of dealing with it.

The data showed that the older generation was less tolerant of nonconformists than the younger generation; also, that within each group the less educated were less tolerant than the better educated.

The fact also was brought out that the older generation tended to have much less education than the younger—reflecting the big change in American school attendance in the past thirty years.

Can we then forecast, we asked, that if external conditions are unchanged the younger people will be more tolerant when they grow older than their elders are now? Is the long-term trend toward greater tolerance of nonconformists?

Much evidence points in this direction. Not only are more of the people who are moving from youth to middle age better educated than their elders, but also they are products both of child-rearing practices and of a school system which is more apt to foster tolerance. These inferences could be drawn from an analysis of a series of psychological questions which suggested that products of modern rearing and schooling are less likely to be rigid categorizers and less likely to favor authoritarian or conformist child-rearing practices.

On the other hand, even if the people who are now 30 may still be more tolerant when they reach 60 than their elders, they may, on the average, be somewhat less tolerant than they are now. This is suggested by the tendency, among people at the *same* educational level, for the older ones to be not only less tolerant but also less optimistic about their personal future. This lack of optimism often reflects anxiety about such matters as health and old-age security. It was suggested that the presence of such anxiety is not as conducive to tolerance as its absence.

The detailed analysis presented in this chapter was carried out primarily on that portion of the national cross-section most interested in the particular issues, because it is this group which is most likely to be informed and to translate opinions into action. Further analysis, reported but not exhibited, indicated that the pattern of relationship of education and age to tolerance was essentially the same in the less interested and more politically indifferent segment of the population.

Finally, a replication of the analysis on the special sample of types of community leaders revealed that, among 12 possible comparisons of college graduates and others, all 12 showed the better educated to be more tolerant of nonconformists than the less educated. Of 13 possible comparisons of those over and under the age of 50, 12 showed the younger leaders of a given kind to be more tolerant than the older, while in one instance there was no difference in tolerance by age.

This chapter disavows a flat prediction that the next generation will be more tolerant than the present one. If the Communist threat should become greater, pressures against tolerance might increase; if the threat should become less, pressures against tolerance might decrease. Rather, this chapter seeks to weigh some of the underlying forces in American society making for or against a *tendency* toward growth of tolerance. On balance, the direction in which these underlying forces have been going should be encouraging to those who are concerned with preserving the American heritage of freedom.

Chapter Five

DOES IT MATTER WHERE PEOPLE LIVE?

Is tolerance of nonconformists scattered at random over the American map? Or do we find certain areas which have a larger proportion of intolerant people than others? If so, where?

The answers are not obvious. It would be an interesting exercise sometime to learn what kind of evidence is used to make guesses about regional distributions of attitudes.

Because all Southern Senators voted in favor of censuring their colleague from Wisconsin, it may be thought that the South is more likely than other parts of the country to be alerted to the support of the Bill of Rights, at least as implied in that particular action.

Because some very important Middle Western newspapers are conspicuously anti-liberal in editorial policy, it may be thought that the Midwest is much more anti-liberal in sentiment than the rest of the country.

Because rural people may be more likely to attend church regularly, it may be thought that they are more likely than others to practice the gospel message of tolerance.

Because the small hard core of Communists may have concentrated in our larger metropolitan centers, it may be thought that the reaction against the Communist menace and concern about its dangers would be strongest among city people.

Guesses such as these may be wrong, and some of them may be right. Or they may be right for the wrong reasons. Actually, the variables involved are many and complex. For example, some people who are unwilling to extend civil rights to Socialists and atheists also may have anti-Catholicism as part of their syndrome of intolerance. Hence, they would not be found among the supporters of a Catholic crusader against Communists or other radicals. On the other hand, some people who share one or two beliefs of a public figure or even who merely share his party label may support him even if they may dislike things he stands for. It would strain credulity, for example, to think that a Georgia farmer, a Polish auto maker in Detroit, and a schoolteacher in Harlem all shared the same sentiments because they voted for the Democratic candidate for President in 1952.

With our scale of tolerance of nonconformists we can hope to cut through the tangled brush of allegiance to particular individuals or party labels, and observe how some quite basic attitudes actually differ in different types of communities. The attitudes reflected in this scale are not of the type likely to change drastically overnight with the waxing or waning of the star of any particular public figure.

Let us look at the data from our national cross-section when broken down by four broad regions of the country—West, East, Middle West, and South. Census definitions are followed in classifying states by region. The states included in a given region may be seen from the map in Chart I.

Based on the 15-item scale of willingness to tolerate nonconformists, Chart II tells the story. The West, including the Mountain

CHART I

UNITED STATES REGIONS AS DEFINED
IN THIS CHAPTER

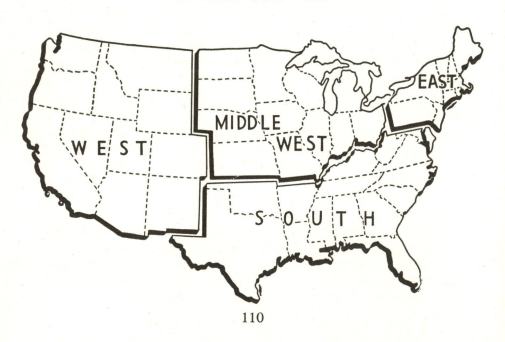

States and Pacific Coast, has the largest proportion of relatively tolerant people; next come the East and Middle West; and last comes the South.

The top set of bars in Chart II shows this for the complete national cross-section. When we select only those people who are more interested in issues raised by the Communist threat and by methods of meeting it, all of the percentages for the relatively tolerant go up, but *the rank order by regions is unchanged*. This is shown by the second set of bars in Chart II.

The two survey agencies, the American Institute of Public Opinion and the National Opinion Research Center, agree quite closely in their independent findings. The percentages for those classed as "more tolerant" on the scale, by each agency for each region, in the complete national sample were:

	AIPO		*NORC*	
West	46%	*(338)*	49%	*(321)*
East	40	*(632)*	39	*(630)*
Middle West	31	*(741)*	33	*(724)*
South	14	*(772)*	18	*(774)*

The numbers in parentheses show the size of the samples. The two agencies also rank regions in the same order when sub-samples of "more interested" and "less interested" people are treated separately.

Let us continually keep in mind the fact that we are not here measuring tolerance, in general. Rather, we are measuring willingness to grant certain rights to people whose views might be disapproved, such as the right to speak, the right to hold certain kinds of jobs, etc. The kinds of people used as test cases are Socialists, atheists, Communists, and people whose loyalty has been criticized but who avow they were never Communists. We are not measuring willingness to tolerate other kinds of people whose views may be disliked. In particular, there is no mention of problems associated with race relations.

But region is only one way of cutting the geographical pie. Another way is to ask: Who are more likely to be tolerant of nonconformists, people who live in cities or people who live in the country?

Chart II also gives us an answer to this question—*the city people* tend to be more tolerant.

111

CHART II

WHERE AMERICANS LIVE IS RELATED TO THEIR WILLINGNESS TO TOLERATE NONCONFORMITY

PERCENTAGE DISTRIBUTION OF SCORES
ON TOLERANCE SCALE

BY REGIONS

	LESS TOLERANT	IN-BETWEEN	MORE TOLERANT	

ALL CASES IN NATIONAL CROSS-SECTION

WEST	13	39	48	659
EAST	15	46	39	1262
MIDDLE WEST	16	53	31	1465
SOUTH	27	57	16	1546

THOSE PERSONS MORE INTERESTED IN ISSUES

WEST	9	40	51	410
EAST	12	43	45	738
MIDDLE WEST	13	52	35	823
SOUTH	21	58	21	806

BY TYPE OF COMMUNITY

ALL CASES

METROPOLITAN AREAS	14	47	39	1891
OTHER CITIES	19	51	30	1362
SMALL TOWNS	20	55	25	917
FARMS	29	53	18	762

THOSE PERSONS MORE INTERESTED IN ISSUES

METROPOLITAN AREAS	10	45	45	1101
OTHER CITIES	15	50	35	777
SMALL TOWNS	18	52	30	538
FARMS	22	56	22	361

Numbers inside the bars show percentages; numbers at the ends of the bars show the size of the samples.

City people are in two groups, those living in cities of 100,000 population or suburbs (using Census definitions of metropolitan area) and those living in all other cities of 2500 or above in population.

Rural people are in two groups, those living in small towns or villages (under 2500) and those living on farms.

Chart II shows, both for the complete national cross-section and for the "more interested" people, that the metropolitan areas tend to have the largest number making relatively high scores in tolerance on our scale. Other cities are second, small towns third, and farms last.

We get the same picture essentially for each of the survey agencies. For example, the comparative percentages classed as "more tolerant" on the entire cross-section were:

	AIPO		*NORC*	
Metropolitan Areas	39%	*(936)*	40%	*(955)*
Other Cities	28	*(619)*	32	*(743)*
Small Towns	26	*(509)*	23	*(406)*
Farms	16	*(419)*	19	*(343)*

The two agencies differed rather seriously in the total size of their urban and rural samples, but this does not materially affect the picture presented in Chart II. When two independent sets of percentages are in as close agreement as those shown in the table above, or as in the earlier comparison of Northern and Southern regions, we may be quite confident of the general reliability of the results.

WILL RURAL-URBAN DIFFERENCES "ACCOUNT FOR" THE NORTH-SOUTH DIFFERENCES— OR VICE VERSA?

It hardly requires an intimate knowledge of American geography to think of additional questions which might be asked with respect to our data. The South and the Middle West tend to be less tolerant on our scale than other regions. But Chart II also shows us that rural areas in general are less tolerant. Can it be that the explanation for the differences by region lies merely in the differences in the urban-rural distribution? Or vice versa?

113

CHART III

HOW MUCH MORE RURAL ARE THE MIDDLE WEST AND SOUTH THAN OTHER REGIONS?

PERCENTAGE, WITHIN A REGION, WHO LIVE
IN GIVEN TYPE OF COMMUNITY

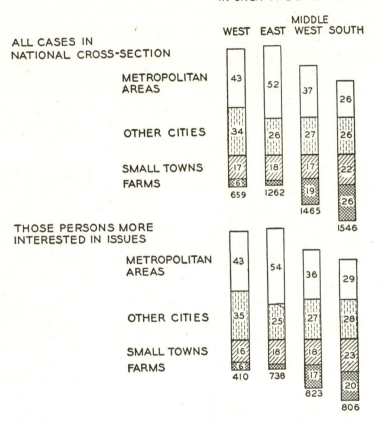

ALL CASES IN
NATIONAL CROSS-SECTION

	WEST	EAST	MIDDLE WEST	SOUTH
METROPOLITAN AREAS	43	52	37	26
OTHER CITIES	34	26	27	26
SMALL TOWNS	17	18	17	22
FARMS	6		19	26
	659	1262	1465	1546

THOSE PERSONS MORE
INTERESTED IN ISSUES

	WEST	EAST	MIDDLE WEST	SOUTH
METROPOLITAN AREAS	43	54	36	29
OTHER CITIES	35	25	27	28
SMALL TOWNS	16	18	18	23
FARMS	6		17	20
	410	738	823	806

114

First, let us check the extent to which the South and Middle West are more rural than other regions. Chart III shows the data from our samples. (It may surprise some who rove over the vast area of the map covered by the Mountain and Pacific States to learn what a large proportion of our sample in these states is urban. But cities, according to the Census, are where most Westerners live—notably in great metropolitan agglomerations in southern California, around San Francisco Bay, and in lesser urban centers such as Seattle, Portland, Denver, and Salt Lake City.)

Next, let us take all of the people in our national cross-section living in metropolitan areas and compare them alone for regional differences in tolerance. Similarly for those in other cities, taken alone, etc. Chart IV shows that in every such comparison Northerners are more likely to make high tolerance scores than Southerners. This also is borne out in Chart V, where the same comparisons are shown, but only for those people who are more interested in the issues of concern to this study.

We conclude, then, that the presence of so many rural people in the South is *not* enough to account for relative lack of tolerance in the South toward nonconformists.

As among the three Northern regions, however, the picture which was clear before we introduced type of community becomes less clear as we inspect Charts IV and V.

Among metropolitan and other urban populations, the West seems still to have the highest percentages of more tolerant people. Except in metropolitan areas, differences between the East and Middle West are now small and inconsistent. Especially in view of the very small samples of farmers in the East and West, the verdict probably should be "no striking differences" in attitudes of farmers and small-town dwellers as between the East, Middle West, and Far West.

In summary, we cannot erase the influence of regionalism as far as the South is concerned by considering rural and urban people separately. Some of the distinction between the West and other Northern regions in tolerance remains. But East-Middle West distinctions are mixed, and some may indeed have appeared initially to be as large as they did *because* the Middle West is more rural.

Now let us give the data in Charts IV and V the reverse treatment.

Can we explain why small-town people and farmers are less tolerant by the fact that so many of them are Southerners or Middle Westerners?

CHART IV

AMONG URBAN AND RURAL PEOPLE, TAKEN SEPARATELY, NORTHERNERS ARE MORE WILLING THAN SOUTHERNERS TO TOLERATE NONCONFORMISTS

PERCENTAGE DISTRIBUTION OF SCALE SCORES

FOR ENTIRE NATIONAL CROSS-SECTION

		LESS TOLERANT	IN-BETWEEN	MORE TOLERANT	

METROPOLITAN AREAS
- WEST — 12 | 34 | 54 | 282
- EAST — 11 | 42 | 47 | 663
- MIDDLE WEST — 12 | 54 | 34 | 543
- SOUTH — 23 | 53 | 24 | 403

OTHER CITIES
- WEST — 15 | 39 | 46 | 227
- EAST — 19 | 50 | 31 | 332
- MIDDLE WEST — 17 | 50 | 33 | 406
- SOUTH — 26 | 58 | 16 | 397

SMALL TOWNS
- WEST — 19 | 47 | 34 | 110
- EAST — 16 | 49 | 35 | 223
- MIDDLE WEST — 19 | 54 | 27 | 243
- SOUTH — 24 | 62 | 14 | 341

FARMS
- WEST — 15 | 50 | 35 | 40
- EAST — 25 | 57 | 18 | 44
- MIDDLE WEST — 19 | 55 | 26 | 273
- SOUTH — 37 | 53 | 10 | 405

116

CHART V

AMONG URBAN AND RURAL PEOPLE, TAKEN SEPARATELY, NORTHERNERS ARE MORE WILLING THAN SOUTHERNERS TO TOLERATE NONCONFORMISTS

PERCENTAGE DISTRIBUTION OF SCALE SCORES

FOR THOSE PEOPLE MORE INTERESTED IN ISSUES		LESS TOLERANT	IN-BETWEEN	MORE TOLERANT	
METROPOLITAN AREAS	WEST	8	32	60	176
	EAST	10	40	50	397
	MIDDLE WEST	8	53	39	295
	SOUTH	15	53	32	233
OTHER CITIES	WEST	9	41	50	143
	EAST	15	47	38	185
	MIDDLE WEST	12	50	38	223
	SOUTH	24	57	19	226
SMALL TOWNS	WEST	14	53	33	64
	EAST	14	46	40	133
	MIDDLE WEST	18	52	30	152
	SOUTH	21	62	17	189
FARMS	WEST	11	56	33	27
	EAST	22	52	26	23
	MIDDLE WEST	18	55	27	153
	SOUTH	27	58	15	158

If, within each region, the difference in tolerance by type of community tended to disappear, we would have succeeded in showing that type of community was not, in and by itself, as important as region. Again we turn to Charts IV and V. To make this comparison easier for the reader, we rearrange from these charts the percentages of people classed as "more tolerant":

	Farm	Small Town	Other Cities	Metropolitan
Entire Cross-section				
West	35%	34%	46%	54%
East	18	35	31	47
Middle West	26	27	33	34
South	10	14	16	24
For Those People More Interested in Issues				
West	33%	33%	50%•	60%
East	26	40	38	50
Middle West	27	30	38	39
South	15	17	19	32

Reading the figures horizontally, we see that in all cases the percentage "more tolerant" is higher in the metropolitan areas than in the small towns or on the farms. "Other cities" tend to be midway between metropolitan and rural, but vary somewhat erratically. The differences between small towns and farms tend also to be somewhat inconsistent.

We can safely conclude that there *are* urban-rural differences in tolerance, irrespective of region. The fact that a given type of community has more Westerners or more Southerners than the average will *not* explain why that type of community is more tolerant or less tolerant than other types. In other words, there must be *something else* about city life or about people who live in cities which tends to make them more tolerant than rural people. Incidentally, it may be reported that we reach the same conclusions if we consider only the data of either of the two survey agencies alone.

Now if there is *something else* about city life or city people which tends to make for greater tolerance, what is it? Could it be a difference in education? We know that city people are more likely to finish high school and go on to college than rural people. Likewise, we know that among farmers, for example, Northern farmers are likely to be better educated than Southern farmers. Could education account for differences in tolerance of nonconformists shown between types of com-

118

munities and between regions? We know from Chapter Four that there is a striking relationship between education and tolerance.

CAN EDUCATIONAL DIFFERENCES ACCOUNT FOR DIFFERENCES IN TOLERANCE BY REGION AND TYPE OF COMMUNITY?

First, let us check the facts asserted in the preceding paragraph. Among people living in a particular type of community—for example, farmers—are there differences in educational level between Northerners and Southerners? Table 1 answers "Yes." Similarly, Table 1 shows that within each region city people tend to get more schooling than farmers.

Next, let us sort our national cross-section into five groups by educational level.

Finally, *within each educational group,* let us repeat all of the analysis of the relationship between region, type of community, and tolerance. The results appear in Table 2 for the national cross-section and in Table 3 for the "more interested" in issues.

Now, what do Tables 2 and 3 tell us? They give us a good deal of information but must be read cautiously. No individual percentage is shown unless based on 20 or more cases, but the numbers behind many of the percentages are still so small in some cases that any particular percentage must be regarded with caution. Rather, what is important are the general patterns:

1. The strong relationship of education to tolerance of nonconformity which we studied in Chapter Four reappears in the present context with unquestionable force. A given percentage at the higher educational levels is almost always higher than the corresponding percentage at lower levels. For example: Consider *metropolitan areas in the East:* Table 2 shows, for the complete sample, the following drop-off in tolerance as we go down the educational ladder:

College Graduates	78%
Some College	63%
High School Graduates	57%
Some High School	39%
Grade School	27%

TABLE 1

EDUCATIONAL LEVEL, BY TYPE OF COMMUNITY WITHIN EACH REGION

	NUMBER OF CASES					PERCENTAGE OF SAMPLE WHO FINISHED HIGH SCHOOL			
	Small Farm	Other Towns	Cities	Metro-politan		Small Farm	Other Towns	Cities	Metro-politan
Complete National Cross-Section									
West	40	108	226	284	West	50%	45%	60%	60%
East	44	222	331	661	East	37	43	44	47
Middle					Middle				
West	272	241	402	543	West	40	54	44	43
South	404	339	395	400	South	14	29	33	44
Those More Interested in Issues									
West	27	63	142	174	West	56%	54%	68%	65%
East	24	133	185	396	East	46	51	55	56
Middle					Middle				
West	152	160	220	295	West	46	56	52	51
South	158	188	224	232	South	24	37	35	54

TABLE 2

HOW WILLINGNESS TO TOLERATE NONCONFORMITY DIFFERS BY REGION AND TYPE OF COMMUNITY AMONG PEOPLE AT EACH EDUCATIONAL LEVEL

(Complete National Cross-Section)

	NUMBER OF CASES					PERCENTAGE CLASSIFIED AS "MORE TOLERANT" ON SCALE OF TOLERANCE			
	Small Farm	Other Towns	Cities	Metro-politan		Small Farm	Other Towns	Cities	Metro-politan
College Graduates									
West	3	7	31	30	West	—	—	84%	73%
East	2	13	28	77	East	—	—	54	78
Middle					Middle				
West	15	28	23	31	West	—	68%	65	64
South	5	18	31	34	South	—	—	45	62

(*Table 2 continued*)

| | NUMBER OF CASES | | | | PERCENTAGE CLASSIFIED AS "MORE TOLERANT" ON SCALE OF TOLERANCE | | | |
	Farm	Small Towns	Other Cities	Metropolitan		Farm	Small Towns	Other Cities	Metropolitan
Some College									
West	6	10	28	51	West	—	—	69%	67%
East	3	11	27	54	East	—	—	59	63
Middle West	21	28	44	54	Middle West	52%	32%	61	59
South	19	28	34	47	South	—	29	21	55
High School Graduates									
West	11	31	78	88	West	—	32%	41%	57%
East	11	72	93	178	East	—	44	41	57
Middle West	73	76	103	147	Middle West	43%	29	45	42
South	34	52	63	97	South	15	19	18	26
Some High School									
West	8	22	40	52	West	—	41%	40%	52%
East	9	39	88	137	East	—	26	27	39
Middle West	39	35	102	123	Middle West	13%	17	23	31
South	70	72	100	86	South	10	13	23	20
Grade School									
West	12	38	49	63	West	—	18%	35%	27%
East	19	87	95	215	East	—	17	11	27
Middle West	124	74	130	188	Middle West	14%	11	18	18
South	276	169	167	136	South	9	6	4	7

No percentages shown unless based on 20 or more cases.

This table is to be read as follows: There were, in our national cross-section, 30 college graduates who live in metropolitan areas of the West. Of these 30, 73% qualified for our "more tolerant" category. In contrast, among the 63 grade school people who live in metropolitan areas of the West, only 27% qualified for the "more tolerant" category, etc.

Similarly, Table 3 shows the same kind of progression among the "more interested."

2. The main comparisons by regions available in Tables 2 and 3 are within urban areas because of the small rural samples from the East and the West, which all but disappeared when cut five ways by education. But Table 2 makes one fact unmistakably clear. *There is not a single percentage figure for the South which is as high in tolerance as the corresponding figure in any Northern region.* There are 17 percentages shown for the South in Table 2; the unanimity of this finding is convincing: *amount of education alone cannot explain the North-South differences.* The picture in Table 3 is only a little less convincing. Among the "more interested" people only, the South is lowest of all regions in tolerance of nonconformists, in 14 out of 17 matched comparisons. One should not, however, overlook the finding in Tables 2 and 3 that *well*-educated Southerners tend to have more tolerant attitudes than *less*-educated Northerners.

3. Among the three Northern regions, the West tends still to have the highest percentage of tolerance when education and type of community are held constant. In 13 possible comparisons in Table 2, the West leads all other regions in nine and is tied for first in two others. Likewise, the West is well in the lead in Table 3. Differences between East and Middle West, however, are found in both directions; one cannot say confidently that any important difference in tolerance remains when urban-rural and educational levels are held constant. Actually, we will recall from Chart IV that the East-Middle West difference tended to become inconsistent or wash out when we first took into account type of community. In other words, we suspect that the main reason why the Middle West is less tolerant than the East is the presence of its large rural population, which tends, like rural people everywhere, to be less tolerant than urban populations.

4. With education held constant, Tables 2 and 3 permit complete rural-urban comparisons only for the Middle West and South. The metropolitan people are quite consistently more tolerant than rural people. However, the differences between large and small cities are mixed and probably not significant. And the same inconclusive answer must be given to small towns as compared to farms.

In sum, Tables 2 and 3 show once again what a big factor education is in tolerance of nonconformists. But they also show that difference in amount of education alone is *not enough* to account for North-South differences, for the greater frequency of tolerance in the West,

TABLE 3

HOW WILLINGNESS TO TOLERATE NONCONFORMITY DIFFERS BY REGION AND TYPE OF COMMUNITY AMONG PEOPLE AT EACH EDUCATIONAL LEVEL

(Those More Interested in Issues)

	NUMBER OF CASES					PERCENTAGE CLASSIFIED AS "MORE TOLERANT" ON SCALE OF TOLERANCE			
	Small Farm	Other Towns	Metro-Cities	politan		Small Farm	Other Towns	Metro-Cities	politan
College Graduates									
West	1	6	25	25	West	—	—	84%	72%
East	3	12	21	62	East	—	—	52	76
Middle					Middle				
West	11	26	21	26	West	—	69%	62	65
South	5	17	20	28	South	—	—	55	61
Some College									
West	6	9	21	31	West	—	—	71%	68%
East	2	8	16	38	East	—	—	—	66
Middle					Middle				
West	15	20	27	34	West	—	30%	67	59
South	12	23	19	38	South	—	26	—	53
High School Graduates									
West	8	19	51	56	West	—	—	40%	66%
East	6	48	65	121	East	—	50%	42	56
Middle					Middle				
West	44	44	67	89	West	45%	32	43	40
South	21	30	39	59	South	24	13	18	29
Some High School									
West	6	10	17	34	West	—	—	—	56%
East	6	24	44	84	East	—	33%	38%	37
Middle					Middle				
West	24	20	58	71	West	13%	10	22	37
South	32	32	65	49	South	13	22	25	22
Grade School									
West	6	19	28	28	West	—	—	32%	36%
East	7	41	39	91	East	—	12%	15	30
Middle					Middle				
West	58	50	47	75	West	9%	10	23	21
South	88	86	81	58	South	14	8	6	14

No percentages shown unless based on 20 or more cases.

or for the greater frequency of tolerance in metropolitan areas than in rural communities.

In concluding this section, one further note is needed.

North and South comparisons involve another variable which should be considered explicitly; namely, racial differences in attitudes. Negroes as a whole are not as likely as whites to be found in our "more tolerant" groups. This is true when Northern whites and Northern Negroes are compared or when Southern whites and Southern Negroes are compared.

The sample of Northern Negroes is too small to permit detailed breakdowns, but such tabulations as are possible show that the Negro-white difference in tolerance within the North tends to vanish when education is held constant. Negroes who have not finished high school (two thirds of the Northern Negroes) do not appear to differ significantly in their attitudes from whites with comparable schooling in the same type of community. The same may be true of the better-educated Negroes when compared with their white counterparts, but samples are much too small for confident tests.

The Northern Negroes as a whole tend oftener to be in our "more tolerant" groups than Southern Negroes, 25% as compared with 10%. A big factor here may be education, since nine out of ten of the Southern Negroes in our sample had not finished high school; but rural-urban differences count, too, since Northern Negroes live mainly in large cities.

Where enough cases exist to compare Southern whites with Southern Negroes at what is formally the same educational level, and within the same type of community, differences in tolerance between the two races are small. Consequently, whether we base the tabulations shown in Charts IV and V and Tables 2 and 3 on the entire Southern population, as we did, or on white respondents only, the over-all picture is essentially unaltered.

WHAT ABOUT OUR LOCAL COMMUNITY LEADERS—DO THEY VARY BY REGIONS IN THEIR TOLERANCE?

Briefly, the answer is "Yes." The special sample of local community leaders is not, as will be remembered, a part of the national cross-section and was not used in any of the foregoing analysis in this chapter. These arbitrarily selected leaders live in cities of 10,000 to 150,-000, most of which are independent cities, though some of them are suburbs within a metropolitan area. For comparison with the leaders we shall show attitudes among the cross-section *from the same cities as the leaders,* just as we did in Chapter Two, but now with one addition: the data will be broken down by regions.

Chart VI presents a quite important finding. It shows that *in each of the four regions,* West, East, Middle West, and South, the local community leadership as represented on our arbitrarily selected list *was consistently more willing to tolerate nonconformists than was the rank and file in the same communities.*

Moreover, Chart VI shows for our special sample of leaders, quite independently of our cross-sectional samples, the same *direction of differences by regions* we encountered earlier. The leaders in the West would appear to be on the average the most tolerant, though perhaps not significantly so; those in the South the least, with Easterners and Midwesterners in-between but more like the Westerners than like the Southerners in attitude.

There are in our study 14 different types of community leaders, such as mayors, presidents of chambers of commerce, etc. When we study each type separately by region, our sub-samples get very small. But so consistent is one of the findings shown in Chart VI that among 13 of the 14 different types of leaders the Southern leaders were less tolerant than the average of their Northern counterparts. (The exception is presidents of women's clubs, where the Southern women were, by a not significant 3%, more likely to be tolerant.)

On the other hand, there was no sustained pattern of consistency distinguishing leaders from the West, East, and Middle West from one another. Among the 14 types of leaders, there were seven among whom Westerners were the most tolerant; five among whom Midwesterners were the most tolerant; and two among whom the Easterners were the most tolerant. Most such differences were small and within chance expectations.

HOW THESE RESULTS MAY THROW LIGHT ON A THEORY ABOUT TOLERANCE

The findings in this chapter, like those in the preceding one, reflect the operation of a factor which may be essential to tolerance; namely, that of contact with people with disturbing and unpopular ideas.

125

CHART VI

IN EACH REGION COMMUNITY LEADERS ARE MORE WILLING THAN RANK AND FILE IN SAME CITIES TO TOLERATE NONCON-FORMISTS

PERCENTAGE DISTRIBUTION OF SCORES ON SCALE OF TOLERANCE

	LESS TOLERANT	IN-BETWEEN	MORE TOLERANT

WEST
- SELECTED COMMUNITY LEADERS: 5 / 22 / 73 / 200
- CROSS-SECTION IN SAME CITIES AS LEADERS: 14 / 39 / 47 / 109

EAST
- SELECTED COMMUNITY LEADERS: 4 / 30 / 66 / 405
- CROSS-SECTION IN SAME CITIES AS LEADERS: 17 / 42 / 41 / 226

MIDDLE WEST
- SELECTED COMMUNITY LEADERS: 4 / 27 / 69 / 502
- CROSS-SECTION IN SAME CITIES AS LEADERS: 18 / 51 / 31 / 313

SOUTH
- SELECTED COMMUNITY LEADERS: 7 / 36 / 57 / 393
- CROSS-SECTION IN SAME CITIES AS LEADERS: 22 / 57 / 21 / 249

126

In Chapter Four we showed how education was related to tolerance, and these findings were strengthened in the present chapter by the evidence that within each region and type of community education tended to make for tolerance.

A number of reasons why education should make for tolerance were explored in Chapter Four and illustrated with data. Some of these are related to a more general reason which might be proposed; namely, that schooling *puts a person in touch with people whose ideas and values are different from one's own.* And this tends to carry on, after formal schooling is finished, through reading and personal contacts. Now, we can plausibly argue that this is a necessary, though not the only, condition for tolerance of a free market place for ideas. To be tolerant, one has to learn further not only that people with different ideas are not necessarily bad people but also that it is vital to America to preserve this free market place, even if some of the ideas traded there are repugnant or even dangerous for the country. The first step in learning this may be merely to encounter the strange and the different. The educated man does this and tends not to flinch too much at what he sees or hears.

Similarly, as we have already suggested in this chapter, the citizen of a metropolitan community is more likely to rub shoulders with a variety of people whose values are different from his own and even repugnant to him than is the man or woman in a village. The city man has to learn to live and let live in his heterogeneous community to an extent not necessary for the villager.

But there is a dynamic as well as a static impact to this phenomenon. Owing to the relatively high rural birth rate and to changes in technology which shrink the percentages of rural population with every successive Census, the population flow is mainly from the country to the city and the city suburb. Consequently, many city dwellers have lived in two worlds of values—those of their childhood in the country and those of their adulthood in the city. The reverse is rare. The shock of exposure to two value systems could have an effect on tolerance not unlike the effect of formal schooling as described above. It is precisely in those parts of the country where most people are natives of their type of community, if not actually of the same county in which they now reside—such as farm areas, especially in the South —that tolerance of "dangerous" ideas seems to be most difficult. This same effect may help to explain why the cities of the Far West, which

127

have grown at such an astonishing rate by recruiting from all parts of this country, are the highest of all in our scale of tolerance.

It should be noted that contact alone is inadequate to explain tolerance. There must be something more; otherwise, the South would be the most tolerant part of this country with respect to the Negro. The contact must also be at something like a level of equality; for example, going to school or college with fellow students who have different values or working side by side in the same factory with such people.

COMPARISON WITH OTHER STUDIES

While there is a scattered body of past survey data, the present study appears to be a pioneering enterprise with respect to exploring differences in tolerance by region and type of community, with education also taken into account.

In 1947, Roper found residents of large cities more tolerant than rural dwellers concerning the employability of Communists and suspected Communists in various kinds of jobs (19). A Gallup poll in the same year reported that farmers more than city dwellers favored the punishment of Hollywood screen writers who refused to testify on past Communist connections (17). But in 1953, the NORC found no consistent differences by size of community in attitudes toward free speech (16).

Regional breakdowns of the 1953 NORC data support the present findings that tolerance of nonconformists may be greater in the Far West than in other parts of the country. On specific questions relating to free speech for Socialists and Communists, the South was not consistently different from the North. But the survey also showed the South to contain the largest proportion of people with "authoritarian" attitudes, as defined by questions similar to those used in Chapter Four, and the Far West the smallest proportion (16).

With respect to ethnic and religious attitudes there are also inconsistencies. All surveys show the South to be more intolerant than the North on questions relating to the Negro. But on anti-Semitism, Roper found in 1946 that Southerners were less anti-Semitic than Northerners, except for those from the Far West (19). On the subject of anti-Catholicism, the Al Smith campaign as far back as 1928 indicated that the Northern rural areas, which are predominantly Protestant, as well as the South may have been the most hostile. Gallup in 1940 asked, "Would you vote for a Catholic for President who was qualified for the position?" He found that in every region of the country the rural people were much more likely to say "No" and that the largest percentage of "No's" was found in the rural South (2). The NORC surveys in 1950 and 1953 also found a disproportionate number of anti-Catholics in the rural areas, and especially in the South (16), as did a national survey by Gaffin in 1952 (6).

It is hardly a surprise that the regional distribution of Senator McCarthy's most intense support does not correspond with the regional distribution of tolerance or intolerance of nonconformists, as reported in this chapter. For example, Gallup found in June 1954 that 14% of the national cross-section expressed "intense approval" of the Senator and that his support was strongest among the older and less educated people. But the proportion expressing "intense approval" was slightly lower in the rural regions than in the urban. Among the farmers as a whole it was 12%. In the South as a whole it was 13% (1). Differences of 1% or 2% from a national average are not likely to have statistical significance, but it is to be noted that they are opposite from what might be expected from a superficial examination of the findings reported in the present chapter. This serves to illustrate the point made at the beginning of this chapter, that a variety of special factors, including religious attitudes and political loyalties, may at any given moment inhibit or stimulate the basic tendencies with respect to tolerance of nonconformists as studied in this book. A variety of important studies show how sets of "cross-pressures" operate. For example, see Lazarsfeld et al. (15), Berelson et al. (3), Campbell et al. (4), and Harris (7). For further data from the present study see Chapters Eight and Nine.

Why do the kinds of differences in tolerance exist which we have found by region and type of community? Better answers to this question are needed, based on tests of explicit hypotheses. This is a challenge to future research in social science.

SUMMARY

This chapter has asked: *Do Americans differ in tolerance of nonconformists, depending on where they live?*

With respect to *regions,* the West seems to have the largest proportion of relatively tolerant people on the scale of willingness to tolerate nonconformists, and the South the smallest proportion. The East and Middle West are in-between.

With respect to *types of community,* metropolitan areas and other cities tend to have a larger proportion of relatively tolerant people than rural areas.

Southerners are more rural than Northerners. Southerners also tend to have less education. But neither of these facts alone will explain the North-South differences in tolerance of nonconformists. There is something in Southern culture that tends to differentiate Southerners, in cities as well as rural areas, at all educational levels, from all other regional groups.

Midwesterners are more rural than other Northerners. But rural Midwesterners are not less tolerant than other rural people, though they are less tolerant than city people. Analysis shows that the reason the Middle West as a whole is less tolerant than the East or West may be mainly the fact that so many of its people live in small towns and on farms.

Rural people in every region are less likely to be tolerant of nonconformists than city people, even when we compare urban and rural people with the same amount of schooling. There is something about life in a small community that makes it less hospitable to divergent opinions than is the case in our urban centers. In the anonymity of city life it is much easier for deviant behavior to flourish than in the goldfish bowl of a small community. In the large community there are sometimes so many goldfish that nobody bothers to look at them. In the small town a lone exotic specimen can be viewed with careful, critical, and occasionally devastating attention.

Civic leaders in cities of 10,000 to 150,000 within every region—West, East, Middle West, and South—are more likely than the cross-section to be among those who are relatively tolerant of nonconformists. But the leaders also tend to differ somewhat in attitude, by regions. In particular, the Southern community leaders—though far more tolerant than the average person in their own communities—are consistently less likely to be among the relatively tolerant than are their counterparts in the North.

130

Chapter Six

DO WOMEN HAVE VIEWPOINTS DIFFERENT FROM MEN?

The child first learns to respect the rights of other people, as these rights are defined by our culture, in the home. And more than any other person, his first teacher must be his mother.

Day by day, in countless little ways, the values and traditions of the American way of life are transmitted. It is not so much the formal ideologies that are taught as the kinds of actual conduct which reflect those ideologies.

Central, therefore, to the problem of preserving through successive generations our country's traditions of justice and respect for the rights of others stands the American woman.

This chapter explores the attitudes of women and considers various ways in which their actions and attitudes differ from those of men. In the political sphere women, whose franchise is hardly a generation old, tend to be less interested than men. Their knowledge of public issues and their concern about political action are less. But there is another sphere in which women tend to be more involved than men— in the practice of religion. The church shares with the home and the school the responsibilities as a transmitter of values to the younger generation.

Faced with the Communist threat to the American way of life and faced with reactions to this threat from those who would sacrifice historic liberties, how do women respond? How well have they thought through the implications of the dilemmas which have to be resolved? If the traditional respect for the rights of other people is to be preserved or changed, what women think can be of equal or even greater significance than what men think.

We ask, then, how do women answer the questions on tolerance of nonconformity, measured by our scale, as compared with men?

131

Chart I presents three basic facts:

1. Women tend to be less tolerant of nonconformists than do men.

2. Women tend to be less interested than men in the news about Communists and methods of dealing with Communists. (Other tabulations, such as those dealing with topics of conversation, all show the same tendency.) Moreover, as we have seen in earlier chapters, less interested people tend, on the average, to be less tolerant than others.

3. But lower political interest will not account for the greater intolerance on the part of women. Even among those people who are classed as "more interested" in the issues relevant to this study, *the interested women tend to be more intolerant than the interested men.*

Let us keep constantly in mind that we are using the word "intolerance" here, as everywhere in this study, in a strictly limited sense. We are dealing with the limitations of civil liberties which people would place on Socialists, atheists, Communists, or persons whose loyalty has been questioned but who swear they have never been Communists. It is tolerance of such nonconformists or suspected nonconformists which we are investigating—and only that. Indeed, it is possible that there are many subjects about which women would be *more* tolerant than would men. Therefore, when, to avoid tedium in this chapter as in others, we do not redefine our term "tolerance" every time it is used, we trust that the reader will continue to hold this definition in mind.

The difference between men and women in scores on our scale of tolerance of nonconformists is not great, percentage-wise, but it is quite remarkable in its consistency in almost all kinds of sub-groupings that we can set up.

Look at Chart II. At all educational levels, women tend to be less tolerant than men. True, the difference by sex is small as compared with difference by education, but it is consistent. If we sort by age instead of education, as on the lower half of Chart II, we get the general picture in most age groups.

Or look at Chart III. In each of our four broad regions—West, East, Middle West, and South—women are less tolerant of nonconformists than are men. And as shown in the lower half of Chart III, the same conclusions can be drawn if we sort by type of community, with the single exception of people in farming areas.

Charts II and III are based on those people in our national cross-section who are called "more interested in the issues" of our study.

CHART I

WOMEN TEND TO BE LESS WILLING THAN MEN TO TOLERATE NONCONFORMISTS

PERCENTAGE DISTRIBUTION OF SCALE SCORES

	LESS TOLERANT	IN-BETWEEN	MORE TOLERANT	
MALES	16	49	35	2300
FEMALES	21	52	27	2632

WOMEN TEND TO BE LESS INTERESTED THAN MEN IN U.S. COMMUNISTS AND WHAT IS BEING DONE ABOUT THEM

PERCENTAGE WHO SAY THEY FOLLOW SUCH NEWS

	HARDLY AT ALL	FAIRLY CLOSELY	VERY CLOSELY	
MALES	36	49	14	2300
FEMALES	47	42	9	2632

EVEN THOSE WOMEN MORE INTERESTED IN SUCH ISSUES TEND TO BE LESS WILLING THAN MEN TO TOLERATE NONCONFORMISTS

PERCENTAGE DISTRIBUTION OF SCALE SCORES

	LESS TOLERANT	IN-BETWEEN	MORE TOLERANT	
INTERESTED MALES	13	48	39	1436
INTERESTED FEMALES	15	53	32	1442

Numbers inside the bars show percentages; numbers at the ends of the bars show the size of the samples.

133

CHART II

WOMEN, AT EVERY EDUCATIONAL LEVEL AND IN MOST AGE GROUPS, ARE LESS WILLING THAN MEN TO TOLERATE NONCONFORMISTS

(Among Those More Interested in Issues)

PERCENTAGE DISTRIBUTION OF SCORES
ON SCALE OF TOLERANCE

LESS TOLERANT | IN-BETWEEN | MORE TOLERANT

BY EDUCATION

COLLEGE GRADUATES
- MALES — 21 — 75 — 163
- FEMALES — 6 — 33 — 61 — 135

SOME COLLEGE
- MALES — 7 — 32 — 61 — 147
- FEMALES — 11 — 42 — 47 — 172

HIGH SCHOOL GRADUATES
- MALES — 9 — 43 — 48 — 361
- FEMALES — 14 — 50 — 36 — 406

SOME HIGH SCHOOL
- MALES — 14 — 53 — 33 — 297
- FEMALES — 19 — 55 — 26 — 279

GRADE SCHOOL
- MALES — 21 — 62 — 17 — 459
- FEMALES — 23 — 62 — 15 — 333

BY AGE

21 TO 29
- MALES — 9 — 36 — 55 — 237
- FEMALES — 10 — 49 — 41 — 288

30 TO 39
- MALES — 8 — 45 — 47 — 356
- FEMALES — 14 — 47 — 39 — 327

40 TO 49
- MALES — 12 — 48 — 40 — 349
- FEMALES — 19 — 48 — 33 — 270

50 TO 59
- MALES — 21 — 49 — 30 — 218
- FEMALES — 15 — 54 — 31 — 210

60 AND OVER
- MALES — 20 — 59 — 21 — 275
- FEMALES — 23 — 62 — 15 — 247

134

CHART III

WOMEN, IN EACH BROAD REGION AND MOST COMMUNITY TYPES, ARE LESS WILLING THAN MEN TO TOLERATE NONCONFORMISTS

(Among Those More Interested in Issues)

PERCENTAGE DISTRIBUTION OF SCORES ON SCALE OF TOLERANCE

		LESS TOLERANT	IN-BETWEEN	MORE TOLERANT	
BY REGIONS					
WEST	MALES	11	30	59	198
	FEMALES	8	49	43	212
EAST	MALES	11	42	47	394
	FEMALES	13	45	42	344
MIDDLE WEST	MALES	10	53	37	434
	FEMALES	16	52	32	389
SOUTH	MALES	20	56	24	409
	FEMALES	23	58	19	397
BY TYPE OF COMMUNITY					
METROPOLITAN AREAS	MALES	10	41	49	572
	FEMALES	11	48	41	529
OTHER CITIES	MALES	14	46	40	388
	FEMALES	17	53	30	389
SMALL TOWNS	MALES	16	53	31	273
	FEMALES	19	55	26	269
FARMS	MALES	19	61	20	202
	FEMALES	24	51	25	159

135

These people are especially important to study because, as Chapter Three showed, they include most of those who are well informed or who are politically minded in the sense of voting or otherwise translating attitudes into actions.

When, however, we base our tabulations on the entire national cross-section, we get almost exactly the same patterns for the total population as for the more interested. In almost every comparison, females tend to be less tolerant of nonconformists than do men. To avoid too much repetitious detail, the tabulations are not presented here. Moreover, separate tabulations of the samples obtained independently by each of our survey agencies, the American Institute of Public Opinion and the National Opinion Research Center, yield the same general picture.

SOME POSSIBLE CLUES TO SEX DIFFERENCE IN TOLERANCE OF NONCONFORMISTS

Why do women tend to be less tolerant of nonconformists than do men? We see that women are less interested in following the news about the issues involved than men are, but we see also that difference in interest does not provide the answer.

One possible explanation would follow the lead of Chapter Four, where it was suggested that the greater the personal anxiety, the greater may be the need for an external symbol—like the Communist or radical in general—to blame for one's woes. We did see in Chapter Four that there was a certain amount of suggestive, if not completely convincing, evidence favoring such an explanation, particularly as it compared older people and less educated people with others. But to apply to sex differences, we would need to show that women are, in fact, more pessimistic or worried than men. What are the findings?

Consider the question: **On the whole, do you think life will be better for you or worse, in the next few years than it is now?** On the average, 59% of the men said "better," as compared with 57% of the women. Differences by sex are negligible compared with the differences in response by age:

AGE	NUMBER OF CASES		PERCENTAGES IN NATIONAL CROSS-SECTION ANSWERING "BETTER"	
	Men	*Women*	*Men*	*Women*
21 to 30	*384*	*520*	72%	78%
30 to 39	*534*	*640*	67	65
40 to 49	*534*	*524*	65	58
50 to 59	*378*	*415*	51	50
60 and over	*467*	*531*	36	33

As was reported in Chapter Three, the replies to the question: **What kinds of things do you worry most about?** were overwhelmingly in terms of personal or family problems. Men were somewhat more likely than women to mention financial or business problems; women were more likely to mention problems of health (of children or of relatives as well as themselves), together with a miscellany of problems of the family not classifiable under economics or health. The percentages of males and females, respectively, in the national cross-section who said they were worried about these types of personal or family problems are as follows:

	Men	Women
Worried about finances	51%	38%
Worried about health	19	30
Worried about other personal or family problems	25	39
Number of cases	*2300*	*2630*

These categories are not mutually exclusive; some responses were coded twice or even three times. After discussion of his or her worries, the question was asked: **Would you guess that you worry or are concerned about such things more than most people, or less?** Women oftener than men answered "more"—22% among women, 17% among men. The difference is consistent at all age groups except the oldest. But it cannot be accepted as convincing evidence that women are more anxious than men. For one thing, our culture may merely make it more permissive for a woman to say she is worried than for a man to say so, just as our culture makes it more permissive for a woman to express troubles by shedding tears.

CHART IV

BOTH GAINFULLY EMPLOYED WOMEN AND THOSE WHO ARE HOUSEWIVES ONLY TEND TO BE LESS TOLERANT OF NONCONFORMISTS THAN ARE MEN

(For Those More Interested in Issues)

PERCENTAGE DISTRIBUTION OF SCORES
ON SCALE OF TOLERANCE

		LESS TOLERANT	IN BETWEEN	MORE TOLERANT	
WHITE-COLLAR OCCUPATIONS	MEN	7	39	54	772
	WORKINGWOMEN	12	45	43	302
	HOUSEWIVES ONLY	14	44	42	505
OTHER NON-FARM OCCUPATIONS	MEN	19	51	30	685
	WORKINGWOMEN	17	60	23	187
	HOUSEWIVES ONLY	16	57	27	398

Men and Workingwomen classified by their own occupations; Housewives classified by their husbands' occupation.

Many women have a dual role, that of a gainfully employed woman as well as that of a homemaker. A separate study of the working-women suggests that, while some differences in tolerance of nonconformists are found as between workingwomen and those who are housewives solely, they are small and inconsistent differences. This is summarized in Chart IV, for those more interested in issues, but the same pattern appears for the entire national cross-section.

The data in Chart IV can be broken down further. Among the major white-collar occupations, the comparative percentages classed as "more tolerant" are as follows:

	Number of Cases	Percentage "More Tolerant"
Professional and		
Semi-Professional		
Men	159	66%
Workingwomen	102	50
Housewives only	106	47
Proprietors, Managers,		
and Officials		
Men	223	51%
Workingwomen	51	41
Housewives only	150	41
Clerical and Sales		
Men	200	49%
Workingwomen	129	39
Housewives only	106	41

In all cases, "housewives only" are classified according to the occupations of their husbands.

A comparison of workingwomen with those who are housewives only is also quite inconclusive for other occupations. Among crafts-men and foremen, workingwomen tend to be more tolerant than wives of men in these occupations; among service workers and unskilled laborers, the reverse is the case; among operatives or semi-skilled workers, the percentage classed as "tolerant" among workingwomen and housewives is a tie. No one of the differences is by itself large enough to be statistically significant.

Thus far we have shown that women tend quite consistently to be somewhat less tolerant of nonconformists than do men. Women also

139

are less interested in the news about the issues we are considering. But the sex differences in interest do not seem to explain the sex differences in tolerance. For even among the more interested the women tend to be less tolerant than the men. Psychological explanations in terms of the possibly greater anxieties of women do not receive very strong support from our data, although a somewhat greater percentage of women than men say that they worry about personal or family problems. Women, on the other hand, tend to be almost as optimistic as men about their personal future. Further comparisons, of gainfully employed women and those who are housewives only, show no consistent differences, though both classes of women tend to be less tolerant than men in corresponding occupations.

In looking for other factors which might be associated with sex differences, we must consider the striking difference in the percentage of men and women, respectively, who say that they attend church. Let us explore this variable.

HOW CHURCHGOING, BY MEN AND WOMEN, IS RELATED TO TOLERANCE OF NONCONFORMISTS

One must be hesitant to accept at face value any figure purporting to show the number of churchgoers. In the present survey, following a question on religious preference, it was asked: **Have you attended church or religious services in the last month?** There is a tendency for too many people to answer such a question "Yes," just as too many people report performance of a socially approved act like voting. In Chapter Three we noted that the inflation in voting was about 5%; this could be checked by references to official voting figures. There is no corresponding check on the error, whatever it may be, in estimating church attendance, but some error probably exists.

For our purposes, however, the figures need not be exact. We can be sure that those who say they attended church in the last month include most of the regular churchgoers, in addition to a few nonregular churchgoers who happened to attend some ceremonial affair, such as a neighbor's wedding. While those saying they did not attend church within the past month may include some regular churchgoers who were kept away by illness, we can be pretty sure that most such respondents are not regular churchgoers.

140

CHART V

WOMEN ARE MORE LIKELY THAN MEN TO REPORT ATTENDING CHURCH IN LAST MONTH

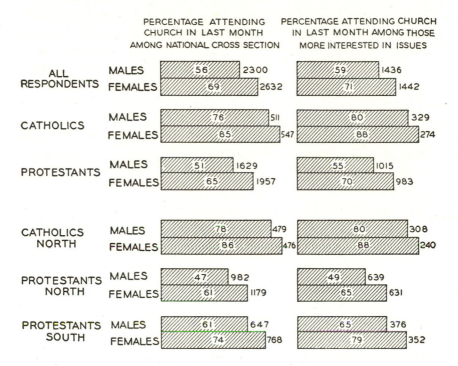

		PERCENTAGE ATTENDING CHURCH IN LAST MONTH AMONG NATIONAL CROSS SECTION	PERCENTAGE ATTENDING CHURCH IN LAST MONTH AMONG THOSE MORE INTERESTED IN ISSUES
ALL RESPONDENTS	MALES	56 — 2300	59 — 1436
	FEMALES	69 — 2632	71 — 1442
CATHOLICS	MALES	76 — 511	80 — 329
	FEMALES	85 — 547	88 — 274
PROTESTANTS	MALES	51 — 1629	55 — 1015
	FEMALES	65 — 1957	70 — 983
CATHOLICS NORTH	MALES	78 — 479	80 — 308
	FEMALES	86 — 476	88 — 240
PROTESTANTS NORTH	MALES	47 — 982	49 — 639
	FEMALES	61 — 1179	65 — 631
PROTESTANTS SOUTH	MALES	61 — 647	65 — 376
	FEMALES	74 — 768	79 — 352

Chart V shows that women are more likely than men to say they attended church in the month preceding this survey (made in May, June, and July 1954). Sex differences in church attendance are especially large among those who say their religious preference is Protestant. Southern Protestants of both sexes are considerably more likely than Northern Protestants to say they attended church, though neither group compares with the high percentages for Catholic men and women. The data in Chart V are presented in duplicate—for the entire national cross-section and for those persons more interested in issues relevant to this study. The two sets of pictures are very much the same.

141

The data in Chart V are important to us for the following reason: *Regular church attenders are less likely than other people to be tolerant of the kinds of nonconformists or suspected nonconformists about whom we are inquiring.*

Looking at our complete national cross-section, we have the following comparative percentages of people classified as "more tolerant" on our scale of tolerance of nonconformists:

	Number of Cases	*Percentage Classed as "More Tolerant"*
Attended church in last month	*3095*	28%
Did not attend church in last month	*1833*	36

These percentages, we must remember, are based on our scale of tolerance toward very special kinds of nonconformists, including atheists. It would hardly be a surprise if church members, in spite of the tolerance which is implicit in the gospels if not always in the historic practices of Christianity, were less tolerant than others toward enemies of religion. But there are 15 items involved in the scale of tolerance toward nonconformists, and only two of the items involve directly and explicitly enemies of churches and religion. Two of the items, for example, involve Socialists who advocate government ownership of railroads and big business. But on these items, as well as the others, the church members were less tolerant than the non-church members. For example: **If a person wanted to make a speech in your community favoring government ownership of all the railroads and big industries, should he be allowed to speak, or not?**

The percentages answering "Yes" were:

Among church attenders	60%
Among non-church attenders	67%

There would appear to be something about people who go to church regularly that makes fewer of them, as compared with non-churchgoers, willing to accord civil rights to nonconformists who might be Communists, suspected Communists, or merely Socialists.

Since women, as we have seen earlier in this chapter, are less likely to be tolerant than men, and since women, as Chart V has shown, are more likely to be churchgoers, can churchgoing be a key to the difference? Do women appear to be more intolerant of nonconformists *merely* because women practice religion more faithfully?

142

The answer would seem to be "No." The basic data are shown in Chart VI. Among those attending church in the previous month, women tend to be less tolerant than men. Among those not attending church, women also are less tolerant than men. The sex differences in tolerance are, however, too small to be significant among Catholics. They are not large but clearly significant among Protestants. Chart VI is based only on that fraction of our population which is classed as "more interested" in issues. Table 1 summarizes information for the complete national cross-section with essentially the same results as Chart VI, except that the sex difference in tolerance among Catholics is much larger in Table 1 than in Chart VI. The sample of Jewish men and women was not large enough to permit very detailed breakdown, but it may be noted parenthetically that Jewish respondents tended, as a whole, to be much more tolerant of nonconformists than were either Catholics or Protestants in the entire cross-section; 79% of the Jewish males (based on 76 cases) and 68% of the Jewish females (based on 82 cases) are classed as "more tolerant" on our scale. Where comparisons are possible, as in the North, Protestants differ somewhat from Catholics, but differences are not consistent among various sub-samples. More detailed tabulations than are shown in Chart VI also show Protestants higher than Catholics in tolerance in some groups, and Catholics higher than Protestants in others.

Table 2, based like Chart VI on those "more interested" in the issues of concern to this study, compares the tolerance of men and women churchgoers and non-churchgoers, at each educational level. (North and South are shown separately.) The reader may enjoy checking through this table, which actually is very simple to read when he gets the idea of it. All of the percentages are based on such small numbers that they would be expected to fluctuate considerably by chance alone. But the table is important as a test of *consistency*, based on what we call *matched comparisons*. For example, on the top line we have 77 males and 81 females, matched on three characteristics—they live in the North, they are college graduates, and they attended church in the past month. We see that 67% of the males are among the more tolerant; 58% of the females. Going all the way down the table, we find that we can make 17 such matched comparisons. (No percentage is shown unless based on at least 20 cases.) The reader can verify the fact that 14 of the 17 possible matched comparisons show women to be less tolerant, two show the reverse, and there is one tie.

143

CHART VI

MEN AND NON-CHURCH ATTENDERS ARE MORE WILLING TO TOLERATE NONCONFORMISTS THAN FEMALES AND CHURCH ATTENDERS

(Among Those More Interested in Issues)

PERCENTAGE DISTRIBUTION OF SCORES ON
SCALE OF TOLERANCE OF NONCONFORMISTS

			LESS TOLERANT	IN-BETWEEN	MORE TOLERANT	
ALL RESPONDENTS	WENT TO CHURCH	MALES	15	50	35	848
		FEMALES	16	54	30	843
	DID NOT GO TO CHURCH	MALES	11	43	46	588
		FEMALES	15	47	38	445
CATHOLICS LIVING IN NORTH	WENT TO CHURCH	MALES	12	54	34	249
		FEMALES	11	57	32	212
	DID NOT GO TO CHURCH	MALES	10	42	48	59
		FEMALES	14	39	47	28
PROTESTANTS LIVING IN NORTH	WENT TO CHURCH	MALES	11	48	41	314
		FEMALES	15	49	36	410
	DID NOT GO TO CHURCH	MALES	10	40	50	325
		FEMALES	15	49	36	221
PROTESTANTS LIVING IN SOUTH	WENT TO CHURCH	MALES	23	55	22	241
		FEMALES	22	60	18	278
	DID NOT GO TO CHURCH	MALES	15	61	24	135
		FEMALES	23	57	20	74

144

TABLE 1

MEN AND NON-CHURCH ATTENDERS ARE MORE WILLING TO TOLERATE NONCONFORMISTS THAN FEMALES AND CHURCH ATTENDERS

(Entire National Cross-Section)

	NUMBER OF CASES		PERCENTAGE "MORE TOLERANT" ON SCALE OF TOLERANCE OF NONCONFORMISTS	
	Male	Female	Male	Female
All Respondents				
Went to church	1289	1806	30%	27%
Did not go to church	1009	824	40	31
Catholics Living in North				
Went to church	370	408	34%	26%
Did not go to church	109	68	42	37
Protestants Living in North				
Went to church	461	718	37%	33%
Did not go to church	521	461	43	34
Protestants Living in South				
Went to church	389	570	16%	14%
Did not go to church	258	198	19	10

TABLE 2

AT MOST EDUCATIONAL LEVELS, MEN AND NON-CHURCHGOERS ARE MORE WILLING TO TOLERATE NONCONFORMISTS THAN ARE WOMEN AND CHURCHGOERS

(For Those More Interested in Issues)

	NUMBER OF CASES		PERCENTAGE "MORE TOLERANT" ON SCALE OF TOLERANCE OF NON-CONFORMISTS	
	Male	*Female*	*Male*	*Female*
North				
College Graduates				
Went to church	77	81	67%	58%
Did not go to church	47	33	91	72
Some College				
Went to church	71	82	58%	46%
Did not go to church	38	36	90	67
High School Graduates				
Went to church	166	234	44%	38%
Did not go to church	127	91	65	47
Some High School				
Went to church	108	122	32%	28%
Did not go to church	103	65	42	31
Grade School				
Went to church	163	126	18%	18%
Did not go to church	120	70	27	20
South				
College Graduates				
Went to church	27	27	67%	37%
Did not go to church	12	4	—	—
Some College				
Went to church	26	51	39%	32%
Did not go to church	12	3	—	—
High School Graduates				
Went to church	42	64	29%	17%
Did not go to church	26	17	23	—
Some High School				
Went to church	48	71	19%	20%
Did not go to church	38	21	31	14
Grade School				
Went to church	114	98	10%	7%
Did not go to church	62	39	10	18

In just the same way we can compare churchgoers and non-church-goers. Again, looking at the top of Table 2, we see that there are 81 Northern female college graduates who went to church matched with 33 who did not. The proportion classed as "more tolerant" among the churchgoers is 58%; among the non-churchgoers, 72%. In the entire table, for both sexes, we can make 15 such matched comparisons, and 12 of the 15 show churchgoers less likely to be among the relatively tolerant, while there are two reversals and one tie, all in the South.

In spite of the untrustworthiness of particular percentages based on such small sub-samples, a fairly consistent and stable *pattern* emerges. The reader also can see how consistent are the North-South differences for groups matched by sex, education, and church attendance. And he can note how the powerful relationship between education and tolerance is once again manifested in this table.

Table 3 is to be read exactly like Table 2. The only difference is that here we sort by age instead of by education. Seventeen comparisons can be made of men and women from Table 3. In 15 comparisons women are less tolerant; there is one reversal and one tie. Seventeen comparisons of churchgoers and non-churchgoers show 12 in which churchgoers are less tolerant, four reversals, and one tie, three of which are in the South and involve very small samples. Also noteworthy is the consistency of the pattern of decreasing tolerance with increasing age.

Table 4 is analogous to Tables 2 and 3. It sorts by type of community. Fifteen comparisons by sex show women less tolerant than men in nine, with five reversals and one tie. Fifteen comparisons by church attendance show churchgoers less tolerant than non-churchgoers in 11, with four reversals. Also, one observes a tendency for the urban places to be more tolerant than the rural, among women as well as among men, among churchgoers as well as among non-churchgoers.

What, then, has this section of the chapter shown? First, that women go to church oftener than men. Second, that more churchgoers are intolerant of the kinds of nonconformity we are dealing with than are non-churchgoers, and that this holds for males and females separately. Third, that mere differences in churchgoing will not alone suffice to explain the fact that women tend to be less tolerant than men. Fourth, that these facts hold when education, age, region, and type of community also are taken into account.

147

TABLE 3

AT MOST AGE LEVELS, MEN AND NON-CHURCH-GOERS ARE MORE WILLING TO TOLERATE NONCONFORMISTS THAN ARE WOMEN AND CHURCHGOERS

(For Those More Interested in Issues)

	NUMBER OF CASES		PERCENTAGE "MORE TOLERANT" ON SCALE OF TOLERANCE OF NONCONFORMISTS	
	Male	Female	Male	Female
North				
21 to 29				
Went to church	89	129	51%	46%
Did not go to church	85	66	71	56
30 to 39				
Went to church	152	166	44%	42%
Did not go to church	109	65	64	52
40 to 49				
Went to church	152	132	44%	37%
Did not go to church	95	61	52	43
50 to 59				
Went to church	91	99	37%	37%
Did not go to church	59	45	41	31
60 and over				
Went to church	104	124	18%	15%
Did not go to church	90	58	33	24
South				
21 to 29				
Went to church	40	70	40%	23%
Did not go to church	23	23	35	26
30 to 39				
Went to church	59	73	36%	26%
Did not go to church	36	23	33	17
40 to 49				
Went to church	66	65	21%	15%
Did not go to church	36	12	25	—
50 to 59				
Went to church	41	52	10%	19%
Did not go to church	27	14	15	—
60 and over				
Went to church	53	53	11%	6%
Did not go to church	28	12	11	—

TABLE 4

IN MOST TYPES OF COMMUNITY, MEN AND NON-CHURCHGOERS ARE MORE WILLING TO TOLERATE NONCONFORMISTS THAN ARE WOMEN AND CHURCHGOERS

(For Those More Interested in Issues)

	NUMBER OF CASES		PERCENTAGE "MORE TOLERANT" ON SCALE OF TOLERANCE OF NON-CONFORMISTS	
	Male	Female	Male	Female
North				
Metropolitan Areas				
Went to church	258	276	43%	43%
Did not go to church	196	138	63	49
Other Cities				
Went to church	162	183	44%	30%
Did not go to church	114	92	54	41
Small Towns				
Went to church	96	125	35%	33%
Did not go to church	83	45	41	22
Farms				
Went to church	72	66	22%	27%
Did not go to church	45	20	29	45
South				
Metropolitan Areas				
Went to church	67	91	36%	24%
Did not go to church	51	24	45	17
Other Cities				
Went to church	79	89	20%	18%
Did not go to church	33	25	18	20
Small Towns				
Went to church	57	72	16%	17%
Did not go to church	37	23	19	22
Farms				
Went to church	56	61	21%	15%
Did not go to church	29	12	—	—

WHAT ABOUT THE CIVIC LEADERS?

The findings thus far in this chapter have been based on the national cross-section only. Our special sample of local community leaders, however useful it may be for certain kinds of comparisons, is not suitable for a comparison of men and women. If the categories of male leaders leave much to be desired in terms of coverage or representativeness, the female leaders taken by themselves cannot be defended as representative at all.

The D.A.R. regents and women's club presidents were selected as interesting special categories for the purpose of this study, but certainly not as representative of a wide variety of female civic leaders. What about the League of Women Voters, for example, and other women's groups which we reluctantly omitted? It does happen to be a fact that the female civic leaders in our sample are not as likely as men to be found in our group classed as "more tolerant." But this fact is not necessarily meaningful and must not be taken as corroborating other findings in this chapter.

A better case can be made for an analysis of the attitudes of civic leaders in terms of religion. Three fourths of the leaders selected for our study are men, and these occupy a much more diverse, though not of course truly representative, collection of roles in the community.

The leaders are, in fact, considerably more likely to say they attended church in the past month than is the national cross-section. For all leaders the proportion is 78%; for male leaders alone, 75%. In the national cross-section, the corresponding figures are 69% and 63%. Now, we know from Chapter Two that our civic leaders, as a whole, are much more likely than the cross-section to be among the more tolerant people. Do we not have something here that contradicts what has been reported earlier in this chapter about the negative relationship between tolerance and churchgoing? Indeed, may not attitudes associated with more frequent churchgoing be one of the reasons why the civic leaders are more likely to be tolerant than the rank and file?

The answer is that it is not a contradiction, and that, whatever distinguishes the tolerance of leaders and others, it is almost certainly not the greater extent of religious practice among the leaders. The evidence is shown in Table 5.

TABLE 5

CHURCHGOERS AMONG CIVIC LEADERS ARE LESS LIKELY TO BE CLASSED AS "RELATIVELY TOLERANT" THAN NON-CHURCHGOERS

	PERCENTAGE "MORE TOLERANT" ON SCALE OF TOLERANCE OF NONCONFORMISTS	
	Males Only	*Males & Females*
All Cases		
Attended Church Regularly	67% (*870*)	62% (*1162*)
Did Not Attend Church Regularly	74 (*287*)	73 (*338*)
Northern Catholics		
Attended Church Regularly	67% (*170*)	65% (*196*)
Did Not Attend Church Regularly	— (*16*)	— (*17*)
Northern Protestants		
Attended Church Regularly	71% (*417*)	66% (*597*)
Did Not Attend Church Regularly	75 (*198*)	74 (*237*)
Southern Protestants		
Attended Church Regularly	58% (*237*)	57% (*313*)
Did Not Attend Church Regularly	64 (*44*)	63 (*51*)

Number of cases in parentheses.

Considering all leaders, male and female, we see that the proportion shown as more tolerant is 62% among those who attended church in the past month; 73% among others. Among males only, the figures are 67% and 74%. Some of this difference may be attributable to more frequent church attendance by Southern civic leaders, whose attitudes differ somewhat from Northerners. But even if we consider Northern Protestants and Southern Protestants separately we see in Table 5 that churchgoers are less likely to be among those classed as "more tolerant" than the non-churchgoers.

Churchgoing is so high among civic leaders, generally, that the number of cases of non-churchgoers is very small in any one of the 14 categories of civic leaders. However, among the 14 types of leaders, when each type is analyzed separately we find that in 10 of the 14 categories it is the non-churchgoers who have the highest proportion of relatively tolerant people.

None of the differences cited in this section is large enough to justify making much of a point. But when the *pattern* is as consistent as it is in Table 5 we are compelled to accept it as not contradicting our earlier findings with respect to the national cross-section. The relatively greater tolerance among civic leaders clearly does not occur *because* of the fact that they are somewhat more faithful churchgoers.

Incidentally, the differences in the direction noted occur not only when the scale, as a whole, of tolerance of nonconformists is used but also when a single item, such as free speech for Socialists, is considered. For example, 15% of the churchgoers among the civic leaders say they would not favor letting a Socialist make a speech in their community, as compared with 10% of the non-churchgoers.

WHAT DO THESE DATA MEAN?

Few results in this book are more susceptible of easy misinterpretation than the data on tolerance of nonconformity as related to sex and to religion.

First, let us remind the reader once again, at the risk of boredom, that we are not studying tolerance in general, but rather tolerance of particular nonconformists like Socialists, atheists, and Communists, or people whose loyalty has been challenged but who swear they are not Communists. The bond which seems to unite all of these objects of hostility in the eyes of the undiscriminating, and which makes it possible for all to fit into our single scale of measurement of tolerance, is their perceived relation to the Communist threat in general.

Second, we shall need data not yet presented, but forthcoming in Chapter Seven, to see how much of a role the threat of Communism to religious values plays in the total complex of concepts which people have of the danger which America faces. Until these data have been seen, it is best to withhold judgment as to the meaning of the relative unwillingness of churchgoers as compared with others to extend full civil rights even to Socialists.

The same comments apply to consideration of the sex differences in attitude. But some further notes should be offered with respect to the women.

It might plausibly be argued that, as between the average male and average female who attend church equally often, the female may be more devout. (Obviously, mere church attendance is only the most superficial index of devotion.) This might conceivably account for sex differences in attitudes among churchgoers, but it is hardly likely to be the sole explanation. For how, then, would we fully account for the quite consistent evidence in Chart VI and Tables 1, 2, 3, and 4 that among those *also* who did *not* go to church in the past month the women tended to have less tolerant attitudes than the men?

One could speculate on the possibility that our findings bear some relationship to differences in the child-rearing of boys and girls, respectively, in American culture. The hypothesis would be that boys are allowed more freedom than girls to meet assorted kinds of odd characters and in the course of this experience acquire a little more tolerance for people with peculiar or different ideas. This might be true, but, if so, one would expect women to differ considerably from men on the psychological variables discussed in Chapter Four. Take, for example, the statement: **If a child is unusual in any way, his parents should get him to be more like other children.** If women are more rigidly intolerant of deviance, *in general,* we should expect women to agree with this statement more frequently than do men. In fact, the reverse is the case. The percentage of men agreeing with this statement is higher (63%, based on 2139 cases with an opinion) than that of women (59%, based on 2450 cases).

On the other hand, consider the *adult* role of the woman. Especially during the childbearing and child-rearing period it is one which almost certainly limits her social environment more than that of the man. Her husband may be more likely to meet radicals in his labor union

153

or his business or professional relationships and learn better to "live and let live." This may be true, but, if so, how do we account for the lack of difference in tolerance as between workingwomen and those who are housewives only, shown in Chart IV?

A NOTE ON FINDINGS FROM OTHER STUDIES

As with the material on region and urban-rural differences, the present study goes farther than prior studies in exploring attitudinal difference between men and women, particularly in so far as religious practices may be involved.

But previous data are in accord with many of the findings. Thus, as far back as 1945, NORC surveys showed women to be moderately, yet consistently, more likely than men to place restrictions on Communists, Socialists, and the rights of free speech and a free press, and this same finding was repeated in 1953 **(10, 16)**. These and many other surveys by Gallup and Roper have shown that women are generally less informed than men on public affairs, a fact which is attested also by smaller percentages of women who vote in national elections **(16, 18, 3, 4)**. Gallup polls have shown consistently that women attend church more frequently than men **(1)**. There do not seem to be data, however, on the relative attitudes of male and female churchgoers and non-churchgoers.

The caution that the findings of this chapter may be quite specific to attitudes viewed in the context of the Communist threat is based, in part, on the inconclusive evidence from other studies as to whether women tend to be more intolerant than men on related subjects. NORC survey data show no differences between sexes, for example, on questions designed to elicit "authoritarian" attitudes **(16)**. After reviewing the findings from a wide variety of studies of ethnic prejudice and other forms of intolerance, in the *Nature of Prejudice,* G. W. Allport concluded that the evidence was too conflicting to support any single broad generalization as to the sex differences **(24)**.

SUMMARY

This chapter has shown that women tend, with small but consistent difference, to be less tolerant than men with respect to nonconformists like Socialists, atheists, or Communists, or suspected nonconformists.

Women are less interested than men in the news about Communists and what is being done about them. In general, the less interested people are, the less tolerant they are on our scale. But this fact does not explain sex differences in tolerance. We see that among interested people only, as well as in the entire cross-section, women tend to be less tolerant than men.

Women are somewhat more likely than men to say they worry about personal or family problems, but there is only a slight sex difference in tendency to be optimistic; not enough to support a convincing psychological explanation of differences in tolerance.

Women who are gainfully employed tend to be less tolerant than males in similar occupations. Housewives tend to be less tolerant than men in occupations similar to their husbands'. There is no consistent pattern of differences in tolerance between women who are gainfully employed and other women.

Women are more faithful church attenders than are men. Church attenders are more likely to be intolerant of Socialists, atheists, Communists, or suspected Communists than non-churchgoers, and this finding holds for each sex separately. But greater fidelity to the church would not seem to account for the sex differences, since female churchgoers are quite consistently less tolerant than male churchgoers; and the same holds among non-churchgoers considered separately.

Women are, if anything, less likely than men to agree with such a statement as "If a child is unusual in any way, his parents should get him to be more like other children." This finding suggests that women may not be more intolerant *in general* than men, but that the differences reported in this chapter are quite specific, as related to varying perceptions of the Communist menace.

Chapter Seven

WHAT ASPECTS OF COMMUNISM DO AMERICANS DISTRUST MOST?

In this chapter we shall examine certain of the images in the minds of Americans about the internal Communist threat. Here our concern will be primarily with a qualitative description of the contents of beliefs. A study of the important matter of how perception of the internal Communist threat relates to tolerance of nonconformists is reserved mainly for the next chapter.

The subject of the internal Communist threat was introduced with the question: **How great a danger do you feel that American Communists are to this country at the present time—a very great danger, a great danger, some danger, hardly any danger, no danger?** It has already been noted in Chapter Three that among the national cross-section 19% answered "very great," 24% "great," 38% "some danger," 9% "hardly any danger," and 2% "no danger." There were 8% with no opinion. More detailed statistical analysis of these responses will come in Chapter Eight.

This question was followed by asking:

Why do you think this?

What kind of people in America are most likely to be Communists?

What kinds of things do Communists believe in?

Have you ever known a person who you thought might be a Communist? If "Yes": How could you tell? What made you think this?

The unguided, uncoached responses to these four questions constitute the main source material for this chapter. The free answers were carefully coded by the survey agencies but are often so vague and overlapping that they do not lend themselves readily to statistical treatment. In selecting some comments for quotation, any editor runs the risk of distortion. Particularly, there is a temptation to quote the more colorful. Even a rough summarization into types and a count of each type are helpful in keeping perspective. Such counts will be reported.

Before we look at our present data, it is important that we keep in mind the crucial fact, presented in detail in Chapter Three, that very few people are deeply and personally anxious about the internal Communist threat. It will be recalled that less than 1% in the national cross-section mentioned Communists spontaneously when first asked what they worried most about, and not over 2% mentioned it upon further non-directive probing. Yet, as we also saw in Chapter Three, a considerable proportion—somewhat over half of the cross-section— said that they followed very closely or fairly closely the news about American Communists and what is being done about them. These we have been calling the "more interested" people.

MORE PEOPLE ARE BOTHERED ABOUT COMMUNISTS CONVERTING OTHER AMERICANS THAN ABOUT POSSIBLE ESPIONAGE OR SABOTAGE

Most of the 11% who felt that there was hardly any danger or no danger from American Communists at the present time said that the F.B.I. or other police agencies had the problem well under control.

When those who said that Communists were at least some danger at the present time—81% of the national cross-section—were asked why they thought this, their replies tended to fall into two main categories:

First, very numerous general statements like: "The Communists are out to take over America"; "They're working for Russia"; "They want a revolution"; "They are awful people."

Second, more specific statements which might in turn be coded into one of three categories—namely, references to sabotage, espionage, or subversion, this last in the sense of either converting others to Communism or spreading Communist ideas or both. In some instances, two or even all three types of threats were mentioned by the same person, in which case his response was coded more than once.

Perhaps the most remarkable finding is that so few people mentioned sabotage or espionage as compared with the proportion mentioning the conversion of others to Communism, or the spreading of Communist ideas. A rough and not too exact count of the responses in the national cross-section shows specific mentions as follows:

Sabotage	8%
Espionage	8%
Conversion and Spreading Ideas	28%

All of these figures may be a little too high or a little too low, as it was sometimes difficult to infer just what the respondent meant. This difficulty is reflected in a spread of 7% between the findings on "conversion" as reported by the two survey agencies:

	American Institute of Public Opinion	National Opinion Research Center
Sabotage	7%	8%
Espionage	8	9
Conversion, Spreading Ideas	24	31
Total Sample	2483	2450

But there can be no doubt that the latter was most frequently mentioned of the three. This is even more manifest in the sample of local community leaders, where the corresponding percentages are: sabotage, 5%; espionage, 6%; conversion or spreading ideas, 36%.

First, let us sample some comments on *sabotage:*

"They could sabotage our railroads and factories; could ruin our country."
—*Housewife,* New York.

"Seems like they have a hand in some of our big strikes which stop defense production."
—*Accountant,* Texas.

"They can do a fabulous amount of damage if they become a fifth column the same as in France; that caused the collapse of France."
-—*Salesman,* Michigan

158

"The Communists cause strikes in our factories and they might use bombs."

—*Secretary* (female), Florida.

"They're mostly underground now and sabotage is the real danger."
—*Paper-mill employee*, Pennsylvania.

"Plants blowing up, fire, strikes, are all being done by Communists."
—*Housewife*, Ohio.

"They are scattered all over our big factories and are working underground in all of them. Looking for chances of sabotage."

—*Farmer*, Illinois.

"One of their objectives is to infiltrate government, and armed forces, and other vital spots with a view to destruction and sabotage when the need for it strikes."

—*Mayor*, Massachusetts.

"All the plane wrecks we have—there couldn't be that many without a reason. They want to scare people so we won't trust our government."

—*Housewife*, Pennsylvania.

"They are traitors to our country secretly trying to subvert the government. When they are not known they might do things to injure the country, but there's not very much chance of their hurting us now. If we were on the verge of war, then we would be in real danger of sabotage from them."

—*Newspaper editor*, Indiana.

Some sample comments about *espionage:*

"They get positions in our defense plants, where they are hard to uncover. They take our secrets and this causes the government to put more into police work than spending money on our defenses."
—*Housewife*, New Jersey.

"They have positions in the government, especially in science. They steal our secrets and give them to Russia."

—*Florist*, Pennsylvania.

"In some research centers they're in a position to cause real trouble through espionage."

—*Research scientist*, Michigan.

159

"The various agencies like the F.B.I. are controlling them. Yet there is some danger that they have stolen secrets, especially when they have gotten into labor unions in defense plants."

—*Clergyman*, New York.

"They have a terrific spy setup and now's a good time to move in on us with all of us fighting among ourselves."

—*Automobile salesman*, Missouri.

"Infiltrating into Army and research laboratories, getting our secrets. And they may be in the State Department."

—*Housewife*, New York.

"The real danger is the possibility, if we get into a war, that secrets both from industrial and science laboratories could be passed to other countries by the Communists who infiltrate our country."

—*School superintendent*, Texas.

"The episode of Russia getting the atom bomb secrets tells the story of what can happen."

—*Cost estimator*, Massachusetts.

A quite convincing case can be made for the proposition that the most lethal danger facing America today from internal Communists is their potentiality for spying or, above all, for crippling sabotage in case of war. Yet the vulnerability of communications, bridges, tunnels, ports, factories, etc., to sabotage is apparently not the main threat in people's minds. In any event, it was seldom verbalized in this survey, as indicated by the fact that only 8% mentioned anything that could be thus catalogued. What was on the minds of a much larger number was *the danger of Americans today becoming converts to Communism or Communist ideas.* They saw perils of subversion of our youth in schools and colleges and of adults such as workers in factories, Negroes, and other minority groups, government employees, etc. Some sample comments:

"Relatively little has been done to stop the Communists. They can still teach in our schools. Nothing stops them from planting their ideas. If they can teach, they mold the ideas of youth, make them think world government is a wonderful thing, when youth doesn't know that world government means slavery from the top."

—*Housewife*, California.

"I think that there is a danger because Communists try to undermine our ideals, our ways of thinking. I believe this can be combated, not by some of the means that are being used now, but by a better knowledge by everyone of the advantages of our type of government and the disadvantages of Communism—definitely through education."

—*Junior high school teacher,* District of Columbia.

"Many of our schools have Communist teachers."

—*Bakery employee,* Illinois.

"They are in our schools and do a lot of harm."

—*Lumber trimmer,* Kentucky.

"They are agitating the Negroes. They always try to work on the man that hasn't had a chance or equal rights with most people."

—*Student* (male), Alabama.

"They are infiltrating and must be uprooted. They are teaching government ownership, government control, and government share the wealth."

—*Housewife,* Wisconsin.

"They can do damage to our youth by influencing opinion, by imposing their own opinions. In this way they try to change our youth's ideas into Communistic ones."

—*Foreman, steel mill,* Illinois.

"So many young persons believe in Communism, there must be some persons teaching it."

—*Housewife,* Michigan.

"I think some elements of Communist ideology have been sold to people in the newspaper field and they peddle it daily in their columns. So people in influential places have adopted some of those ideas, especially the idea the state should control the instruments of production."

—*Government official,* District of Columbia.

"If we let them go they'll try to turn everybody against religion and the way we live in this country."

—*Roofer,* Alabama.

"They're creeping in in places and poisoning the minds of young people in education with things that are contrary to the Bible."

—*Housewife,* Indiana.

161

"Looks like so many foreigners who have settled in this country have been Communists and lowered the morale of people by propaganda."
—*Housewife*, Alabama.

"I don't think there's too much to worry about, but any group that is working against the government is dangerous, large or small. Their damage is in teaching children the wrong doctrines. Communists either have a distorted twist of their minds or don't have much of the American way in their life."
—*Auto mechanic*, Iowa.

"Our country is fairly well protected with the F.B.I. They and the Secret Service are alert and on the job to prevent much danger. But we really aren't as well aware of the Communists as we should be, especially those who hope to inflict their beliefs on young people."
—*Housewife*, Pennsylvania.

"It's like a germ. It can spread. Communists are a danger when they talk to ignorant people. Ignorant people can be used by Communists to get more converts. I think ignorant people are most likely to become Communists, but, still, I always had a feeling that Mr. and Mrs. Roosevelt may have been Communists."
—*Housewife*, New Jersey.

"They influence so many people. They have no religion. They don't believe in God. They believe in destroying the faith of those that have religion. I think they get into colleges and influence students."
—*Housewife*, Wisconsin.

"Communists get children into cellars, educating them in warfare, and training them to go into secret places."
—*Housewife*, Massachusetts.

"They are working mostly among Negroes. That Paul Robeson caused a lot of trouble."
—*Housewife*, Oklahoma.

"They are poisoning the minds of our kids in school."
—*Physician*, California.

"They teach people against Christianity, ungodly things, and this is against our country. We believe in Christianity."
—*Clergyman*, Texas.

162

"In different communities I've heard there are Communist school-teachers and ministers. Young minds catch onto these things through their influence. Hitlerism proved that it's the youth of the country who can be instilled with these ideas."

—Housewife, Pennsylvania.

"With all the youngsters growing up, they can get them to listen. The younger generation seems more ready to listen."

—Housewife, Minnesota.

"They are getting into schools and teaching the children things and it's the young minds that are easy to influence."

—Housewife, Nebraska.

"Communists have infiltrated into the school system. We know that teachers in Harvard are avowed Communists. They are spreading Communism in every way they can."

—Housewife, Texas.

"They are trying to take over our thinking and teach the overthrow of the government and public control of everything."

—Housewife, Minnesota.

"There are always a few people who are easily led and these forget too easily the advantages of this country. You see I'm foreign-born myself. Quite a few people are shaky about world problems and willing to listen to anyone who'll tell them they'll have better things for them."

—Housewife, New Jersey.

"They're in our books, our movies, much more enmeshed in the life of the country than people realize. They started years ago—look at your I.W.W.'s and so on—one tiny facet. Education and identification is the only way to clear this thing, to bring it out into the open."

—Housewife, Connecticut.

"I have had contacts with Communists for ten years as a labor leader. I know their methods—how a few individuals can take control of 7000 or 8000 people."

—President, C.I.O. local, New Jersey.

"Communism and Socialism are the same thing and are being taught in this country."

—Lawyer, Michigan.

163

"They are so clever and so numerous that people who are very innocent get involved. They teach the government and state first, no religion, and everybody equal."

—*Housewife,* Missouri.

"They are undermining the youth of the country and if it isn't stopped we may have a generation of Communists in America."

—*Housewife,* Ohio.

"Just like Socialism—they are teaching no God, no hereafter, no rich, no poor, which is a big lie."

—*Merchant,* New York.

"So many people in America are eager like those soldiers of ours in Korea to fall in the trap set by Communist propaganda and even give up their own country for it. Maybe some of those who fall in the trap are scared to fight in war and join the Communists to get out of fighting for their country."

—*Housewife,* California.

"They don't believe in religion and they work on people who don't have a very good character to begin with."

—*Stenographer* (female), Kansas.

"Every Communist is trying to convert others and is likely to bring in some. When one gets in the government that happens. We don't need them."

—*Physician,* Ohio.

"They prey on unfortunate and maladjusted personalities and sound convincing to them."

—*Nurse,* Oklahoma.

"They preach against Christ. People who don't believe in Christ are so warped they can do almost anything."

—*Housewife,* Texas.

"There's always a danger to have someone preaching against our form of government. Eventually someone's going to believe him. The trouble is most people don't even know what a Communist is. It's good to read books about Communism—you get a better view of it. If you understand, you don't like it at all."

—*Grill man in restaurant,* Illinois.

The frequency with which the idea of converting Americans to Communism recurs in the comments may come as a surprise to those who believe that the era of making any appreciable number of Communist converts in this country has long since passed. The unmasking of Russia as an implacable enemy of the democratic way of life, together with the post-war thriving of the American economy, should be creating a climate very different from that of the period when most American Communists and fellow travelers were recruited.

In so far as the ideas so widely prevalent about *current* subversion of thought, especially of our youth, are exaggerated or untrue, a tremendous challenge is presented to leaders of American public opinion to correct the misapprehension. But it would be shortsighted, indeed, to assume that the mistaken ideas, however wild some of them may seem, are devoid of what psychologists call "reality testing."

First, there can be no denying that some Americans *in the past,* including some well-educated people, were victimized by Communist ideology. It does not necessarily follow, as some Americans seem to think, that the same thing is happening today and that our youth in schools and colleges or our government workers or factory employees are being successfully subverted to become traitors to the United States and secret agents of world revolution.

Second, there can be no denying that certain propositions which some Communists believe in, or profess to believe in, are also sincerely believed by some Americans today who are loyal to America and bitterly opposed to Russia. The difficulty, of course, is to counteract the belief that the holding or propagation of any such beliefs, especially as they deviate from traditional American thinking, is "playing Russia's game."

Before we consider such beliefs more specifically, let us turn to another question asked in our survey. The question is: **What things do Communists believe in?**

As with the previous question, there are considerable difficulties in classifying the answers. The two survey agencies, however, were in closer agreement on these responses than on the earlier ones. Table 1 provides a summary for the national cross-section as a whole and for the more interested and less interested portions separately, as well as for the local community leaders. It will be noted that the percentages in Table 1 add to more than 100, since some responses had to be coded in more than one category.

The classification in Table 1 is not too satisfactory, and the categories are obviously not mutually exclusive. It will serve, however, as a rough guide.

TABLE 1

WHAT DO COMMUNISTS BELIEVE IN?

(Responses to this question from national
cross-section and selected community leaders)

	Selected Community Leaders	National Cross-Section		
		More Interested in Issues	Less Interested in Issues	Total Cross-Section
Against religion	27%	29%	19%	24%
Political dictatorship	35	22	12	18
Government ownership of property	25	24	10	18
Promoting domination of world by Russia	13	21	10	17
Abolition of class distinction (e.g., "keep everybody poor")	20	18	10	15
Abolition of individual rights (other than property rights)	20	11	6	8
Immoral, amoral, anti-family, etc.	7	5	5	5
Miscellaneous (includes slogan-type answers, such as "overthrow the government," or "revolution," or general statements like "they are cruel," or other comments not classifiable above)	38	29	20	24
No answer	7	12	38	24
Number of Cases	1500	2778	2155	4933

Percentages add to more than 100% because of multiple responses.

166

Now, in the light of this table, let us ask: Which of the concepts listed there are believed in by considerable numbers of Americans who are themselves definitely anti-Russian and anti-Communist? It is doubtful whether any Americans, except for the small core of Communists and a scattering of right-wing Fascist extremists, believe in or preach political dictatorship. It is likewise doubtful whether any but a handful of disciplined Communists favor or advocate the domination of the world by Russia. The overt or covert advocacy of restriction of civil liberties is actually seen more often among the professional anti-Communists than among American Communists, who for tactical purposes profess zealous concern for rights which are, of course, denied in Russia. If we also exclude categories like "immoral" and "overthrow the government" as too vague or general, we are left with three categories in Table 1.

First, "against religion," which heads the list in frequency of mention in Table 1. It is quite doubtful whether there is any more evidence of militant atheism in the United States today than in the past. There is, for example, no such public atheist today as conspicuous as was Robert G. Ingersoll in his generation. But from the standpoint both of the devout Catholic and Protestant—the Protestant fundamentalist, particularly—there is an assault on traditional religious tenets. The youth in our schools—especially in secular colleges and universities—often emerge with doubts about the inspiration of the Bible or the infallibility of religious beliefs learned in early childhood. Indeed, a case can be made for thinking that reactions against these phenomena are among the main sources of anti-intellectualism in America, in so far as "intellectualism" stands for a free market place of ideas. And it is nothing new. One can look back, for example, to the Scopes trial in Tennessee. The fact to be reckoned with is that teachers, books, and magazines do threaten certain kinds of traditional religious certitude.

The leap to the conclusion that this is the insidious influence of atheistic Communism, directly or indirectly, is a long leap, indeed, but it will continue to be made by many good people who are predisposed to believe it. The majority of Americans probably do not believe it. Actually, only 16% of the national cross-section answered "Yes" to a check-list question: **If an American opposed churches and religion, would this *alone* make you think he was a Communist?** while another 7% answered "Don't know." Presumably, even a smaller number would have answered "Yes" if "a man with liberal religious views"

167

had been substituted for the outright opposer of churches and religion.

Second, "government ownership of property." Certainly there are Americans, including some of the most militant anti-Communists in the country, who favor an extension of government ownership and control beyond the point it has reached in America today. Deliberate effort to confuse the Socialist with the Communist, or even to brand the non-Socialist New Dealer as a Communist, may be expected to continue as long as there is political advantage in so doing. This kind of obfuscation is no less in the tradition of American politics than that which twenty years after the depression still seeks political advantage in blaming the depression solely on Herbert Hoover. But the point to be made here is this: The man who sincerely believes the advocates of government ownership to be under Communist domination is not at all illogical if he concludes that conversion to Communist ideology is a great danger. From the point of view of his value system, he has drawn a correct conclusion. The weakness of his position must therefore lie in his premise; namely, that advocates of government ownership *are* under Communist domination or even indirectly the dupes of Communism. In our survey we asked a check-list question: **If an American favored government ownership of all the railroads and big industries, would this alone make you think he was a Communist?** In the national cross-section, 17% answered "Yes" and 12% answered "Don't know."

Third, "abolition of class distinctions." It will be noted in Table 1 that 15% of the national cross-section, commenting on what Communists believe in, made remarks which were coded in this category. Most such remarks were not, however, intended to be complimentary —quite frequent were phrases like "keep everybody poor," "wipe out everybody who has any money," etc. Indeed, most respondents probably intended their remarks as another way of describing government ownership of property, including farms. In so far as the category really conveys any meaning different from that just discussed in the paragraph above, we may note that there are many Americans whose advocacy of high income taxes for the prosperous can be seen as subversive by those who believe that such "leveling" is a Russian importation. Likewise, opposition to discrimination against minority groups with respect to housing, education, employment, or recreation can be branded as pro-Communist subversion. This, too, is understandable, since "anti-discrimination" has been highly vocal and conspicuous in the American Communist Party line.

Of course there are other categories of people, in addition to those listed above, who can be and are branded by some as Communist subversives. Those who dare to oppose the techniques of politicians who capitalize on anti-Communism; those whose views on foreign policy or the United Nations are disliked; those who are simply guilty of association with anybody in any suspected categories—such persons can be believed to be spreading Communism if they are in a position where they can influence other people.

In connection with the first two categories which we have discussed —namely, anti-religion and pro-government ownership—there is one minor tabulation which is of some interest, particularly because it may throw some further light on our findings in Chapter Six with respect to sex and religion. Let us compare the differences between men and women, those who attended church in the month prior to the survey and those who did not, in what they choose to mention as Communist beliefs. Data for the national cross-section are shown in Table 2. This table brings out these points: (1) That among churchgoers and non-churchgoers alike a female is more likely than a male to perceive Communist beliefs in terms of hostility to religion. (2) That the *reverse* is true about government ownership of property. Males are more likely than females to pick this out as a tenet of Communist belief. (3) That churchgoers are more likely than non-churchgoers to point both to anti-religious beliefs and government ownership of property. However, the differences between churchgoers and others, as might be expected, are much larger in connection with noticing anti-religion.

Table 3 adds another point to these same data. When we apply to each of these groups in Table 2 our scale of tolerance toward nonconformists, utilized in the preceding chapters of this volume, we find in *every one* of the eight groups that the percentage rated as "more tolerant" on our scale is *lower* among those who have their eyes fixed on anti-religion than among those who have their eyes fixed on government ownership of property. This finding needs to be interpreted cautiously, because the classifications of "anti-religious" and "favoring government ownership" are based on free answers and subject to considerable error in coding. But it does underline the possibility that it may not be simple or easy for those who see in Communism a religious threat to raise their level of tolerance.

TABLE 2

MEN AND WOMEN, CHURCH ATTENDERS AND NON-CHURCH ATTENDERS, COMPARED AS TO THEIR STATEMENTS AS TO WHAT COMMUNISTS BELIEVE IN

(National Cross-Section)

		PERCENTAGES DESCRIBING COMMUNISTS AS:	
	Number of Cases	Anti-Religious	Favoring Government Ownership
More Interested in Issues			
Went to church in last month			
Women	963	35%	23%
Men	847	28	27
Did not go to church in last month			
Women	380	24%	17%
Men	588	21	24
Less Interested in Issues			
Went to church in last month			
Women	843	24%	9%
Men	442	18	13
Did not go to church in last month			
Women	446	18%	7%
Men	422	11	11

TABLE 3

HOW TOLERANCE OF NONCONFORMISTS IS RELATED TO STATEMENTS AS TO WHAT COMMUNISTS BELIEVE IN

(National Cross-Section)

| | PERCENTAGE CLASSED AS "MORE TOLERANT" ON SCALE OF TOLERANCE AMONG THOSE DESCRIBING COMMUNISTS AS: | |
	Anti-Religious	Favoring Government Ownership
More Interested in Issues		
Went to church in last month		
Women	29% (*339*)	33% (*221*)
Men	33 (*236*)	40 (*229*)
Did not go to church in last month		
Women	31% (*90*)	59% (*66*)
Men	40 (*124*)	59 (*139*)
Less Interested in Issues		
Went to church in last month		
Women	23% (*194*)	41% (*78*)
Men	17 (*89*)	39 (*59*)
Did not go to church in last month		
Women	28% (*78*)	54% (*30*)
Men	23 (*48*)	43 (*48*)

Number of cases in parentheses.

WHAT KIND OF PEOPLE DO AMERICANS THINK ARE LIKELY TO BE COMMUNISTS IN THIS COUNTRY?

The question, **What kind of people in the United States are most likely to be Communists?** was not especially productive as initially asked. Many tended to give very general answers, such as "almost any kind of person," "dupes," "unpatriotic people," and the like, or simply said they hadn't thought much about it. The interviewer was especially instructed to use "non-directive" methods to encourage respondents to talk further. Finally, unless the subject was brought up earlier, the questions were asked: **What racial or religious groups are they most likely to be in?** and **What kind of jobs are they most likely to be in?**

The answers fall into several types:

First, responses in terms of *broad social class or education*. About half of the respondents answered in these terms. *The vote was about 2 to 1 that the less educated and working-class people were more likely to be Communists than the better-educated and white-collar people.* Better educated respondents were much more likely to express an opinion than the less educated respondents. But, as Table 4 shows, each educational level in the sample was more likely to think Communists relatively uneducated than relatively educated. Among those more interested in issues, the vote was about 2 to 1 among respondents *at each* educational level. Among the less interested, the vote varied by educational level, from 58% and 22%, respectively, among those with the most schooling, to 14% and 12% among those with the least schooling.

Most of the local community leaders were willing to express an opinion on this point. Their vote, like that of the national cross-section, also was nearly 2 to 1 that Communists are more likely to be found among the less educated and working classes, 32% saying "better educated," etc., and 55% saying "less educated," etc.

Second, there was *no marked tendency to single out a particular racial or religious or other ethnic group as especially likely to harbor Communists*. A fourth of the sample explicitly said there were no differences in this respect.

TABLE 4

WHAT KIND OF PEOPLE ARE MOST LIKELY TO BE COMMUNISTS?

(National Cross-Section)

	Number of Cases	PERCENTAGE WHO SAY THAT U.S. COMMUNISTS ARE LIKELY TO BE:	
		White-Collar, Better Educated, etc.	*Working Class, Less Educated, etc.*
Total Sample	*4933*	18%	35%
Respondents in Cross-Section by Interest and Education:			
More Interested in Issues			
College graduates	*308*	31%	59%
Some college	*319*	27	57
High school graduates	*768*	22	47
Some high school	*576*	19	37
Grade school	*792*	15	31
Less Interested in Issues			
College graduates	*68*	22%	58%
Some college	*141*	22	49
High school graduates	*440*	16	38
Some high school	*446*	14	26
Grade school	*1050*	12	14

Among those expressing an opinion, 25% answered in general terms like "foreign"—but many of these comments may have represented an intention to say "people who are un-American" or people who "fall for a foreign ideology" rather than explicitly connoting people of foreign birth or extraction. Respondents in our sample who themselves are foreign-born or natives of foreign parentage were only slightly less likely than natives of native parentage to give a response which was coded in this category—21% as compared with 27% among natives of native parentage.

In spite of anti-Semitic propaganda which has made it a point to identify Jews with Communist infiltration, and in spite of the numerous Jewish names which actually have appeared in the news about suspected Communists brought before investigating committees, it is of interest to note that only 5% of the national cross-section said that Communists were especially likely to be Jewish. The proportion of such mentions was somewhat larger, 11%, among the local community leaders. Among respondents in the cross-section who are themselves Jewish, the corresponding proportion who mentioned a special likelihood of Communists being Jewish was 7%.

The proportion mentioning Negroes as especially likely to become Communists was 9% in the national cross-section and 5% among the local community leaders. Among Southern white respondents, 15% thought Negroes especially likely to become Communists, but only 4% of respondents who themselves were Negroes thought so.

When asked: **What kind of people in America are most likely to be Communists?** 12% in the cross-section and 5% among the community leaders volunteered, "people who are not religious" or are "against religion." Among the more interested segment of the cross-section, this was volunteered by 15% of the males who had gone to church in the last month and by 18% of the females. From those not attending church, the number of mentions dropped to 8% among males and 12% among females. Corresponding figures for the less interested were 13%, 12%, 8%, and 8%, respectively.

Third, with respect to *kinds of jobs* in which Communists are most likely to be found, *jobs in industry and in government take top place in frequency of mention* by the cross-section, with 24% and 21%, respectively. Among local leaders, corresponding figures are 16% and 26%. In both samples, schools and colleges were mentioned spontaneously by a smaller number, by 6% in the cross-section and 11% in the sample of leaders.

Fourth, this inventory would not be complete without noting that 19% of the cross-section and 38% of the sample of leaders offered spontaneous comment derogatory to the personalities of Communists, such as "the kinds of people who are most likely to become Communists are crackpots," or "queer people," or "warped personalities."

Such a hodgepodge of images is significant to us only because it was volunteered with a minimum of coaching. In the next chapter we shall see the results of some more specific check-list questions—for example, on the Communist threat in government, defense plants, and schools and colleges—and see, as we might expect, that the number *volunteering* any kind of answer to the question we are discussing is far less than the number who would agree to an explicit question about the magnitude of the threat when asked.

ONLY 3% OF CROSS-SECTION SAY THEY EVER KNEW AN ADMITTED COMMUNIST

A reading of that portion of the questionnaire which has been described in this chapter gives one a feeling that responses are not so much in terms of fearing American Communists as of bewilderment that some people have in fact become Communists, and of anger as expressed in such statements as, "What makes me mad is these people standing on the Fifth Amendment after doing all they can to tear down our government."

Like the operations of crime syndicates in our large cities or of international spy rings, there is a mystery about the secret ways of Communists which can sharpen the audience interest in news or tales about them and also can free the imagination to see dangers without limit. "There are thousands of secret Communists all over, so secret they never even go to cell meetings." "They've filtered everywhere." "They are worming their way secretly into all positions where they can cause a great deal of trouble." "They have a cunning way of getting into key positions and eating at the foundations of our government." "They are in a lot of places none of us realize."

The secrecy and mystery of Communist operations are almost as remote from the daily life of the average American as the intrigues within the Kremlin itself. The remoteness is illustrated by the following finding: When asked, **Have you ever known a person you thought might be a Communist?** only 3% of the cross-section said they knew a person who *admitted* he was a Communist. Another 10% said they knew somebody who acted suspiciously enough to make them think he might be.

Those who reported a ground for suspicion of somebody were asked to tell what the ground was. In practically all cases it was an inference from things the suspect said, though in a few instances it was people he associated with, things he read, or just deviant or queer behavior in general. It may throw some further light on the image of Communists which some people hold if we quote a few sample comments. But *we must keep in mind that these quotations are not typical,* since 87% claimed they never knew anybody whom they even suspected to be a Communist.

"He was always talking about world peace."

—*Housewife,* Oregon.

"Would not attend church and talked against God. He was always against local politics."

—*Housewife,* Pennsylvania.

"I saw a map of Russia on a wall in his home."

—*Locomotive engineer,* Michigan.

"I suspect it from his conversation and manner. He was well educated and had a high disregard for the mentality of others."

—*Lawyer,* Georgia.

"Her activities in distributing literature about the United Nations."

—*Housewife,* Indiana.

"Didn't believe in the Bible and talked about war."

—*Laborer,* Arkansas.

"He wrote his thesis in college on Communism."

—*Dentist,* Illinois.

"He aimed all his talk toward betterment of people through government ownership of property."

—*Foreman,* Florida.

"In my college days in the depression a group of young men and women lived together in a large home and called themselves Socialists."

—*Schoolteacher,* California.

176

"He was a radical who wanted to change everything in the country—it fits the picture."

—*Rancher,* Wyoming.

"Just his slant on community life and church work. He was not like us."

—*Bank vice-president,* Texas.

"The literature they read and the way they talk—atheists."

—*Farmer,* Rhode Island.

"They were strongly in favor of the Hollywood group who were taken up as Communists and objected to their conviction."

—*Stockbroker,* California.

"I just knew. But I wouldn't know how to say how I knew."

—*Farmer,* Kansas.

"He didn't believe in Christ, heaven, or hell."

—*Building contractor,* Mississippi.

"He brought a lot of foreign-looking people into his home."

—*Housewife,* Kansas.

"He's against almost everything done in the United States. His ideas are not those of a liberal but a fanatic. He voices ideas with abandon."

—*Accountant,* California.

"When I was collecting for the United Fund Drive and asked a man for a donation, he began raving about war and Korea."

—*Housewife,* Michigan.

"Avidly defends the underdog and explains the reasoning behind Communist moves."

—*Manager of business,* Maryland.

"I just don't trust her. She seems to be living behind a false front. I think she is smart enough so she could, as it were, live two lives. She has more money to spend and places to go than seems right. But I could be mistaken."

—*Housewife,* Iowa.

"A distant relative of mine. Is a scientist, an atheist, and down on everything."

—*Housewife,* Michigan.

177

"During the war I used to say Russia was our enemy and he got mad at me."

—*Merchant,* New York.

"A preacher. He gave me a radical-sounding paper to read—that we should all be equal such as the leaves on a tree are equal."

—*Housewife,* Maryland.

"Very aggressive along certain lines. Wanted to be a leader but not interested in money."

—*Insurance agent,* New Jersey.

"He had a foreign camera and took so many pictures of the large New York bridges. A young man but never associated with people his own age."

—*Housewife,* New York.

"The way he talked. He is dead now so he can't make any trouble."

Punch-press operator, New York.

"My husband's brother drinks and acts common-like. Sometimes I kind of think he is a Communist."

—*Housewife,* Ohio.

Even if only 10% in our cross-section belong in the category from which these quotations are taken, and even if there are few typhoid Marys in this sample who would spread mischievous rumors, the picture is not a pleasant one. It illustrates how the label "Communist" may become a convenient synonym for "that which I dislike or distrust." Indiscriminate use of the label by public figures as an offensive weapon against measures or ideas which they oppose can hardly discourage the ordinary person from doing likewise in more limited and personal ways.

Now let us lay aside this 10% whose acquaintances may or may not have been Communists or even fellow travelers. What about the 3% who reported having known a self-admitted or self-proclaimed Communist? It is particularly interesting to see, if we can, what portions of the public are most likely to have had personal exposure to such a person.

Table 5 shows how this 3% is distributed by type of community and region. City people in the North are most likely to say they have known an admitted Communist. It is rare, indeed, to find a farmer or a Southerner who reports such a contact.

TABLE 5

CITY PEOPLE IN THE NORTH ARE MOST LIKELY TO SAY THEY HAVE KNOWN A COMMUNIST

PERCENTAGE, AMONG THOSE LIVING IN A GIVEN TYPE OF COMMUNITY AND GIVEN REGION, WHO SAY THEY HAVE EVER KNOWN A SELF-ADMITTED OR SELF-PROCLAIMED COMMUNIST:

	Metropolitan Areas	Other Cities	Small Towns	Farms
West	7%	5%	6%	3%
East	6	3	4	—
Middle West	2	4	3	2
South	2	1	3	—

NUMBER OF CASES ON WHICH PERCENTAGES ARE BASED:

	Metropolitan Areas	Other Cities	Small Towns	Farms
West	284	226	108	40
East	661	331	222	44
Middle West	543	402	241	272
South	400	395	339	404

179

Does this pattern of contacts mean that Communists are more likely to have been active in Northern cities than elsewhere? Perhaps. But one must be extremely cautious in interpreting Table 5 in terms either of absolute or relative percentages. The absolute percentages may be inaccurate in either direction. They may be too high in so far as some respondents may have thought a man admitted he was a Communist when all that he admitted may have been that he was, for example, a Socialist. They may be too low in so far as some respondents may have been reticent about telling the interviewer, even in an anonymous interview, that they had ever had any contact with a Communist. If such reticence existed, however, it was well concealed from the trained interviewers, who report no special signs of hesitation or suspicion in answering this question. Even assuming that there was no bias in response, or that whatever bias in response existed was the same throughout the country, one cannot conclude that the probability of knowing a Communist in the Far West was necessarily greater than, say, in the Middle West. It must be remembered that a major fraction of the adults in the West migrated there from other parts of the country. There may be much more chance that a person who has lived in several regions will have met a Communist somewhere at some time in his life than will a person who has lived all his life in a single place, especially in a single small town or rural county.

The sheer fact of meeting more people of all kinds may, indeed, account in part for the finding that better educated people are much more likely than others to say they knew a self-admitted Communist. Percentages by education are:

College graduates	7%	*(376)*
Some college	7%	*(460)*
High school graduates	4%	*(1198)*
Some high school	3%	*(1022)*
Grade school	1%	*(1842)*

(Number of cases on which percentages are based is shown in parentheses.) The better educated also tend to be located in greater proportions in the cities than in small towns and on farms, but further cross-tabulation demonstrates that residence alone will not account for differences by education in likelihood of meeting a Communist. This table suggests the obvious possibility that better educated people are more likely to meet Communists because Communists themselves

180

are more likely to be better educated. This may very well be true, on the average, and if true would indicate that many people who were shown in Table 4 to assume the contrary may be wrong in their impressions.

One further observation. The above findings might be taken to suggest that many among this 3% *in our own cross-section of respondents* may themselves be Communists or fellow travelers. It is easy to dispute this on two counts.

First, from internal evidence in the questionnaire. In the national cross-section of 4933 cases, there are 158 cases, or 3%, who claimed to have known a self-admitted or self-proclaimed Communist. Let us look at their answers to certain other questions:

Do you think a man can believe in Communism and still be a loyal American, or not? A total of 124, or 78%, of these 158 cases answered a flat "No." Among the 34 others, 20 answered "Yes," eight gave qualified answers, and six expressed no opinion. (The 20 included respondents like the man who said he had a friend from Yugoslavia who was a Communist and strong for Tito, but a good American.) These 34 cases can be broken down further on answers to other questions:

To reduce taxes, do you favor cutting down the size of our Air Force now? Only one person out of the 34 said "Yes."

To reduce taxes, do you favor cutting down our atom bomb production now? Only four persons out of the 34 said "Yes."

Suppose it turned out that the only way to stop the Communists from taking over the rest of Europe was for the United States to fight Russia. Should we let the Communists take over the rest of Europe or fight Russia? Only six answered "Let the Communists take over."

Exactly the same question was asked about Asia, with nine answering "Let the Communists take over."

Or consider a question supported by a fourth of the entire national cross-section, including, presumably, all of the extreme isolationists: **Would you favor cutting down our aid to our allies now?** Isolationists and Russian sympathizers alike should agree on this one. But only nine of our special group of 34 took the isolationist position.

A large number of other breakdowns, which take off from different starting points and are not merely restricted to people who say they knew Communists, yields much less than 1% who can be considered "fellow travelers" by whatever criterion one wishes to use. This is

181

further confirmed by reading entire questionnaires from such marginal cases.

This is not to deny the possibility that some people concealed their real feelings or even lied. Communists would be expected to lie. Moreover, real Communists, if any were drawn for the sample, may have refused to answer at all. There is no basis whatever for thinking that such evasion could account for major patterns of findings reported in this study.

But we do not have to rely on internal evidence in the cross-section to show that most people who said they knew self-admitted Communists were extremely unlikely themselves to be Communists. For a second line of evidence we can turn to our sample of local community leaders. Like our better educated in the national cross-section, *the local leaders were not only more likely than others to be tolerant of nonconformists but also were more likely than others to have been in a position to know a Communist.* Eleven per cent of the community leaders, as compared with 3% in the cross-section, said they had known a self-admitted or self-proclaimed Communist. As Table 6 shows, every one of the 14 selected types of leaders was more likely to have known a Communist than was the average in the cross-section.

Further tabulations of the national cross-section show that men are more likely than women to say they ever knew an admitted Communist—4% as compared with 2%. Jews are more likely than Protestants or Catholics—10% as compared with 3% for Catholics and Protestants alike. Differences by age are negligible, the very youngest and the very oldest being slightly, though perhaps not significantly, less likely to say they ever knew an admitted Communist.

The findings in this section tend to emphasize further the remoteness of the Communist threat from the *personal* experience of most Americans. Where personal contacts with admitted Communists have occurred, they tend to have been experienced most often by city people, especially in the North, by the better educated generally, and by local community leaders. The relationship between remoteness and intolerance of nonconformists will be examined, along with other variables, in the next chapter.

182

TABLE 6

HOW LIKELY ARE LOCAL COMMUNITY LEADERS TO HAVE KNOWN COMMUNISTS?

	Number of Cases	Percentage Who Said They Had Ever Known a Self-admitted or Self-proclaimed Communist
Public Officials		
Mayors	112	10%
Presidents, School Board	111	10
Presidents, Library Board	109	16
Political Party Chairmen		
Republican County Central Committee	110	16%
Democratic County Central Committee	103	14
Industrial Leaders		
Presidents, Chamber of Commerce	113	12%
Presidents, Labor Union	106	11
Heads of Special Patriotic Groups		
Commanders, American Legion	114	9%
Regents, D.A.R.	100	5
Others		
Chairmen, Community Chest	100	13%
Presidents, Bar Association	99	15
Newpaper Publishers	92	19
Presidents, Women's Club	109	5
Presidents, Parent-Teachers' Association	112	5
Average of Community Leaders	1500	11%

Roper surveys in 1947 and 1950 showed that large majorities believed that American Communists were in key positions where they could harm the country **(5, 19)**.

Two NORC surveys, conducted during 1950 and again in 1953, confirm that the public tends to regard the internal Communist danger chiefly in terms of infiltration and influence rather than espionage or sabotage. The questions were identical to one in the present survey: **In what way do you feel American Communists are a danger?** and while the classification of responses was subject to the same occasional ambiguities noted in the current study, both surveys clearly revealed larger proportions mentioning propaganda and infiltration of government, schools, labor, etc., than mentioning spying, stealing secrets, sabotage of industry, etc. **(16)**.

The area of public conceptions of Communist beliefs has been largely ignored in earlier research, though incidental evidence of the frequent equation of irreligion with Communism is available from another NORC poll in the spring of 1953. In that survey, 16% of the public said they would be "very suspicious" that a person "who goes around talking against religion" is a Communist, and 28% would be "a little suspicious" of him. The proportion who would be very suspicious happens, incidentally, to be the same as the proportion in the present survey who say that opposition to churches and religion would be enough in themselves to indicate that a person is a Communist **(16)**.

Survey data in the literature substantiate the present findings concerning conceptions as to what people are most likely to be Communist. Jews and Negroes, for example, have never been singled out by more than 4% or 5% of the population. Unless people were probed extensively, or unless particular groups were suggested to them, majorities of the public have generally replied that Communists are likely to be found anywhere and are not concentrated in any particular class or type of people. Nevertheless, as in the present survey, Communists are usually *more* likely to be thought of as poor, uneducated people in manual or trade-labor occupations rather than as educated, wealthy, white-collar, or intellectual types—although there is some evidence that the latter image of the Communist is becoming somewhat more prevalent than it was a few years ago **(16)**.

The only past data concerning personal acquaintance with possible Communists come from two state polls conducted in California in 1948 and in Minnesota in 1947. Even when their questions were put in the broad terms of "ever knowing anyone you suspected might be a Communist," only 22% in California and 14% in Minnesota answered "Yes." The higher proportion in California provides indirect support for the findings presented here, that city people and Far Westerners are more likely to have encountered Communists personally. In both the state polls, however, as here also, those who admitted they knew probable Communists included large numbers who explained their belief in such terms as "He was always playing Russian music," or "He used to have the lights burning at two o'clock in the morning" (17).

SUMMARY

This chapter has reported on the image of internal Communism in the minds of the American people interviewed in this survey.

More people are bothered about the possibility that Communists will convert other Americans to Communism than about espionage or possible sabotage in case of war.

Preoccupation with subversion, it was suggested, might seem outdated now that Russia's intentions are fully unmasked and now that the American economy is on a sounder basis than in depression days. To understand this preoccupation with subversion, we must remember two points:

1. That a few Americans, including some well-educated people, were converted to Communism in the past, and that some were fellow travelers. What happened in the past can easily be believed to be happening now.

2. That some things which Communists believe in, or profess to believe in, are also believed and propagated by Americans who themselves are loyal to America and bitterly opposed to Russia. Three such areas of belief are with respect to religion, extension of government ownership of property, and leveling of class lines. It is not too hard for the "anti-intellectual" to suspect that Americans who propagate doctrines which are a threat to his church or religious beliefs are under Communist domination or at least indirectly influenced by Communist ideology. So with other economic, political, and social views.

When asked what Communists believe in, the national cross-section most frequently mentioned "anti-religion," while "government ownership of property" was also high on the list. Churchgoers and women were somewhat more likely to be sensitized to the religious area than non-churchgoers and men. Men were somewhat more likely than women to note the economic threat. Tolerance of nonconformity was shown to be especially low among those who thought most about the anti-religious threat.

People thought that U.S. Communists are more likely to be less educated or working-class people than better educated or white-collar people. There was no marked tendency to isolate particular ethnic or religious groups—only small minorities of respondents, for example, mentioned Jews or Negroes. As to types of jobs in which the most

Communists are found, industry and government were mentioned most frequently, with schools and colleges third.

Only 3% of the cross-section said that they had ever known an admitted Communist. Another 10% had known a person whom they suspected of being a Communist, and their grounds for suspicion contribute to the picture of American beliefs about what Communists are like.

Since the Communist threat is so seldom a matter either of personal experience or, as Chapter Three showed, of deep personal concern, it is of interest to see what kinds of people are more likely to have met and known admitted Communists personally. These tend to be city people, Northerners, males, and the better educated. Moreover, the special sample of local community leaders is considerably more likely to have encountered an admitted Communist than the cross-section. These findings bear importantly on the question of how remoteness from contact with a problem may distort conceptions about it and heighten intolerance. This question will be reviewed, along with others, in the next chapter.

Chapter Eight

HOW FAR DOES THE COMMUNIST THREAT ACCOUNT FOR INTOLERANCE OF NONCONFORMISTS?

The foregoing chapter has described the picture of the internal Communist threat in the minds of Americans across the country.

Previous chapters showed what kinds of people were most willing and what kinds of people were least willing to extend civil liberties to Socialists, atheists, Communists, or people who, though accused of disloyalty, denied they had ever been Communists.

Now we shall apply the findings of the last chapter to the findings of earlier chapters. We shall consider two main questions:

1. How closely is perception of great internal Communist threat related to intolerance of nonconformists?

2. How completely do the two variables, perception of threat and general tolerance or intolerance of nonconformists, account for attitudes toward specific governmental actions—for example, toward the work of Congressional committees investigating Communism?

The first question is of central theoretical and practical importance. If the answer is that there is a very close 1-to-1 relationship between perception of great internal Communist threat and intolerance of nonconformists, there are predictable consequences.

One is that if the internal Communist danger should increase or should be perceived as increasing, intolerance may be expected to increase at the same time. An increase in the internal Communist danger is by no means an impossible contingency, especially if war becomes more imminent. An increase in concern about the internal danger also is by no means impossible, particularly if the public should become much more concerned or frightened than it is now about sabotage in case of war.

An opposite consequence of a 1-to-1 relationship between perception of great threat and intolerance could be expected if the internal threat should decrease or should be perceived as decreasing. A decrease in the internal Communist danger, like an increase, is by no means impossible. If the conversion of other Americans to Communism is, as many people now think, slowed down practically to a stop, and if the hard core of disciplined Communists is under ever more effective surveillance of the F.B.I. and other agencies of the executive arm of the government, the threat would in fact be diminishing. And the confidence of the American people in the F.B.I. and its allied forces should be such that the *perception* of threat also would diminish. It would follow, therefore, from a 1-to-1 relationship between perception of great threat and intolerance, that intolerance would decrease and that this decrease could be accelerated by stressing, in public information programs, the fact of the decline of the threat.

But suppose there is not so close a relationship between the perception of great threat and intolerance.

That is, suppose that a good many people are tolerant *despite* the fact that they see the internal Communist threat as very dangerous. If this were true, it would suggest that even if the threat increased, great increase in intolerance of nonconformists would not necessarily follow.

And suppose that a good many people are intolerant *despite* the fact that they do not see the internal Communist threat as very dangerous. Then a decrease in the Communist threat or perception of the threat would not necessarily, *of and by itself,* make them more tolerant. Only a long-sustained program of public education through the press, radio, and television, and more direct local influences, based not primarily on the negative theme of "pooh-poohing" the Communist threat but principally on the positive theme of the supreme importance of civil liberties, could be expected to have an effect.

Hence the significance of our first question: How closely is the perception of great internal Communist threat related to intolerance of nonconformists?

Our second question also is of importance: How completely do the two variables, perception of threat and general tolerance or intolerance of nonconformists, account for attitudes toward specific governmental actions—for example, toward the work of Congressional committees investigating Communism? Whether perception of threat

189

and tolerance or intolerance are very closely related to each other or are not too closely related, they still may not be the only factors or even the most crucial factors determining attitudes toward a particular event, especially in the political arena. We need to examine this problem and can use the attitudes toward the work of Congressional investigating committees as a case study.

HOW CLOSELY IS PERCEPTION OF THE INTERNAL COMMUNIST THREAT RELATED TO TOLERANCE OR INTOLERANCE OF NONCONFORMISTS?

The first direct question about American Communists asked in this survey was as follows: **How great a danger do you feel that American Communists are to this country at the present time—a very great danger, a great danger, some danger, hardly any danger, or no danger?**

Chart I shows how this question was answered by our special sample of selected community leaders, by the more interested fraction of the national cross-section, and by the less interested. We see that the leaders are somewhat *less likely* than the more interested in the rank and file to say "very great danger" or "great danger." Only 2% in either group, however, answered "no danger at all." Among the less interested people in the cross-section, it will be seen that 14% expressed no opinion, while the percentage responding "a very great danger" or "a great danger" was less than among the more interested.

Now let us examine the relationship between answers to this question and our scale of tolerance of nonconformists used in the earlier chapters of this volume. The findings are shown in Chart II and merit close inspection.

First, the bars in Chart II show that there is *a definite relationship between perception of the risk and tolerance as measured by our scale.*

Consider the local community leaders. Among the 230 who perceive a very great danger, the proportion "more tolerant" is 53%; among the 223 who perceive hardly any danger, the percentage is very much higher, 75%; and the percentage is 77% among the handful, 35 cases in all, who perceive no danger.

190

CHART I

HOW COMMUNITY LEADERS AND THE CROSS-SECTION VIEW THE INTERNAL COMMUNIST THREAT

QUESTION: How great a danger do you feel that American Communists are to the country at the present time?

NATIONAL CROSS-SECTION

PERCENTAGE ANSWERING:	SELECTED COMMUNITY LEADERS	THOSE MORE INTERESTED IN ISSUES	THOSE LESS INTERESTED IN ISSUES
A VERY GREAT DANGER	15	23	15
A GREAT DANGER	22	25	21
SOME DANGER	45	38	37
HARDLY ANY DANGER / NO DANGER	15	9	10
DON'T KNOW			14
	1500	2778	2155

Numbers inside the bars show percentages; numbers at the ends of the bars show the size of the samples.

CHART II

RELATIONSHIP BETWEEN SENSE OF INTERNAL DANGER AND WILLINGNESS TO TOLERATE NONCONFORMANCE

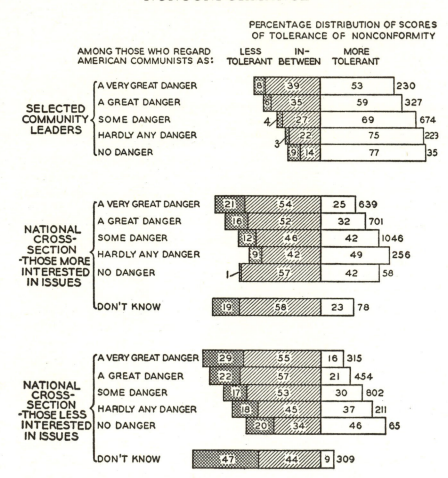

PERCENTAGE DISTRIBUTION OF SCORES OF TOLERANCE OF NONCONFORMITY

AMONG THOSE WHO REGARD AMERICAN COMMUNISTS AS: — LESS TOLERANT — IN-BETWEEN — MORE TOLERANT

SELECTED COMMUNITY LEADERS

	LESS TOLERANT	IN-BETWEEN	MORE TOLERANT	N
A VERY GREAT DANGER	8	39	53	230
A GREAT DANGER	6	35	59	327
SOME DANGER	4	27	69	674
HARDLY ANY DANGER	3	22	75	223
NO DANGER	9	14	77	35

NATIONAL CROSS-SECTION -THOSE MORE INTERESTED IN ISSUES

	LESS TOLERANT	IN-BETWEEN	MORE TOLERANT	N
A VERY GREAT DANGER	21	54	25	639
A GREAT DANGER	16	52	32	701
SOME DANGER	12	46	42	1046
HARDLY ANY DANGER	9	42	49	256
NO DANGER	1	57	42	58
DON'T KNOW	19	58	23	78

NATIONAL CROSS-SECTION -THOSE LESS INTERESTED IN ISSUES

	LESS TOLERANT	IN-BETWEEN	MORE TOLERANT	N
A VERY GREAT DANGER	29	55	16	315
A GREAT DANGER	22	57	21	454
SOME DANGER	17	53	30	802
HARDLY ANY DANGER	18	45	37	211
NO DANGER	20	34	46	65
DON'T KNOW	47	44	9	309

Likewise, among either the interested or the less interested people in the cross-section, the percentages increase as the perception of threat increases. The only exception to a straight line progression of these bars is the case of the more interested people who perceive "no danger." Only 1% of them are classed as "less tolerant," but the proportion "more tolerant," 42%, is below that among those who answer "hardly any danger." The "no danger" group is very small, however, comprising only 58 cases, and the discrepancy could well be a sampling error.

It will be noted that those who answer "don't know" about the danger, among the interested and less interested alike, tend to include fewer of the more tolerant people than any other groups.

Second, while a clear and unambiguous relationship between perception of threat and tolerance exists, *it is a far cry from a 1-to-1 relationship*.

Chart II makes this finding unmistakably evident.

Look again at the 230 local community leaders who perceive a very great danger. A *majority* of them, 53%, are classified as "more tolerant" on the scale, and this proportion is higher than that of any category whatever of the rank and file, *whatever their perception of danger*.

Within any one of the three main samples shown in Chart II, it is evident that the correlation between perception of threat and tolerance, though existing, is no 1-to-1 relationship. There are many people who perceive a very great danger yet are among the more tolerant. There are some who perceive hardly any or no danger yet are among the less tolerant. And there is the group called "in-between" on the tolerance scale who are found in substantial proportions among all groups of people sorted by their perception of danger. If these findings can be trusted, we are forced to the following conclusion:

There is a relationship between perception of internal Communist danger and tolerance, but not high enough to suggest that changes in perception of danger alone would automatically and simultaneously result in changes in tolerance. The two variables do have something in common. But tolerance or intolerance may be a disposition too deeply rooted in a man's or woman's personality structure to be responsive to a merely *negative* information program which minimizes the internal Communist risk, even if the facts should justify such an interpretation of the risk.

We can get further confirmation of the findings from Chart II if we

TABLE 1

TYPES OF COMMUNITY LEADERS COMPARED ON
HOW THEY VIEW INTERNAL COMMUNIST
THREAT AND ON HOW THIS VIEW RELATES
TO TOLERANCE OF NONCONFORMISTS

	Perceived Threat			Tolerance	
	NUMBER WHO SAY DANGER IS		PERCENTAGE WHO SAY	PERCENTAGE CLASSED AS MORE TOLERANT	
	"very great" or "great"	*all other answers*	*"very great" or "great"*	*among those who say "very great" or "great"*	*among all others*
Public Officials	(1)	(2)	(3)	(4)	(5)
Mayors	38	74	34%	55%	63%
Presidents, School Board	30	81	27	60	62
Presidents, Library Board	36	73	33	72	82
Political Party Chairmen					
Republican County Central Com.	52	58	47%	69%	71%
Democratic County Central Com.	21	82	20	48	69
Industrial Leaders					
Presidents, Chamber of Commerce	32	81	28%	56%	69%
Presidents, Labor Union	35	72	33	57	64
Heads of Special Patriotic Groups					
Commanders, American Legion	60	54	57%	45%	48%
Regents, D.A.R.	69	31	69	45	55
Others					
Chairmen, Community Chest	31	69	31%	71%	89%
Presidents, Bar Association	35	74	33	74	78
Newspaper Publishers	22	70	24	68	90
Presidents, Women's Club	57	53	52	42	58
Presidents, Parent-Teachers' Assoc.	40	62	39	57	85
Average of Community Leaders	558	942	37%	57%	70%
Cross-Section of Leaders' Cities	400	497	45	26	38
National Cross-Section	2109	2824	43	27	41

This table is to be read as follows: Among mayors, 38 said the internal Communist threat was "very great" or "great." These 38 constituted 34% of all mayors. Among these 38, there were 55% who were scored as "more tolerant" on our scale of tolerance of nonconformists. Among the 74 who had other, milder views of the internal Communist threat, 63% were scored as "more tolerant."

look at Table 1. This tables shows the picture for individual types of local community leaders. Consider the top line, mayors. Of those in our sample, 38 mayors, or 34%, said that the internal Communist danger was "very great" or "great." Column 4 in Table 1 shows that, among these 38 mayors, 55% were scored as "more tolerant" on our scale of tolerance of nonconformists. Column 5 in Table 1 shows that among the 74 mayors who thought there was "some," "hardly any," or "no" danger the proportion "more tolerant" is 63%.

Comparing columns 4 and 5 all the way down in Table 1, we see that among each type of local leader, *without exception,* those who perceived the least internal Communist danger were more likely to be classed as "more tolerant."

But the differences, though completely consistent, are never very large. It is quite evident that a substantial number of these leaders can maintain attitudes of tolerance *in spite of* their estimate of the internal Communist danger. Moreover, there are some, though proportionally far fewer than among the rank and file, who are not among the more tolerant *in spite of* the fact that they do not view the internal Communist risk as great.

The number of cases on which the percentages in columns 4 and 5 in Table 1 are based is so small that any individual percentages must be viewed with extreme caution. (One time out of 20 we would expect differences of as much as 15% between any two percentages in this table, by chance alone.) But the *consistency* of the differences between columns 4 and 5 is sufficient to establish the significance of the *general pattern.*

The third column in Table 1 is also of some interest, in that it shows that 10 of the 14 types of community leaders were *less likely* than the average in the national cross-section to call the internal Communist threat "very great" or "great." The exceptions are the D.A.R. regents, the American Legion commanders, the women's club presidents, and the Republican County Central Committee chairmen.

The findings which we have reported thus far in this chapter have such important implications that we need to cross-check them in every way possible.

First, we can test the conclusions by comparing the results of the samples collected independently by our two survey agencies, the American Institute of Public Opinion and the National Opinion Research Center. In Table 2 we check the essential findings of Chart II. We see that both agencies agree quite consistently in their findings that the percentage "more tolerant" increases progressively as we go down from those who perceive very great danger to those who perceive little danger. Both agencies also agree in the fact that there is no 1-to-1 relationship. Individual percentages differ somewhat as between the two agencies, but the essential patterns are the same.

Second, we can check our findings by substituting more specific questions for the single general question used as an index of the perceived severity of the internal Communist threat.

For example, respondents were asked to guess *how many Communists they think there are in the United States*. A fourth of the leaders, a third of the more interested cross-section, and half of the less interested portion of the cross-section were not prepared even to venture a guess. The guesses varied wildly—all the way from over a million to under a thousand. The percentage classified as "more tolerant" on the scale of tolerance of nonconformists was highest among those guessing numbers somewhere between 50,000 and 250,000. Those who guessed still larger numbers were less likely to have relatively tolerant attitudes—as also were those who guessed very small numbers. In the more interested cross-section, for example, there were 156 who guessed less than a thousand—and these tended to have the least proportion of more tolerant people of any category of respondents. "Only a handful are enough to take over the country," commented a New York storekeeper.

More specific questions were asked about the number of Communists in government, in defense plants, teaching in colleges, and teaching in public schools. Answers were classified in terms of thousands, hundreds, a few, or none. Those who said "thousands" were less likely to be classed as tolerant of nonconformists than those who said "hundreds" or "a few," but the differences in tolerance scores were not great.

Further questions were asked in each case about the degree of danger. This type of question differentiated the more tolerant and less tolerant much more sharply than questions about mere numbers of Communists. For example, among the more interested cross-section:

How much danger is there that Communists within the Government can hurt the country?

	Percentage classed as "more tolerant"
Among those who answered "great danger"	28% (*1090*)
Among all others	41% (*1688*)

196

TABLE 2

HOW TWO SURVEY AGENCIES COMPARE ON RELATIONSHIP BETWEEN SENSE OF INTERNAL DANGER AND WILLINGNESS TO TOLERATE NONCONFORMISTS

Those classed as "more tolerant" on our scale of tolerance, among persons with different perceptions of danger

How great a danger do you feel American Communists are to the country at the present time?	Selected Community Leaders		NATIONAL CROSS-SECTION			
			More Interested in Issues		Less Interested in Issues	
	AIPO	NORC	AIPO	NORC	AIPO	NORC
A very great danger	52%	53%	22%	29%	14%	18%
A great danger	58	61	33	32	22	21
Some danger	68	71	42	43	28	31
Hardly any danger	76	72	44	54	38	35
No danger	—	—	45	37	47	45
Don't know	—	—	27%	21%	7%	12%

Number of cases on which above percentages are based

	AIPO	NORC	AIPO	NORC	AIPO	NORC
A very great danger	119	110	290	349	170	145
A great danger	149	178	336	365	212	242
Some danger	327	347	502	534	341	461
Hardly any danger	125	98	122	134	108	103
No danger	16	19	27	31	34	31
Don't know	6	5	48	30	166	143

This table is to be read as follows: In the AIPO sample of leaders, among those who say that American Communists are a very great danger, 52% are classed as more tolerant on our scale; in the corresponding NORC sample, 53%.

197

Incidentally, the tenacity with which those who answer "great danger" probably hold their views is suggested by the fact that, in answer to a direct question, 54% said they would not believe President Eisenhower if he should say that there is no longer any danger from Communists within the government. Even though the facts should now or later justify deflating the popular image of the Communist threat, and even though the most respected public figures should assert these facts, some people would be hard to convince.

How much danger is there that Communists in defense plants can hurt the country?

	Percentage classed as "more tolerant"
Among those who answered "great danger"	27% (*1260*)
Among all others	43% (*1518*)

Among those answering "great danger," 66% said they would not believe it if both the management and labor-union officials in a large defense plant were to say someday that Communists in that plant were no longer a danger.

How much danger is there that the Communists in colleges and universities can hurt the country?

	Percentage classed as "more tolerant"
Among those who answered "great danger"	26% (*1104*)
Among all others	43% (*1674*)

Sixty-three per cent of those answering "great danger" claimed that they would not believe it if a head of a college were to say someday that there were no Communists teaching in that college.

How much danger is there that the Communists in public schools can hurt the country?

	Percentage classed as "more tolerant"
Among those who answered "great danger"	29% (*983*)
Among all others	40% (*1793*)

Among those seeing a great danger, 54% said they would not believe it if the school board in their community were to say someday that there were no Communists teaching in their schools.

Differences in tolerance between those who perceive great danger and those who do not are of about the same magnitude for the less interested portion of the cross-section. Although the absolute levels of tolerance are much higher in our special sample of civic leaders than in our cross-section, the differences in tolerance between those who see great threat and others are quite similar to those shown above.

The responses to the questions which we have just reviewed with respect to government, defense plants, colleges and universities, and public schools have been combined with the responses to the general question which was graphed in Charts I and II, to form a *scale* of perception of the internal Communist danger. (For technical description, see Appendix C.) This scale, like our scale of tolerance of nonconformists, should be more reliable and stable than any single component item. Like the tolerance scale, it has been broken into three categories for simplicity of reporting; namely, those who "see relatively great threat," those who "see relatively little threat," and those who are "in-between."

Let us now use this scale to test the consistency of the findings reported thus far in this chapter, within a variety of sub-groups of the population.

For example, how is *education* related to perception of threat and how, in turn, within each educational group, is perception of the threat related to tolerance?

Table 3 shows how education is related to perception of threat. Among the more interested people in the cross-section, the percentage who see relatively great threat tends to be highest among high school graduates or those with some high school. There is a hint that the perception of great threat may tend to have a curvilinear relationship with education. The percentage who see relatively little threat tends to be greatest among college people. Among less interested people there is an even more consistent tendency for the proportion who see relatively little threat to increase with education. The pattern of percentages of those who see a relatively great threat is inconsistent. Table 3 shows that there is some relationship between education and perception of threat but that it is not a simple one, as was the clear and unmistakable relationship between education and tolerance of nonconformists presented in earlier chapters.

TABLE 3

HOW SCALE SCORES ON PERCEPTION OF THE INTERNAL COMMUNIST THREAT DIFFER BY EDUCATION —FOR NATIONAL CROSS-SECTION

PERCENTAGE DISTRIBUTION OF SCALE SCORES

	Grade School	Some H.S.	H.S. Graduate	Some College	College Graduate
More Interested People					
See relatively great threat	37%	40%	40%	35%	28%
In-between	47	42	45	46	46
See relatively little threat	16	18	15	19	26
Total	100%	100%	100%	100%	100%
Number of cases	792	576	758	319	308
Less Interested People					
See relatively great threat	19%	26%	22%	28%	22%
In-between	62	56	54	47	47
See relatively little threat	19	18	24	25	31
Total	100%	100%	100%	100%	100%
Number of cases	1050	446	440	141	68

200

CHART III

AT EACH EDUCATIONAL LEVEL, PERCEPTION OF INTERNAL COMMUNIST THREAT IS RELATED TO TOLERANCE OF NONCONFORMITY

PERCENTAGE CLASSIFIED AS "MORE TOLERANT"
ON SCALE OF TOLERANCE OF NONCONFORMISTS

CLASSIFICATION ON SCALE OF PERCEPTION OF COMMUNIST THREAT		AMONG THOSE LESS INTERESTED IN ISSUES	AMONG THOSE MORE INTERESTED IN ISSUES
COLLEGE GRADUATES	SEE RELATIVELY GREAT THREAT	*	50 / 87
	IN-BETWEEN	56 / 32	66 / 140
	SEE RELATIVELY LITTLE THREAT	80 / 21	85 / 81
SOME COLLEGE	SEE RELATIVELY GREAT THREAT	41 / 39	40 / 111
	IN-BETWEEN	50 / 67	52 / 148
	SEE RELATIVELY LITTLE THREAT	74 / 35	76 / 60
HIGH SCHOOL GRADUATES	SEE RELATIVELY GREAT THREAT	36 / 98	32 / 307
	IN-BETWEEN	35 / 237	47 / 347
	SEE RELATIVELY LITTLE THREAT	42 / 104	56 / 114
SOME HIGH SCHOOL	SEE RELATIVELY GREAT THREAT	19 / 115	21 / 231
	IN-BETWEEN	21 / 251	31 / 240
	SEE RELATIVELY LITTLE THREAT	34 / 80	44 / 105
GRADE SCHOOL	SEE RELATIVELY GREAT THREAT	10 / 198	11 / 289
	IN-BETWEEN	10 / 651	17 / 372
	SEE RELATIVELY LITTLE THREAT	23 / 201	26 / 130

*Only 15 cases of less interested college graduates.

201

Chart III shows how the perception of the Communist threat is related to tolerance at each educational level. This is important because it tells us that the same general conclusions we would draw from Chart II, earlier in this chapter, apply at each educational level of the population. Those who see the least threat tend to be the most tolerant. But there is *something more than perception of threat which is associated with tolerance,* and one such factor is education. For, if we take only those who perceive a relatively great threat, we see how tolerance increases with education. Look at the bars on Chart III for the more interested people. The percentages go up in regular steps— 11% among grade school people, 21% among those with some high school, 32% among high school graduates, 40% among those with some college, and 50% among college graduates. Thus we see how education is related to the capability, if one perceives great internal Communist danger, of being relatively tolerant *in spite of it.* In other words, *there is something about people with more schooling which equips them to make discriminations, to appreciate the principles of civil rights, and to handle a value conflict in a more tolerant way than others.*

We get the same type of evidence of the relation of education and tolerance in all other comparisons which Chart III lets us make.

Information similar to that presented in Table 3 for education is summarized in Table 4 for the following variables:

> Age
> Region
> Type of Community
> Sex
> Church Attendance

Information similar to that graphed in Chart III is likewise presented in Table 5.

We shall spare the reader the minor details and point out the main findings in Tables 4 and 5 very briefly.

Age: Table 4 shows that younger people do not differ appreciably from the older in how they view the severity of the internal Communist threat. Table 5 shows, within each age group, that those who see greatest danger are likely to be the least tolerant. The only exception, the youngest group among the less interested, may be a sampling

202

error. But Table 5 also shows that there is something about the younger generation, *whatever their estimate of threat,* that makes more of them tolerant than the older generation.

Region: Table 4 shows that, among the more interested people, somewhat larger proportions in the South than in the North are likely to see the internal Communist threat as relatively great. Differences are too small to be significant among the less interested. In Table 5 we see the relationship between estimate of danger and tolerance holding in every region. But there is something about region, *whatever the estimate of danger,* that makes Northerners more likely than Southerners to be scored among the more tolerant.

Type of Community: As Table 4 indicates, metropolitan people are more likely to see relatively little threat than are farmers, but other differences in perception of threat are small or inconsistent. Table 5 shows that the correlation of estimate of threat with tolerance is present in each of the types of communities. It also shows that, over and beyond the variable of perceived danger, there is something about city life or about city people that tends to make more of such people relatively high in tolerance than is the case with rural people.

Sex: Women are less likely than men to think the internal Communist threat relatively slight. Table 4 shows that this is true among both the less interested and the more interested. As Table 5 makes clear, males and females are alike in exhibiting the correlation between perception of threat and tolerance. Men are seen to be relatively more tolerant than women in five out of six comparisons in Table 5 *when perception of threat is held constant.*

Church Attendance: Among those more interested in issues, people who attended church regularly in the month prior to the survey are more likely than others to see the Communist danger as severe. Among the less interested, differences in Table 4 are negligible, though in the same direction. Table 5 shows, for church attenders and non-church attenders alike, a relationship between tolerance and estimate of the Communist danger. If we hold constant the estimate of threat, we find churchgoers less tolerant than non-churchgoers in all six comparisons available in Table 5.

TABLE 4

HOW SCALE SCORES ON PERCEPTION OF THE INTER-
NAL COMMUNIST THREAT DIFFER BY AGE, REGION,
TYPE OF COMMUNITY, SEX, AND CHURCH ATTEND-
ANCE—FOR NATIONAL CROSS-SECTION

	PERCENTAGE DISTRIBUTION OF SCALE SCORES				
BY AGE	*21–29*	*30–39*	*40–49*	*50–59*	*60 and over*
More Interested People					
See relatively great threat	39%	34%	35%	39%	39%
In-between	45	49	45	43	44
See relatively little threat	16	17	20	18	17
Total	100%	100%	100%	100%	100%
Number of cases	*525*	*683*	*619*	*429*	*522*
Less Interested People					
See relatively great threat	25%	22%	22%	20%	19%
In-between	53	56	58	58	64
See relatively little threat	22	22	20	22	17
Total	100%	100%	100%	100%	100%
Number of cases	*380*	*491*	*439*	*365*	*476*
BY REGION	*West*	*East*	*Middle West*	*South*	
More Interested People					
See relatively great threat	34%	37%	36%	41%	
In-between	44	43	47	45	
See relatively little threat	22	20	17	14	
Total	100%	100%	100%	100%	
Number of cases	*410*	*738*	*823*	*806*	
Less Interested People					
See relatively great threat	23%	22%	22%	21%	
In-between	53	56	58	60	
See relatively little threat	24	22	20	19	
Total	100%	100%	100%	100%	
Number of cases	*249*	*524*	*642*	*740*	
BY TYPE OF COMMUNITY	*Metropolitan Areas*	*Other Cities*	*Small Towns*	*Farms*	
More Interested People					
See relatively great threat	36%	37%	38%	41%	
In-between	45	45	45	44	
See relatively little threat	19	18	17	15	
Total	100%	100%	100%	100%	
Number of cases	*1101*	*778*	*538*	*361*	

(*Table 4 continued*)

BY TYPE OF COMMUNITY	Metropolitan Areas	Other Cities	Small Towns	Farms
Less Interested People				
See relatively great threat	19%	25%	23%	21%
In-between	55	58	60	61
See relatively little threat	26	17	17	18
Total	100%	100%	100%	100%
Number of cases	*791*	*585*	*379*	*401*

BY SEX	Males	Females
More Interested People		
See relatively great threat	34%	41%
In-between	46	44
See relatively little threat	20	15
Total	100%	100%
Number of cases	*1435*	*1343*
Less Interested People		
See relatively great threat	22%	22%
In-between	54	60
See relatively little threat	24	18
Total	100%	100%
Number of cases	*865*	*1289*

BY CHURCH ATTENDANCE	Went to church in last month	Did not go to church in last month
More Interested People		
See relatively great threat	39%	34%
In-between	46	44
See relatively little threat	15	22
Total	100%	100%
Number of cases	*1810*	*968*
Less Interested People		
See relatively great threat	22%	21%
In-between	58	57
See relatively little threat	20	22
Total	100%	100%
Number of cases	*1286*	*869*

205

TABLE 5

HOW PERCEPTION OF COMMUNIST THREAT IS RELATED TO TOLERANCE OF NONCONFORMITY

COMPARISONS BY AGE, REGION, TYPE OF COMMUNITY, SEX, AND CHURCH
ATTENDANCE—FOR NATIONAL CROSS-SECTION

Classification on Scale of Perception of Communist Threat	Percentage Classed as "More Tolerant" on Scale of Tolerance of Nonconformists				
BY AGE	*21–29*	*30–39*	*40–49*	*50–59*	*60 and over*
More Interested People					
See relatively great threat	40%	31%	27%	21%	9%
In-between	48	47	36	29	21
See relatively little threat	59	59	55	54	33
Less Interested People					
See relatively great threat	36	22	24	15	9
In-between	29	25	21	16	13
See relatively little threat	36	43	39	34	26
BY REGION	*West*	*East*	*Middle West*		*South*
More Interested People					
See relatively great threat	40%	33%	24%		15%
In-between	54	46	37		23
See relatively little threat	60	62	51		36
Less Interested People					
See relatively great threat	29	31	27		8
In-between	37	26	25		8
See relatively little threat	66	49	31		18
BY TYPE OF COMMUNITY	*Metropolitan Areas*	*Other Cities*	*Small Towns*		*Farms*
More Interested People					
See relatively great threat	31%	27%	21%		16%
In-between	47	35	31		25
See relatively little threat	66	51	39		29
Less Interested People					
See relatively great threat	27	21	21		13
In-between	28	21	15		13
See relatively little threat	43	37	34		22

206

(Table 5 continued)

Classification on Scale of Perception of Communist Threat	Percentage Classed as "More Tolerant" on Scale of Tolerance of Nonconformists	
BY SEX	*Males*	*Females*
More Interested People		
See relatively great threat	28%	24%
In-between	40	35
See relatively little threat	55	49
Less Interested People		
See relatively great threat	21	23
In-between	23	19
See relatively little threat	41	32
	Went to church in last month	*Did not go to church in last month*
BY CHURCH ATTENDANCE		
More Interested People		
See relatively great threat	24%	29%
In-between	35	43
See relatively little threat	45	62
Less Interested People		
See relatively great threat	20	25
In-between	19	23
See relatively little threat	31	44

This table is to be read as follows: Consider the more interested people by age. Among those 60 and over who see relatively great Communist threat, 9% are classed as "more tolerant" on our scale; among those in-between on the Communist threat, the percentage classed as "more tolerant" is 21; among those who see relatively little threat, the percentage classed as "more tolerant" is 33.

The number of cases on which each percentage is based is not shown here but can be calculated approximately from the data presented in Table 4.

To sum up, these tabulations converge to demonstrate two facts:

1. *Within various categories of the American population which cross-cut one another, there is consistency in the relationship between perception of the internal Communist threat and tolerance of nonconformists.* The relationship is high enough and consistent enough to suggest that *if* the internal Communist threat is now exaggerated, and *if* the American people were told this and believed it, tolerance of nonconformists would increase. We cannot prove this. It is an inference drawn from a mere association of two variables—sense of threat and tolerance. Such an expectation could be wrong. The only crucial test would be by experiment. For example, attitudes in a community could be measured before and after a sustained campaign of education was carried on in that community. If tolerance scores improved substantially in the after-study as compared with the before-study, we could attribute the improvement to the information program—*provided* that the improvement was significantly greater than in a parallel community which received no program. Similar before and after measures would, of course, be needed in the control community.

2. *The relationship between perception of threat and tolerance, though consistent in almost all sub-groups studied, is far from a 1-to-1 relationship.* This has further important implications. It suggests that merely accenting the negative—merely asserting that the internal threat is exaggerated—would be limited in its effectiveness. For substantial proportions of the American population are intolerant *in spite of the fact* that they perceive relatively little internal Communist threat. Somehow, one would have to bring home to them the value of the fundamental American liberties which are endangered by intolerance—and not just by intolerance of Communists alone, but of others whose opinions are unpopular. This is difficult—even risky. For such a positive program also would presumably be truthful about the internal Communist threat, even if it attacked exaggerations. Some intolerant people who see little or no threat might be made more aware than they are now of the potential danger of an internal Communist conspiracy—especially of sabotage in case of war. Can such people take it? Is there not a danger that such a program, based on truth, would boomerang and actually increase the intolerance?

Such a possibility exists, of course. But against it is the faith that, in the long run, the American people can be entrusted with the truth. The "sober second thought" of the people is the rock on which democracy rests. And there is ample evidence in this survey that knowledge does not breed intolerance. How else explain the *relative tolerance* of so many people, including many of the local community leaders, who are fully aware of the internal Communist threat or may even hold exaggerated views of it?

However, a campaign of information might conceivably boomerang in an opposite direction. If the truth about the internal Communist threat is that it has been exaggerated, such a campaign might overreach its aims and lull people into too much complacency about Communism. This is possible, but it seems unlikely. No findings of this survey support it. Consider, for example, the 3% of the population who, as described in Chapter Seven, say they actually knew an admitted Communist. If we apply to these people our scale of perception of the internal Communist threat, we find that they are *just as likely as others* in the national cross-section to regard the Communist threat as "relatively great."

	Percentage who perceived relatively great threat
Had known an admitted Communist	27% (158)
Had never known an admitted Communist	27% (4775)

Having known a Communist may have made a few people less conscious of the Communist danger than they should be; if so, it may have been fully compensated by making others more than ever conscious of the danger. But the people who were so situated that they had known a Communist were not only, on the average, fully as conscious of the Communist danger as other people but also were much more likely to be tolerant:

	Percentage "more tolerant" on scale of tolerance
Had known an admitted Communist	57%
Had never known an admitted Communist	30%

At every educational level a sharp difference in tolerance between those who knew Communists or did not know them appears. And this is also evident among our special sample of responsible community leaders. Eleven per cent had known a Communist. Just about as many of these leaders see a great threat (26%) as the others (27%). Yet among the 168 who had known a Communist, 85% are classed as "more tolerant" on our scale, as compared with 63% among the 1332 who had not. When, for example, presidents of chambers of commerce and labor leaders alike are more tolerant if they have known Communists, and yet no less perceptive of the Communist danger, we may conclude that knowledge, while it may lead to tolerance, does not necessarily have to lead to complacency.

No other findings in this study contradict the expectation that the "sober second thought" of the American people can be entrusted with the facts, wherever the facts may lie. Indeed, it tends to be the people *most remote* from contact with facts about the Communist threat— some of the less interested and less informed generally, some of the less educated, some of the rural people, some of the women—who are most vague about the shadow shapes of the Communist conspiracy and, at the same time, most ready to approve the sacrifice of our heritage of civil liberties.

THE RELATION OF PERCEPTION OF THREAT AND TOLERANCE OF NONCONFORMISTS TO ATTITUDES TOWARD GOVERN-MENTAL ACTIONS

How completely do the two variables, perception of threat and tolerance or intolerance of nonconformists, account for attitudes toward specific governmental actions—for example, toward the work of Congressional committees investigating Communism?

In this chapter we are dealing with attitudes—particularly with two sets of attitudes. One set involves appraisal of the internal Communist danger. The other set involves tolerance or intolerance of nonconformists. Attitudes are *tendencies* to act. From such general attitudes we should be able to predict, *all other things equal,* what positions certain people will tend to take on certain specific issues. But in the arena of life, and especially of practical politics, all other things are not equal. We have had intimations of this point earlier in this book —for example, in Chapter Five which discussed attitudes by region and type of community. It would be a naïve person, indeed, who would expect that knowledge of how people feel about each of our two sets of variables would alone accurately predict all positions on related specific issues—especially on issues charged with political emotion.

Consider Democrats and Republicans. Each party is a coalition of exceedingly diverse citizens, some inclined, by education, place of residence, and the like, to be tolerant; some not. Actually, people who say they are Republicans in our national cross-section are somewhat more likely to be among the more tolerant on our scale of tolerance of nonconformists than are people who call themselves Democrats:

	Percentage *"more tolerant"*
Republicans	32% (*1378*)
Democrats	27% (*2213*)

Both parties contain many people who view the internal Communist threat as very dangerous. But the current advantage in exploiting this issue politically lies with the Republicans, who have capitalized on events during the long term of Democratic rule, a few extremists even vociferating about "twenty years of treason." This tends to push faithful Democrats on the defensive. Consciously or unconsciously, they are driven to minimize it; the Republicans, to maximize it. For this reason, presumably, we find that Republicans, although on the average somewhat more likely than Democrats to be tolerant on matters measured by our tolerance scale—such as removing "dangerous books" from libraries—are somewhat more likely than the Democrats to perceive the internal Communist threat as "relatively great" on our scale of threat:

	Percentage seeing threat *as relatively great*
Republicans	34% (*1378*)
Democrats	30% (*2213*)

We see the same tendency when we compare chairmen of Republican and Democratic county central committees in our special sample of local leaders:

	Percentage *"more tolerant"*
Republican Committee Chairmen	70% (*110*)
Democratic Committee Chairmen	64% (*103*)

211

The samples on which these two percentages are based (numbers shown in parentheses) are too small to make this difference by itself significant, but the difference between scores on our scale of perception of threat is larger, and significant:

	Percentage seeing relatively great threat
Republican Committee Chairmen	35% (*110*)
Democratic Committee Chairmen	15% (*103*)

Let us now compare Republicans and Democrats on certain specific opinions about Congressional committees investigating Communists. In the national cross-section, only those who had followed the news closely enough to name accurately at least one Senator or Congressman on such a committee are included in this tabulation:

Some people say these Congressional committees are as much interested in getting publicity and votes as in protecting the country from the Communist threat. Others have a different view. What is your opinion?

	Percentage, among those with an opinion, agreeing with first statement
Cross-Section	
Republicans	45% (*855*)
Democrats	54% (*1244*)
Committee Chairmen	
Republicans	37% (*98*)
Democrats	80% (*93*)

It has been said that these Congressional committees investigating Communism are hurting the reputations of some people who really aren't Communists at all. Do you think these committees are or are not hurting the reputations of people who really aren't Communists?

	Percentage, among those with an opinion, who think the committees are hurting reputations of non-Communists
Cross-Section	
Republicans	60% (*901*)
Democrats	67% (*1277*)
Committee Chairmen	
Republicans	68% (*106*)
Democrats	91% (*97*)

212

As far as you know, did a Congressional committee investigating Communism help catch Alger Hiss?

	Percentage, among all respondents, who said "Yes"
Cross-Section	
Republicans	42% *(1020)*
Democrats	35% *(1500)*
Committee Chairmen	
Republicans	80% *(110)*
Democrats	66% *(103)*

Some people think that these [Congressional] committees [investigating Communism] today are actually making it harder for the F.B.I. to catch Communists. Others think that these committees are a real help to the F.B.I. today. What do you think?

	Percentage, among those with an opinion, who say committees help the F.B.I.
Cross-Section	
Republicans	65% *(794)*
Democrats	56% *(1165)*
Committee Chairmen	
Republicans	60% *(85)*
Democrats	34% *(94)*

In general, what is your opinion of these committees investigating Communism?

	Percentage, among all respondents who said:				
	Very favorable	*Favorable*	*Unfavorable*	*Very unfavorable*	*No opinion*
Cross-Section					
Republicans	22%	50%	16%	6%	6%	*(1020)*
Democrats	18	44	20	9	9	*(1500)*
Committee Chairmen					
Republicans	26%	42%	17%	7%	8%	*(110)*
Democrats	6	33	38	18	5	*(103)*

In view of the fact that Republicans tend to be just as tolerant or even more tolerant on our scale than Democrats, do these tables mean that the underlying attitudes of tolerance we have been measuring are *irrelevant* in a specific political decision? No indeed. For it is very easy to show that *among Republicans* the more tolerant take a quite different view of activities of these committees than do the less tolerant. Similarly, *among Democrats*.

Table 6 will illustrate this point, based on one of the questions reported above. Any other question about the committees shows a rather similar *pattern* of relationship. Note that among Democrats the percentage who doubt the single-mindedness of investigating committees drops from 70% to 44%, depending on the perception of the internal Communist danger and on the basic attitudes of tolerance of nonconformists. Among Republicans, the drop is from 68% to 31%. Some of the percentages are based on a small number of cases and could be expected to wobble quite widely by chance. But note in all eight comparisons by political party in Table 6 the Democrats are more likely to be critical.

This table is quite instructive, for it shows how general attitudes operate. They tend to predispose people toward a particular action or judgment, but they do not alone *determine* the action or judgment. Even party membership, in addition, is not enough to determine exactly *which* people will interpret the committees' actions in which way. Other factors, such as the closeness with which news has been followed, will enter in, as well as other attitudes toward the committees, such as belief in the importance of Congressional committees in general as a constitutional safeguard. In Chapter Five we saw how values common to a region, like the South, may cross-cut other attitudes. Similarly with attitudes in regard to religion. Any action in a specific situation may involve a convergence of many different attitudes.

In order to learn more about the way in which such factors as perception of the Communist threat and tolerance combine with other variables, we need further studies explicitly designed to measure these attitudes *prior to* some actual overt behavior like voting, or attending protest meetings, or other civic or political participation. Such studies should be designed to evaluate an individual's role in each of several so-called reference groups, some of whose values he shares and whose approval is important to him. In spite of the growth of research in this field, we have very little systematic knowledge in sociology and social psychology as to how people solve what we call "role conflicts."

214

TABLE 6

HOW JUDGMENTS AS TO SINGLE-MINDEDNESS OF COMMITTEES INVESTIGATING COMMUNISM VARY AMONG REPUBLICANS AND DEMOCRATS, CLASSIFIED ACCORDING TO PERCEPTION OF INTERNAL RISK AND TOLERANCE

THOSE, WITH AN OPINION, WHO SAY COMMITTEES ARE AS MUCH INTERESTED IN GETTING PUBLICITY AND VOTES AS IN PROTECTING THE COUNTRY FROM THE COMMUNIST THREAT

	NUMBER OF CASES		PERCENTAGE	
	Republicans	Democrats	Republicans	Democrats
See Relatively Little *Internal Communist Threat*				
More Tolerant of Nonconformists	85	128	68%	70%
In-between	49	111	42	52
Less Tolerant of Nonconformists	6	17	—	—
In-between on Communist Threat				
More Tolerant of Nonconformists	166	194	54%	59%
In-between	173	297	48	51
Less Tolerant of Nonconformists	46	68	40	47
See Relatively Great *Internal Communist Threat*				
More Tolerant of Nonconformists	107	102	33%	48%
In-between	165	243	31	47
Less Tolerant of Nonconformists	58	84	40	44

Sample comprises those in national cross-section who know the name of at least one committee member.

HOW THE FINDINGS IN THIS CHAPTER COMPARE WITH FINDINGS FROM OTHER STUDIES

The finding that tolerance of nonconformists is lower when the internal Communist threat is perceived as great, and higher when it is perceived as small, is consistent with that in past surveys, and especially with trends on the same questions asked over a period of time.

When the United States and Russia were allies during the war and the danger of Communist subversion was generally regarded as small, tolerance, even in wartime, of such groups as Socialists and support for unlimited free speech and a free press were at a fairly high level.

But as Russian hostility became more apparent after the war, and as surveys showed more and more people concerned with Communist subversion of America, there was growing support for restrictions and sanctions not only against Communists but also against many other groups or individuals who failed to conform to popular opinions. Thus, between 1943 and 1953, for example, the proportion who would suppress Socialist newspapers rose from 25% of the public to 45%; those who would place restrictions on freedom of speech increased from 32% to 45%; those who would forbid any newspaper criticism of the American form of government rose from 30% to 42% **(8, 9)**.

There is also support for the point made in this chapter that intolerance of nonconformists does not *necessarily* accompany belief that the internal Communist danger is great, nor does lack of perception of the Communist threat *necessarily* produce greater tolerance. Long before the cold-war period, and at a time when possible Communist subversion of the United States was taken seriously by only a few, there was still substantial minority support for restrictions and sanctions against deviant groups and individuals. One need only mention again the one American out of four who even then would have banned all "Socialist" publications. Similarly, even today, when four out of five Americans perceive a danger of Communist subversion, other surveys confirm the present findings that a great many Americans do not let this affect their normal tolerance of the right to dissent. Thus, 1953 NORC studies, conducted at a time when popular feeling against Communists was as high as it had ever been, still found a majority of the public giving unqualified support to the principle of "letting people say anything they want to in a public speech" and still found sizable

216

minorities endorsing the civil liberties of deviant groups—including even Communists themselves. Past surveys, too, have found that it is the better educated people who, though alive to the dangers of Communist subversion, are the most tolerant of the rights of all people to express their views (8, 9).

There are also many results from past surveys which illustrate the importance of such "intervening variables" as political party affiliation in affecting opinions concerning specific issues. NORC studies, for example, have revealed little difference between rank-and-file Democrats and rank-and-file Republicans in their assessment of the Communist danger, and no difference at all in their belief that the rights of Communists should be abridged. Yet Gallup polls have consistently reported substantial differences between the supporters of the two parties in their opinion of Senator McCarthy. Such variables as religious affiliation, level of expectation, past personal experience, and many, many others have similarly been shown in past surveys to differentiate the opinions of two groups who otherwise appear comparable in basic attitudes. These basic attitudes predispose one's behavior; they do not determine it (1, 9).

Examples of follow-up studies, with repeated interviews, which provide more searching analysis of the dynamics of attitudes than can any single survey (15, 3).

SUMMARY

This chapter has studied two main kinds of relationships: (1) between perception of the internal Communist threat and tolerance of nonconformists; and (2) between these two variables and more specific judgments—illustrated by opinions about Congressional investigating committees.

1. There is a consistent relationship, within our samples as a whole and within each of a variety of sub-groups, between perception of the internal Communist danger and tolerance. Those who see the danger as greatest tend to be the most intolerant. This correlation appears in almost all sub-samples we have studied. It *suggests* that if the internal Communist threat were to decrease or to be believed to decrease, tolerance of nonconformity might go up somewhat; or, vice versa, with an increase in threat or belief in its increase, intolerance might go up.

However, the relationship, though consistent, is far from a 1-to-1 relationship. Many people who see a great danger are among the more tolerant; many people who see little danger or only a moderate risk are among the less tolerant. Local community leaders are more likely than the cross-section to be able to handle a value conflict with a tolerant solution—that is, *despite* perceiving the internal Communist threat as relatively great, more of them can still be relatively tolerant of nonconformists. Within the cross-section, the same is true of the more interested and better informed; the better educated; the younger; the city people, in the North especially; the males; and those who do not attend church regularly.

The fact that the relationship between perception of threat and tolerance or intolerance, consistent as it may be, is far from a 1-to-1 relationship sets limitations on the possible effectiveness of an information program which merely asserts that the Communist threat is exaggerated, even if it may be exaggerated. The positive values of American freedoms would need also to be brought more effectively into the consciousness of many people.

In presenting the facts about the Communist threat, there may not be too serious danger of boomerang effects in either direction—that is, of scaring people and thereby making them less tolerant, or of lulling them into too much complacency. With respect to the latter point, there was no evidence that people with the closest acquaintance with the Communist threat—for example, those few who had known a Communist personally—were any more complacent than other people, though they were much more tolerant of nonconformists.

2. Perception of threat and tolerance both operate as *predisposing tendencies* which affect judgments about related specific events—such as the activities of Congressional investigating committees. But such tendencies do not alone determine the judgments. Other variables enter in, too, as is likely to be the case in any situation involving judgment, decision, or action. Republicans, for example, are somewhat more tolerant than Democrats with respect to the restrictions on civil liberties measured by our scale, yet are more likely to perceive the internal Communist threat as relatively great. Among Republicans, those who are most tolerant and who see the least threat tend, as would be expected, to be the most critical of the committees. Similarly among Democrats. But when we compare Republicans and Democrats who are alike on these two basic attitudes, we find that the

218

Democrats are somewhat more critical of the committees than are the Republicans. This is merely one of a variety of illustrations which might be offered to show how other factors, *in addition to* perception of the Communist danger or of basic tolerance of nonconformists, necessarily become involved when a concrete, specific issue arises.

Chapter Nine

WHAT THE ANSWERS TO SOME OF THESE QUESTIONS MEAN FOR PEOPLE WHO CAN DO SOMETHING ABOUT THEM

Can we now draw together the findings of this volume as they bear on the strategy of future efforts to enlighten the American people about threats to our freedom, either from the internal Communist menace or from rash and dangerous reactions to this menace?

We shall try. We cannot expect that all of our interpretations will be acceptable. Some of them may be wrong. We have done our best to report accurately the things which the American people are trying to tell us. We shall now do our best to set down some reflections as to what these things broadly imply.

We have found no evidence that the country as a whole is suffering from quivering fear or from an anxiety neurosis about the internal Communist threat. If there is a sickness, the clinical symptoms are more like dietary deficiency.

People have a table fare of vague and distorted information about the Communist danger. They exaggerate present-day conversions of Americans to Communism and they have little awareness, let alone concern, about many of the harmful counteractions to such dangers as do exist.

If a more balanced and palatable diet of information and education were to be made available, what does the study show about the prospects of acceptance?

Although anticipating that some interpreters of the American scene may disagree, the author offers his considered judgment that the prospects, on balance, should be good.

Great social, economic, and technological forces are working on the side of exposing ever larger proportions of our population to the idea that "people are different from me, with different systems of values, and they can be good people, too." This would seem to be a necessary condition to tolerance, but not the only condition. It should be a first step to the recognition that it is good for a country both to respect the civil rights of people whose ideas challenge cherished traditions and to preserve a free market place of ideas even if they seem dangerous. And that the country can and must do this, while still standing firm against its enemies from within and without. In this book we have seen some of these great forces at work.

For example, the findings in Chapter Four show how the almost revolutionary changes in the average level of education within two generations have operated to expose more and more people to values different from those they may have learned at home. The quality of education also has been changing, with a lessening of authoritarian rigidity, and is reflected in turn in changes in child-rearing practices of the young parents of today. Some people fear the effects of education precisely because it does challenge tradition and does stimulate independence of thought. But they tend to be ambivalent, because they see also that education is the main ladder for what sociologists call "vertical mobility." Public opinion polls have found people almost unanimous in saying that they want their children to get a better education so that these children can be more successful than they. This is the American dream.

There is another set of forces operating which dispose people toward tolerance. These are involved in what sociologists call "horizontal mobility." People move around, and increasingly. One of the basic reasons why America is less tradition-bound than the older countries of Europe is the fact that so few young married couples set up their homes in the same village or neighborhood as their parents. Like formal education, movement into new environments exposes people to values different from those they learned at home, and shows that the difference is not necessarily bad or that if it is bad there are ways of handling it without complete intolerance. It is probably no accident that the cities of the Far West, being mostly made up of migrants from other parts of the country, have such a large share of relatively tolerant people, as shown in Chapter Five. Or that rural areas, especially in the South, so many of whose people have never lived anywhere else, are lowest on the tolerance scale. The main population flow is from the country to the city or the city suburb, and there is nothing to suggest that it will be substantially reversed in the future. There are important values of rural life which can be lost or warped in the anonymity of the metropolitan community. But the city dweller does rub shoulders with more people who have ideas different from his own and he learns to live and let live.

The two forces of "vertical" and "horizontal" mobility also produce strains which conceivably can result in intolerance. The higher the level of aspiration of a person, the larger the discrepancy between his aspiration and achievement may become. Though his success may be great by the absolute standards of the whole world, he may have greater anxiety about failure, relative to others, than he would if he lived in a more static and less striving society. Moreover, the mere fact that both "vertical" and "horizontal" mobility serve to confront an adult with values different from those of his childhood also can produce in his mind conflict and strain. One of the ways of coping with personal anxiety, whether it is generated by relative deprivation, by a conflict of values, or by other causes, is to pass the blame along to others. Radicals, especially when they can be assimilated by some people into the concept of traitor as well as heretic, are now convenient targets for such "scapegoating." These tendencies may exist in some people, even if the present study was not able to detect widespread evidence. For the long run, however, it is the author's belief that the mechanisms in American social change which are tending to facilitate tolerance are far more potent than the mechanisms which impede it. The relationships of education, age, and civic responsibility with tolerance, as shown in this book, are more consistent with this conclusion than with its opposite. But we must never forget that we are still living in an industrial revolution which produces strains, and the problems thus generated cannot be swept under the carpet. An adaptive democracy must be made to work or those who are hurt by the social changes may be ready to follow the demagogues of the future. Hence, it is no accident if those thinkers who are most dubious about the ability of our capitalist democracy to master our technological revolution should be the very people who are most pessimistic about the future of civil liberties.

A third force also can operate on the side of tolerance. This is the phenomenal growth of communications. In a single evening television carries the viewer on a magic carpet to all parts of the world. Here, in his farmhouse or city apartment, he meets all kinds of people different from himself. The mere fact that the husband in *I Love Lucy* is a Latin-American understandingly portrayed may have more impact on the American mind than hundreds of books or sermons. The presence on the screen of a talented member of a minority group, not in a special minority-group role but as a natural member of an American entourage, is a powerful lesson in intercultural relations. As a network executive once put it, "What Dodger fan cares whether Jackie Robinson is a Negro as long as he steals second?" Of course it is also possible for television, radio, newspapers, movies, books, and magazines in this new age of manipulation of the masses to teach the wrong lessons, to serve the devil as well as the Lord. But if the first step in tolerance of nonconformists is to meet the new and different, all of the media of mass communications help one make that encounter.

In addition to these great social, economic, and technological forces which are unobtrusively working on the side of tolerance, there is another fact which must never be discounted.

Nobody could sit down and read through the filled-out questionnaire in this study without coming to the conclusion that most of the seemingly intolerant people are good, wholesome Americans. Many of them, as we have seen in this book, are simply drawing quite normal and logical inferences from premises which are false because the information on which the premises are based is false. They have not been as yet sufficiently motivated by responsible leaders of public opinion to give "sober second thought" to the broader and long-range consequences of specific limitations of freedom.

This is not to deny that this country, like any other country, also has its share of hopelessly bigoted, even vicious, people. The rich soil of American democracy can breed some bad plants. Only a few evil or misguided leaders, when ineffectively challenged, can confuse and incite a multitude of other minds. When, for example, national figures say flatly that our schools and colleges are full of teachers of atheistic Communism, can we blame an average citizen who has no firsthand access to the facts if he comes to think a purge of the educational system may be necessary? When politicians for partisan advantage exaggerate the current spread of the Communist conspiracy, can we blame an ordinary person for supporting drastic measures to stop the supposed conversion to Communism of people in key positions in Washington or in our foreign service, armed forces, or defense plants?

To assume that most intolerant people among the rank and file are bad or sick would be to commit an error which, in the author's judgment, is all too common. This error is not unknown even among scholars, for a few of whom, incidentally, the "native fascist" may fulfill the same psychological need of a target upon which to project personal anxieties as may the "liberal" or the "intellectual" for a few other citizens.

It requires no public opinion survey to suggest that most Americans, being decent on the whole, subscribe to certain values which they have learned from earliest childhood. One is a basic sense of fair play—a dislike of the bully who pushes other people around. Second is a respect for the truth and for the right to hear the truth spoken. Third is a concern not to be played for a sucker. Fourth is a deep patriotism which motivates the public to oppose policies when convinced that such policies would weaken America.

Can we not take these values as axiomatic?

Why, then, should not a program of information and education count on motivations, powerful and well-nigh universal, awaiting activation?

People who don't like the fellow who pushes others about in a crowd, or who edges around ahead of others in a line, or who beats up somebody weaker than himself may still approve investigating tactics that take advantage of witnesses. There was only a feeble voice of disapproval, even from self-styled liberals, over the treatment received by the gangster, Costello, on national television. Yet second thoughts do occur. It is no accident that it was a Zwicker case which dramatized the tactics being used in the investigations of Communists and set in motion chain reactions which eventually cost a committee chairman so heavily in public support, as attested by successive Gallup polls. Similarly, while nobody likes a liar, some of the public has to learn that Communist conspirators are not the only liars; that other people, those who would evoke the public's emotions through exposing or claiming to expose Communists, sometimes also trifle with the truth. And the average American surely does not want to be played for a sucker, either by Communists or fellow travelers, or by their prosecutors.

Now what about the motif of patriotism?

Suppose most Americans were to believe that the climate which has been created in our public service is *unnecessarily* preventing loyal citizens, whose skills are needed, from serving the country effectively or from serving it at all. Suppose most Americans were to believe our scientists when they say that the research and development program which must keep us ahead of Russia in the weapons' race may be lagging because of such *unnecessary* harassment. Suppose the public were to believe that some of our foreign-service officers were afraid to tell Washington unpleasant truths in their dispatches for fear of future persecution. If these things were truly believed, can there be any doubt about the response? The function of this book is not to state whether facts alleged in these questions are true, or only partly true, or false. Its function is to report, among other things, that an overwhelming majority of the public does not even know that such allegations are being made.

For example, when asked to describe in their own words the good things and the bad things which Congressional investigating committees have done, only 14 people out of 4933 in our cross-section mentioned any of these allegations. In a later direct question they were asked: **It has been said that some loyal Americans won't take Government jobs today for fear of unjust attacks on their reputations. Have you ever heard this, or read of it?** Only one in five said they had heard this or read of it. Less than a third of these—6% of the entire cross-section—thought the country was being hurt a great deal thereby.

Not all people can face all truths wisely. But analysis of the hopes and fears, the likes and dislikes, the foibles and the faiths of the Americans who took part in this survey strengthens rather than weakens our trust in the kind of people Lincoln loved. Armed with this trust, let us discuss three questions in this closing chapter:

What is the responsibility of the press, radio, and television with respect to these problems?

What is the responsibility of our national political leaders?

What is the responsibility of leaders at the level of local communities?

WHAT IS THE RESPONSIBILITY OF THE PRESS, RADIO, AND TELEVISION WITH RESPECT TO THESE PROBLEMS?

This question is put first among the three, and deservedly so, for a very special reason.

Unlike certain other kinds of national and local problems, it is intrinsic to this problem that the facts which almost all of us must have are *secondhand*.

Only when our own personal interests are immediately and directly involved—if, for example, our own children should be exposed to a Communist teacher, or our own labor union should be threatened by Communist infiltration—is the peril of internal Communism a matter of firsthand awareness. The proportion of the American population

225

likely to have such direct knowledge as of today is minuscule. In the same way, only if we ourselves or someone close to us should sustain an infringement of civil rights or should suffer other injustice and harassment is the threat to civil liberties likely to come into direct vision. However often this may happen to creative thinkers or to people in sensitive positions, such as in the national government, it is still rare in the general population, as Chapter Three has demonstrated.

Contrast this with the impact of a slowdown or shutdown in industrial production. The workers affected know it at once, if not ahead of time, and its repercussions flow throughout an entire community, reaching not only into the home of the worker but out into the home of his grocer, his furniture dealer, his automobile dealer, his banker. Firsthand knowledge, at least about the local situation, is not the exception but the rule. For the national picture, the media of mass communication must be depended on, except for direct news from acquaintances in other parts of the country; but such facts are fitted into a matrix of personal experience and are the topic of daily conversation.

The press, radio, and television must provide the main source—indeed, almost the only source for many people—of information about the internal Communist threat and civil liberties.

Such a contrast is illustrated by answers to two questions in our survey:

Even if people follow the news closely they are likely to form many of their opinions as a result of listening and talking with relatives, friends, and acquaintances. For example, take your own ideas about Communists in the United States and what is being done about them. On the whole, would you say you get your information mostly from what you read or hear on the air, or mostly from what you hear in conversations with other people?

	PERCENTAGE ANSWERING	
	Among Selected Community Leaders	*In National Cross-Section*
Read or hear on air	88%	75%
Conversations with people	8	18
Don't know	4	7
	100%	100%
Number of cases	*1500*	*4933*

226

Now, take a different topic which is on some people's minds: the question of whether we're heading toward more unemployment and harder times. On this subject, would you say you get your information mostly from what you read or hear on the air, or mostly from what you hear in conversation with other people?

	PERCENTAGE ANSWERING	
	Among Selected Community Leaders	*In National Cross-Section*
Read or hear on air	64%	48%
Conversations with people	28	45
Don't know	8	7
	100%	100%
Number of cases	*1500*	*4933*

The absolute percentages must not be taken too literally. People tend to forget the source of most of their information, and there also may be a prestige bias in favor of answering in terms of reading or listening to news. Actually, a considerable proportion who give this answer may have been influenced most in forming their opinions by casual reinforcing remarks expressed in private conversation and long since forgotten. But as far as the supply, if not the effectiveness, of information is concerned, a *difference,* such as that of 75% and 48% observed in the cross-section as between the two tables, is consistent with what the foregoing considerations might lead us to expect.

The singular responsibility of the press, radio, and television goes beyond getting the facts to the people. It involves interpreting and dramatizing the facts—always within the limits of truth. With the new dimension added by television, the potential force for influencing the mind of the nation has never been so great in our history.

And all the skills of the best reporters and interpreters of events are needed. The very remoteness of internal Communism or threats to civil liberties from felt personal experience makes some things very difficult to convey to the popular mind.

Moreover, the subtlety of such a process as a slow erosion of civil liberties could almost defy dramatic presentation, perhaps defy it as stubbornly as did for many years the slow erosion of American top-soil. A few handfuls of loam here, a few there, washed down our rivers, is not news to make banner headlines. Conceivably the greatest threats to our freedom may lie in the cumulative effect of multitudes

227

of little events, each seemingly unimportant in itself, rather than in the dramas of the Senate. The fact, for example, that the Girl Scouts of America quietly made some deletions and changes in their 1954 Handbook, yielding to self-styled pro-American pressure, may or may not be big news, or even a case in point. True, the parents of a Girl Scout might discover by themselves what has happened and make their own interpretation. But very few are likely to do it unless their attention is aroused—either directly through a responsible press, radio, or television, or else through the vigilance of thought-leaders in the local community, who in turn are likely to have been alerted by what they read on the printed page or what they heard or saw over the air.

There may be a place for a properly sponsored special reporting service which would have the duty of spotting all such occurrences and bringing them together in a regularly released fact sheet. Then the working press could see them in their connected significance and magnitude. One event may not make news; a pattern of such events may. This is not to suggest a propaganda organ—prototypes of such a strictly factual reporting service already exist in other fields.

Another side of the picture presents problems of equal difficulty. Much of the secret, sleepless vigilance of the F.B.I. and other agencies in their penetration of the internal Communist apparatus cannot appear in the news at all. It is easily overshadowed in the headlines by public hearings. Even if confidence in the F.B.I. is quite high, we have evidence that there is room for improvement in that confidence. When asked, **Do you think the F.B.I. knows who all of the American Communists are, or do they know most of them, a good many of them, or only a few of them?** the public responded as follows:

| | PERCENTAGE ANSWERING | |
	Among Selected Community Leaders	*In National Cross-Section*
All	5%	3%
Most	56	32
A good many	33	39
Only a few	5	20
Don't know	1	6
	100%	100%
Number of cases	*1500*	*4933*

228

If J. Edgar Hoover were to say that the F.B.I. has most of the American Communists under its eye, would you feel pretty sure it was true, or wouldn't you?

	PERCENTAGE ANSWERING	
	Among Selected Community Leaders	In National Cross-Section
Would feel pretty sure	87%	64%
Would not	11	27
Don't know	2	9
	100%	100%
Number of cases	1500	4933

It was abundantly manifested throughout the year 1954 that the press, radio, and television were increasingly exercising their responsibilities. A history of this effort needs to be written, based on a content analysis of news and editorial comment. Our present survey would add one small footnote to such a study; namely, in its evidence that among the local community leaders in cities of 10,000 to 150,000 the newspaper publishers, in their private attitudes, were high on the list of those who were taking the "sober second thought."

WHAT IS THE RESPONSIBILITY OF OUR NATIONAL POLITICAL LEADERS?

As long as there is partisan political advantage in exploiting the internal Communist threat, just as in capitalizing on any other issue, one can expect such exploitation. Any other expectation would fly in the face of all American political history. But there are boundaries which the more responsible members of both parties do try to observe, in action and in speech.

The present survey was not designed to probe the attitudes of people in the federal government, except as a very few such persons automatically appeared in the national cross-section. But they were far too few to permit any generalizations. A new and searching study of such attitudes is needed, on an adequate sample, especially to test the allegations that a climate of fear has subtly permeated the executive branch of the government, not only in the State or Defense Department, but even in agencies which are not handling classified materials.

For example, it has been alleged that fear of Congressional criticism has led some agencies dealing with outside contractors, even on completely unclassified work, to apply security tests which carry guilt by association to the point of absurdity and deprive the government of valuable services. Curbing excesses in the administration of security regulations, if such excesses actually occur, is just as much a duty of responsible officials in government as is the parallel duty of making sure that the security regulations are as tight as they should be.

Whether or not the alleged climate of fear in Washington is a myth or a reality, there can be no doubt that 1954 marked some kind of turning point. There are those in both the executive and legislative branches who are acting and speaking out forcefully, at least against some of the more overt manifestations of irresponsible behavior.

But how well does the public know what our national leaders really believe? How much have their public utterances influenced American thinking?

The present survey has a bit of data bearing on such questions as of the summer of 1954. The time of the survey must be kept in mind.

A completely open-ended question was asked: **Now, please think of some of the important people or leaders in our country today. Among them would you pick out for me one, in particular, whose opinions on how to handle United States Communists you would especially respect?** The names most frequently mentioned were J. Edgar Hoover and President Eisenhower, with Senator McCarthy third. Other mentions were scattered among a hundred or more names.

| | PERCENTAGE OF MENTIONS | |
	Among Selected Community Leaders	In National Cross-Section
J. Edgar Hoover	52%	27%
President Eisenhower	16	24
Senator McCarthy	5	8
All others	20	14
Don't know	7	27
	100%	100%
Number of cases	*1500*	*4933*

A warning. This study did not seek to measure the current popular strength of any individual. The above figures, based on a single free-

230

answer question, must not be taken as an accurate index of popular support or approval. (For example, it would be unjustified even to suggest that the 8% in the cross-section or the 5% among the local community leaders who chose to mention Senator McCarthy in this context were his only supporters. Gallup polls taken during the time period of the present study indicate that the Senator's support was larger numerically than this, with 14% expressing strong approval and 20% mild or qualified approval.) The question asked above had the purpose of setting the stage for finding out how well people thought they knew the viewpoints of figures whom they especially trusted.

After naming a person whose opinion he would particularly respect, the respondent was handed a card containing two statements:

I know pretty well what his opinions about how to handle Communists are.

I would respect his opinion about how to handle Communists because of the kind of person he is.

The respondent was asked which of the two statements was closer to his view. Answers were as follows:

	PERCENTAGE DISTRIBUTION AMONG THOSE WHO NAMED:		
	J. Edgar Hoover	President Eisenhower	Senator McCarthy
National Cross-Section			
Know his opinion	33%	19%	58%
Kind of person he is	55	65	31
Don't know	12	16	11
	100%	100%	100%
Number of cases	*1331*	*1178*	*403*
Selected Community Leaders			
Know his opinion	38%	24%	62%
Kind of person he is	50	63	27
Don't know	12	13	11
	100%	100%	100%
Number of cases	*773*	*246*	*79*

These percentages probably overstate rather than understate the actual familiarity with a mentor's views. The important point, quite

231

consistent with all other findings in this survey about lack of information, is that only a minority, even among the local community leaders, claimed that they knew what the opinions of J. Edgar Hoover or President Eisenhower on these issues are. In the case of the President, only 19%, among those in the cross-section who said they looked for counsel to him above others, also said that they knew pretty well what his viewpoint is.

Such findings may be somewhat out of date by the time this volume appears. But too much cannot be expected too fast. The task ahead may be long and slow and, at times, anything but rewarding. Those national leaders entrusted with the preservation of the American heritage have a responsibility, not only to act wisely and firmly, but also to speak the truth and speak it often, if any program of public enlightenment is to be effective.

WHAT IS THE RESPONSIBILITY OF LEADERS IN LOCAL COMMUNITIES?

Most of the responsibilities at this level are possibly educational in character rather than those which involve action, especially governmental action. Problems for action, of course, present themselves when it becomes necessary to stop Communist infiltration, as in a labor union, or, on the other hand, when it becomes desirable to block ill-considered methods of immunizing the community against future subversion.

But, at the local level, the greatest challenges are likely to be in terms of longer-range educational needs. Here at the grass roots—in their families, schools, and churches—is the place where children must learn to have faith in the Sermon on the Mount and the Bill of Rights. The survey reviewed in this book has shown that in the cities from which our special sample of local community leaders was drawn there are many responsible adults who themselves have such faith. School board members, presidents of Parent-Teachers' Associations, and chairmen of library committees were well above the general public in tolerance of nonconformity, as this volume has shown. Of course they almost unanimously drew the line against exposing children to Communist teachers, as did practically all respondents. But they also tended to stand firm on not firing a schoolteacher who had been criticized by a Congressional committee as disloyal but swore he was not a Communist. And most of them did not favor purging libraries of "dangerous books."

It is not alone on the negative, but also on the positive actions of such responsible officials, together with the school superintendents, principals, teachers, and librarians, that constructive training in citizenship rests. A reasonable inference from this study is that a large proportion of such citizens have some awareness of their responsibility and the courage to carry it out.

Religious leaders have a particularly heavy obligation in this connection. Chapters Six, Seven, and Eight contained data showing, as would be expected, that churchgoers are more likely than others to perceive the internal Communist threat with its militant atheism as relatively serious. But there also appeared evidence, which might not have been expected, that churchgoers are somewhat more likely than others to be tough on nonconformists—not just on atheists or Communists, but even on Socialists. "Off-beat" ideas are suspect. It has perhaps not been adequately appreciated that a considerable element in the opposition to a free market in ideas in America is religious in origin. And with some justification in fact—since exposure to this free market often does result in a decline of faith in some traditional tenets. The Scopes trial may still be going on, with "defendants" who are now seen as traitors as well as heretics. However much nonorthodox thinking about religion may be detested by some people, tying it up in the same package as Communism surely has no justification, even if seeming ties may have occasionally existed. The responsible leadership of the clergy and laymen, nationally and regionally, has been speaking out ever more clearly on the dangers to America from heedless assaults on our freedom. Protestant, Catholic, and Jewish alike have been active in making public addresses, passing resolutions, and writing articles in religious and secular journals. However important such expressions at a high level may be, even more important should be patient, long-range work within the local parish, quietly and constantly interpreting in terms of the great moral issues of today those ideals, at the very basis of our American liberties, for which our religious institutions stand.

An important special position in connection with the problems with which we are dealing is held by the lawyer. Few groups within our sample of local community leaders contained as many people scored as "tolerant," on our scale of tolerance of nonconformists, as did the presidents of local bar associations. This was shown in Chapter Two.

233

Their free comments, as well, showed how sensitized they were to threats to civil rights. They were divided, however, on the subject of the Fifth Amendment. Fifty per cent of them said they would be almost sure that a man really was a Communist if he refused to tell a Congressional committee whether he ever had been a Communist, while 41% could offer no reason why a person would refuse to tell a committee he had never been a Communist if he really never had been. The question then was asked: **Sometimes a man says he refuses to answer questions about Communism because he does not want to be forced to testify against his former friends. Should he be punished very severely, severely, not too severely, or not at all?** A larger proportion of lawyers tended to be tough on this one than was found among the general public:

| | PERCENTAGE OF RESPONSES | |
	By Lawyers	By National Cross-Section
Very severely	5%	6%
Severely	38	24
Not too severely	28	33
Not at all	19	22
Don't know	10	15
	100%	100%
Number of cases	*109*	*4933*

When lawyers divide as much as this, it is evident that current controversies within the legal profession on the subject of the Fifth Amendment are far from resolved.

The study has shown that heads of patriotic groups like the D.A.R. and the American Legion tend, as might have been predicted, to be less willing to tolerate nonconformists than do our other selected types of local leaders. But it is likewise important to note that nearly half of the local D.A.R. regents and commanders of Legion posts tend to score in the "more tolerant" group—especially the younger and better educated among them. Moreover, they are found to be in the "more tolerant" group even more frequently than the rank and file of people in the general population of their cities or of the nation.

In the case of veterans, we have enough data to permit some further comparisons within our national cross-section. Veterans in the cross-section tend to be found in our "more tolerant" group more often than the average person, male and female, in the general population—43% (based on 433 cases) as compared with 31% in the general population. But those veterans who belong to the American Legion or Veterans of Foreign Wars are somewhat less likely to be tolerant than those who belong to no organization. The comparative percentages are 39% (based on 233 cases) and 47% (based on 185 cases). Veterans belonging to other veterans' groups are not counted here because there were too few cases.

Another interesting finding is the fact that World War II veterans are significantly more likely to be tolerant than World War I veterans:

	Percentage "More Tolerant"
Members of Legion or V.F.W.	
World War II veterans	43% (*174*)
World War I veterans	24% (*59*)
Not Members of any Veterans' Group	
World War II veterans	52% (*185*)
World War I veterans	39% (*75*)

The younger veterans, both in and out of the Legion and the V.F.W., are much better educated than those of World War I, and this factor is associated with the differences in tolerance.

Interesting with respect to education is the suggestion, in our rather small sample, that the Legion and V.F.W. have disproportionally low membership from the two educational extremes of veterans—grade school men and college men. What would happen to the ideology and practices of the major veterans' groups if more of the thoughtful and tolerant veterans, generally, were to exercise their civic responsibility and join up? There must be many progressive local commanders and higher officials who would welcome such support.

Even though the local community leaders, in all roles studied, are more tolerant than the cross-section of people in their own cities or in the nation as a whole, this finding is not necessarily a basis for complacency about leaders' own attitudes. To some people the leaders may appear surprisingly tolerant—or even dangerously so. But to other observers who have a different level of expectation or standard of judgment the leaders themselves are disappointingly less tolerant than might be hoped. The prospect has rosy or somber hues, depending on the spectacles worn. Even an anxious devotee of civil liberties who may be a wearer of darkened glasses should rejoice, however, to see the leaders ahead, not behind, the rest of the people from his point of view. The big question is: Will they *lead?* And lead even better in the future than in the past? This volume cannot answer this question. Only people in their communities can answer it—by their actions in the years ahead.

To sum up: Great social, economic, and technological forces are operating slowly and imperceptibly on the side of spreading tolerance. The rising level of education and the accompanying decline in authoritarian child-rearing practices increase independence of thought and respect for others whose ideas are different. The increasing geographical movement of people has a similar consequence, as well as the vicarious experiences supplied by the magic of our ever more powerful media of communications.

But even among the relatively intolerant people over the land, most subscribe, now as always, to certain basic values of fair play, and their patriotism can hardly be doubted. Some may have warped personalities, but many of them are simply drawing conclusions from premises which are based on false information—for example, the premise that a non-orthodox thinker about religion or economics is either a hard-core Communist or a tool of Communists. A program of information and education which seeks today to correct false premises can count on good motivations in most people, motivations which await activation or need redirection.

If vigilance is the price of liberty, there are certain guardians who have a special responsibility—the press, radio and television, our national political leaders, and our leaders at the level of local communities. This book portrays starkly some of the difficulties which they face. The evils of Communism and the dangerous disregard of civil rights are so intertwined that their disentanglement cannot be easy. Yet disentangled they must be if the heritage of freedom is to be preserved.

True, certain leaders and groups have a special responsibility. But not all responsibility is theirs alone. Every mother, every father, every citizen has a duty to perform.

We now take leave of the interviews to which so many thousands of Americans across the nation patiently confided their thoughts. Our concluding word is to these people: "Thank you. If this book helps, ever so little, to make America see itself more clearly, the time you gave and the confidences you entrusted may not have been in vain."

Appendix A

HOW THE SAMPLES WERE SELECTED AND HOW CLOSELY THEY CONFORM WITH KNOWN POPULATION CHARACTERISTICS[1]

The samples used in this study were described very briefly in Chapter One. We present here a more detailed accounting. Two kinds of samples were used: (1) a national cross-section of the population and (2) a special supplementary sample of local community leaders. Each will be described separately.

THE NATIONAL CROSS-SECTION

The cross-section, using the probability method, sought to be representative of the American population 21 years of age and over, living in private households. Excluded were persons in hospitals, nursing homes, prisons, hotels, and military establishments.

How closely the final sample of respondents who completed interviews corresponded with the national figures is shown by the following tables:

	PERCENTAGE DISTRIBUTION	
	U.S. Adult Civilian Population (Latest estimates from Census data)[2]	*Completed Interviews in Cross-Section Sample*
By Region		
East	27.6%	25.6%
Midwest	29.9	29.8
South	28.9	31.3
West	13.6	13.3
	100.0%	100.0%

[1]For much of the substance of this appendix the author is indebted to Paul Sheatsley of the National Opinion Research Center and Paul Perry of the American Institute of Public Opinion.

[2]The national population characteristics are estimates for June, 1954, based upon the latest Census releases, especially Series P-25 No. 101, dated August 29, 1954, and Series P-25 No. 106, dated Dec. 6, 1954.

	U.S. Adult Civilian Population (Latest estimates from Census data)[3]	Completed Interviews in Cross-Section Sample
By Urban & Rural		
Urban	64.0%	66.0%
Rural	36.0	34.0%
	100.0%	100.0%
By Sex		
Males	47.7%	46.6%
Females	52.3	53.4
	100.0%	100.0%
By Age		
21–29	18.8%	18.4%
30–39	23.5	23.8
40–49	20.9	21.5
50–59	16.4	16.1
60 and older	20.4	20.2
	100.0%	100.0%
By Color		
Negro	9.2%	8.9%
All others	90.8	91.1%
	100.0%	100.0%
By Education		
College	15.4%	17.1%
High School	43.5	45.4
Grade School or none	41.1	37.5
	100.0%	100.0%

It will be seen that the sample is a quite satisfactory reconstruction of the population on these characteristics. There are some biases, but seldom more than 2%. The most serious, possibly, is in the case of education, where there is a deficit of 3.6% in grade school people. This may not be a sampling error, however, for it may reflect a tendency for people to overstate their schooling even more to an interviewer on a poll than to an interviewer on the Census. None of the sampling discrepancies above noted could have made an appreciable

Ibid.

238

difference on the over-all percentages of people reporting a particular opinion.

How the Sample Was Drawn

Methods of drawing the sample differed slightly between the two survey agencies, the American Institute of Public Opinion and the National Opinion Research Center, but the following concise description by one of the agencies outlines the essentials of the process:

The sample was selected by these stages in the following manner:

a. The U.S. was divided into 26 regions consisting of single states (12 of the larger ones) and groups of states. Each such area was processed independently, but the steps taken within each were identical.

b. Within each of these regions the population was ordered by the Census state economic areas, listing metropolitan state economic areas in one group and non-metropolitan state economic areas in another. Within each of these two groups the areas and counties within areas were listed in geographic order.

c. Within each of the counties the population was divided into three rural-urban strata (urban 50,000 and over, urban 2500 to 49,999, and rural).

d. Within counties, cities and minor civil divisions were left in the order in which they appear in Census reports, which is, in most cases, alphabetical order.

e. From this array of the data, from a random starting point, a systematic sample of places (cities and minor civil divisions) in each of the 26 regions was drawn, proceeding through the list in serpentine fashion, with the probability of selection of the places proportional to population in the 1950 Census.

f. Within cities so selected for which household data were reported by minor divisions such as Census tracts or wards, minor divisions were drawn with probability proportional to population. Within the minor division selected, a block was drawn at random.

g. Cities and minor civil divisions selected which were not divided into Census tracts or wards were divided into segments on the

239

basis of maps. These segments were delineated so as to be roughly equal in size of population. Segments were then drawn at random.

h. Rural areas were segmented in the same manner as described under g. and segments drawn at random.

i. When the block or segment had been drawn in the manner described, a random starting point was determined, and the route to be followed in listing dwelling units was laid out.

j. Listers were instructed to start listing dwelling units at the designated point and, in urban areas, to follow the designated route until 75 dwelling units had been listed. Where one block or segment was not large enough to supply 75 dwelling units, designated adjacent blocks or segments were to be taken.

k. In rural areas listers were told to list 50 dwelling units in the same manner. Fewer dwelling units were listed in rural areas because of the greater distance between such units and consequent increased listing cost per unit.

Therefore, the primary sampling units consisted of groups of 75 dwelling units in urban areas and 50 dwelling units in rural areas.

From each primary sampling unit a systematic sample of 10 dwelling units was drawn from a random starting point.

Adults within each occupied dwelling unit drawn into the sample were ordered by age and sex (first males in order of age, then females in order of age) and one chosen by a process of random selection.

If the individual so selected was not reached on the first call, interviewers were instructed to call again and to continue to do so until a total of five calls had been made. Actually some interviewers called back ten or more times.

The other agency followed essentially the same procedure, with minor modifications. For example, all dwelling units within the sampling area were listed, rather than the specified number of fifty or seventy-five; the sampling "take" varied slightly from segment to segment rather than remaining constant, etc.

A total of 537 interviewers from the two agencies conducted the field investigation. The time required for the interview varied from half an hour to over three hours, but the average was about an hour and a quarter.

Analysis of the "Fish Which Were Not Caught"

For this study a total of 4939 interviews were completed, of which 4933 were usable for purposes of analysis. If every person specified in the original sample had been interviewed, the total would have been 5881. It is very important, therefore, to analyze the reasons for non-completion. Actually, the completion rate is one of the best on record and was achieved by instructing every interviewer to make at least five attempts before giving up.

A breakdown of attempted interviews by the two agencies combined is as follows:

	Number	Percentage
Completed interviews	4939	84.0%
Not at home, no contact made	340	5.8
Too sick to be interviewed	64	1.1
Interviewer could not speak respondent's non-English language	52	0.9
Refused to be interviewed	415	7.0
Broke off interview	71	1.2
	5881	100.0%

Even though it is reassuring that the completed interviews in the cross-section sample reproduced the population characteristics of the nation as closely as we have seen they did, we still must be concerned about the introduction of bias because of the "fish which were not caught."

By far the most important fact for our purposes is that only 1.2% broke off the interview after it began. If this number had been very large—say of the magnitude of 10%—we would have real grounds for worry. Why? Because these are the only people who could have failed to co-operate as a consequence of knowing what the questionnaire was driving at. Those who refused to be interviewed at all are a much less serious problem, since they could have had no idea about the contents of the study. Actually, even among the 1.2% who broke off the interview after it began, the majority of reasons were clearly unrelated to the content of the study. For example, a neighbor or friends might drop in during the middle of the interview. The interviewer would stop at this point and make a date for a return engagement, which eventually could not be kept because of circumstances beyond the control of either party.

241

Let us examine each group in turn among those not completing interviews.

Not too much is known about the 5.8% who were not at home or not contacted. We can report that the proportion "not home" was somewhat higher in large cities than in smaller towns and rural areas, and we can surmise that the group is younger rather than older than those interviewed. On the other hand, the combined "not home, no contact" group includes also about 100 sample households which were never called on for an interview at all—and these were chiefly in rural areas—owing to impassable roads or to the lack of a substitute for an interviewer who became unable to finish his assignment. The "big-city" bias of the group who could never be found at home is thus largely compensated for by the rural bias of the group who were never even approached for the interview. This study, however, probably penetrated as fully into the mountain fastnesses and the "Tobacco Roads" of the nation as any survey in recent times, except for the Census itself.

The 1.1% who were too sick to be interviewed are an inevitable loss to any study. This number was kept as low as it was by spreading out the interviewing period long enough to make contact with some of the non-chronic cases after they had recovered.

In areas where no English was spoken, bilingual interviewers were used where possible, but it was thought better to miss a small proportion of cases (0.9%) rather than risk the hazards of a translator.

With respect to the refusal groups—the 7% who would not be interviewed and the 1.2% who broke off the interview after it began —some extraordinary pains were taken to discover whether the failure to get such cases would introduce a serious bias in our analysis. Our considered conclusion is that it would not.

Interviewers were instructed to record verbatim the respondent's stated reason for refusing to co-operate. Interviewers were then asked whether, in their view, this was the real reason he refused, and if not, what they considered to be the true reason. Special attention was given to the possibility of *fear*. The Communist issue directly could not have been a cause of fear among those who refused to be interviewed at all, since none knew that it would be discussed. Also, more than half of the breakoffs came before the subject of Communism was introduced. But some people fear talking even on ordinary market-research surveys, and it is important to know how many such people there are.

242

The reports from the interviewers are analyzed in two columns below; first in terms of reasons given by the respondent for not co-operating, and second in terms of the "real" reasons as inferred by the interviewers:

	Percentage expressing a given reason for refusal or breakoff	Percentage distribution of "real" reasons as inferred by the interviewer
No fear present	6.5%	5.7%
Fear present	.8	1.7
Not ascertainable	.9	.8
Total	8.2%	8.2%

When it is considered that the larger of the figures on fear is only 1.7%, and when it is also considered that very few even of these cases are attributable to the particular content of the questionnaire, the results are most encouraging. There were only seven cases in the entire survey where fear was explicitly expressed in the context of Communism, and only a dozen or so where the interviewer felt that this was an element in non-co-operation. Where no fear was thought to be present, a more detailed breakdown of "reasons" is presented as follows:

	Percentage expressing a given reason for refusal or breakoff	Percentage distribution of "real" reasons as inferred by the interviewer
No interest in surveys, can't be bothered	2.7%	2.3%
Too busy, can't talk now, haven't got the time	3.7	4.0
Not feeling well, don't feel up to it	.7	.5
Not smart enough, don't follow current events	.8	.8
Spouse or parent won't permit it	.3	.4
Miscellaneous	.2	.3
Total	6.5%	5.7%

These figures add to more than 6.5% and 5.7%, respectively, because more than one reason was applicable in some cases.

Analysis of the demographic characteristics of the refusals shows that in the main they do not differ greatly from the population who were interviewed. Interviewers classified the majority of the refusals as "average" in their standard of living, with 15% better than average and 28% lower. This is normal. Somewhat more refusals were obtained from women and from the older age groups, but the differences are not at all striking.

The only respect with which those who refused appears to differ significantly from those who were interviewed is their place of residence, for refusal rates were markedly higher in the largest cities. In rural areas, for example, only 4% of the respondents refused to be interviewed, but in cities of more than 100,000 population the refusal rate was 13%. This phenomenon has been reported in many other surveys as well.

Any loss from a probability sample naturally introduces a possible bias. In general, however, it may be said that the loss rate in the current survey was of no different nature from nor any higher than the loss experienced in any survey inquiry, and that detailed analysis of the groups who contributed to the loss fails to reveal any special characteristics which would affect the over-all interpretation of the findings.

THE SAMPLE OF LOCAL COMMUNITY LEADERS

A unique feature of this study is its special sample of people in certain positions of civic responsibility.

As was stated in Chapter One, the selection of the 14 categories of community leaders was made arbitrarily and was limited by the funds and time available for the research. The major criteria for selection were that the leader be easily and unambiguously *identified,* that he hold some position of *influence* in the community, and that his position hold some *relevance* to the content of the study. These criteria precluded selection of informal leaders who could not readily be identified by the interviewers; of highly informed or experienced individuals who held no formal leadership position; and of leaders in such areas as sports, medicine or finance, which bear no special relevance to the problems studied. Time and cost considerations prevented the interviewing of additional categories of leaders whose views would have been worth while: religious leaders, college presidents, minority-group leaders, etc.

In sampling the leaders it was agreed to eliminate all of the largest cities and also all rural areas. Inclusion of the largest cities would have introduced difficult problems of identification and also of relative weights. Thus, how identify the "local" American Legion commander or P.T.A. head in a city the size of Chicago or Philadelphia? And should the mayor of New York be given equal weight with the mayor of a small town in Idaho; or, if not, what weights should be assigned? The rural areas also posed a problem in that the designated leadership positions were often found only in county seats or other urban places nearby.

For these reasons, community-leader interviews were assigned only in cities of 10,000 to 150,000 population. The randomly selected sampling areas of the two research agencies, which had been used for the larger population study, included a total of 123 such cities. They represent an accurate cross-section of all U.S. urban places of this size. They include cities from all geographical regions, country towns and county seats, suburban communities and large cities, state capitals, industrial cities, college towns.

Within each of these 123 cities, interviewers were assigned to identify the 14 specified leaders and to send their names and addresses to the research agency. Detailed instructions were provided where the identification might prove difficult. In most cases where more than one such leader existed, interviewers were told to select the one with the largest "constituency"; e.g., the publisher of the newspaper with the greatest circulation, the commander of the largest Legion post. Special instructions were provided for determining the labor leader to be interviewed, so that the two or three largest national unions would not be selected in every case. Where the actual category specified did not exist, the nearest equivalent was usually taken. Thus, if there was no Chamber of Commerce in the city, interviewers were asked to choose the head of the largest businessmen's or merchants' association. Most of the 14 leaders had for their constituency only the local community, but a few—the Republican and Democratic county chairmen, for example—represented the county or other larger areas.

245

When the names of the selected leaders had been received by the research agencies, letters were addressed to them explaining the purpose of the study and inviting their co-operation when the local interviewer called for an appointment. As with the general public, the leaders were not informed in advance of the precise content of the questionnaire; it was described only as "a survey of public opinion about current issues." The leaders, furthermore, were not told that they had been selected as representative of a particular group, but rather that they were chosen simply as "prominent members of the community." In this way it was hoped their responses would come in terms of their individual opinions rather than the "official line" of their particular group—labor, business, Republican, Democrat, American Legion, or whatever.

It is obvious from the foregoing that no claims can be made that the present sample is representative of "leadership opinion" in the United States, or even that the 14 separate samples adequately reflect local opinion within each group. We have noted that the largest cities as well as the rural areas are generally not represented in these samples. Some of the leaders interviewed represent only one of several such leaders in the community. And there remains the problem of "weights." In our tabulations, every leader interviewed has been given equal weight, so that the views of the small-city newspaper publisher or school board chairman count just as much as the views of his opposite number in a larger city.

It will be best to evaluate the sample for exactly what it is: the opinions of local leaders of the specified types in a representative cross-section of more than 100 small and medium-sized cities. We cannot say that our sample of Chamber of Commerce heads, for example, represents "American business opinion" or even grass-roots Chamber of Commerce opinion. But we can say that the opinions of those we interviewed in this group accurately reflect the opinions of all leaders of the most influential business association in cities of the designated size. And as such, their views—and the views of the 13 other leadership groups who were interviewed—command some attention and respect.

The rate of interview completion among the community-leader sample surpassed even that achieved among the regular population cross-section. The 123 communities which were selected had a theoretical "leader population" of 1722, but in 34 cases no leader category of the type designated was in existence. Thus, some communities had no Community Chest or united fund, and consequently no chairman of such a group; in some places there was no local D.A.R. chapter, etc. The actual sample, therefore, totaled 1688,[4] yielding the following results:

	Number	Per cent
Completed interviews	1533	90.9%
Out of town, ill, unavailable	73	4.3
Never contacted	31	1.8
Refusal or breakoff	51	3.0
Total	1688	100.0%

It will be noted that the refusal rate among the leaders was only about half that among the population cross-section. While the original refusal rate was considerably higher, every effort was made through personal letters, telephone calls, etc., to overcome the respondent's objection and to obtain his opinions. Considering the fact that these community leaders were in many cases extremely busy individuals, with many demands on their time, their willingness to contribute up to two hours of their time in replying to these questions is most gratifying.

Since interviewing was conducted during the early summer, a small proportion of the leaders were found to be absent from their communities. In most cases it was possible to ascertain their summer address and to interview them there, but inevitably a few were lost for this reason. A small number were too ill to be interviewed, and a few others were unavailable for other reasons. (One was in police custody, under indictment for fraud.) The "never contacted" group represents chiefly interviewer failure. In three areas most of the sample was lost because the interviewer became unavailable and no qualified substitute could be found. In a few cases the deadline expired before any interview attempts could be made, or there was no contact because it was never ascertained which of two or more individuals was the proper one to be interviewed.

[4]In a few instances the same individual held more than one of the 14 leadership positions. Thus, a man might be the local newspaper publisher and also the chairman of the Community Chest. Since the leader sample was designed for separate analysis of each of the 14 groups, such individuals were counted twice and their interviews were duplicated. (If they refused to be interviewed, their refusal was counted twice.) The number of individuals in the total leader sample was therefore slightly less than the 1533 interviews which were tabulated.

The interview completion rates for each of the 14 leadership categories are shown as follows:

	Percentage Completed	Percentage Not Reached	Percentage Refused
Mayors	92%	2%	6%
Community Chest chairmen	93	3	4
School Board presidents	91	7	2
Library Committee chairmen	93	4	3
Republican county chairmen	91	7	2
Democratic county chairmen	87	6	7
American Legion commanders	95	4	1
Bar Association presidents	92	3	5
Chamber of Commerce presidents	94	2	4
P.T.A. presidents	93	5	2
Women's Club presidents	92	6	2
D.A.R. regents	90	6	4
Newspaper publishers	80	8	12
Labor-union leaders	88	6	6

A 90% completion rate was achieved in all but three cases—the Democratic county chairmen, the newspaper publishers, and the labor-union leaders.

From the sampling standpoint, the newspaper publishers are our least satisfactory group. Twelve per cent of them refused to be interviewed, mostly on the grounds that they were too busy to be bothered, while 8% could not be reached, mostly because they were inaccessible on summer vacation. Because the newspaper publishers are particularly important at some points in the analysis in this book, a special effort was made to ascertain the editorial stands, on the subject of Senator McCarthy, of papers whose publishers could not be reached in the sample. Information was obtained in 19 cases, which showed two very favorable to McCarthy, two leaning favorable, eight which took no editorial stand, and seven which were unfavorable. This suggests that, if we had been able to make contact with every publisher, the "true" figures on publishers' attitudes probably would not differ markedly from those reported in the book.

Again, let us repeat, the most dangerous bias which can enter a study like this is through interviews broken off in the middle, *after* the respondent finds out what the study is all about. There were not more than five interviews broken off among all the community leaders—

none among newspaper publishers, incidentally—and in no cases did interviewers think that the breakoff was due to the nature of the subject matter under investigation.

All in all, there is reason to believe that the field workers assigned to the civic leaders did one of the most thorough and conscientious jobs in the annals of public opinion research.

Appendix B

NATIONAL OPINION RESEARCH CENTER

NORC: 356
POS: A–930
5-54

and

AMERICAN INSTITUTE OF PUBLIC OPINION

Time interview started: _____

1. On the whole, do you think life will be better for you or worse, in the next few years than it is now? (If no opinion, ask for "best guess.")

(5)

Better _____ ☐ 1

About the same _____ ☐ 2

Worse _____ ☐ 3

Don't know _____ ☐ 0

2. Everybody of course has some things he worries about, more or less. Would you say you worry more now than you used to, or not as much?

(6)

More _____ ☐ 1

About the same _____ ☐ 2

Not as much __ _____ ☐ 3

Never worry _____ ☐ 4

Don't know _____ ☐ 0

3. What kinds of things do you worry most about?

(7)

4. Would you guess that you worry or are concerned about such things more than most people, or less?

(8)

More _____ ☐ 1

About the same _____ ☐ 2

Less _____ ☐ 3

Don't know _____ ☐ 0

5. Are there other problems you worry or are concerned about, especially political or world problems?

(9)

6. Would you guess you worry about such things more than most people, or less?

(10)

More _____ ☐ 1

About the same ____ ☐ 2

Less _____ ☐ 3

Don't know ___ ___ ☐ 0

7. A. We are interested in what kind of things people talk about. Offhand, what problems do you remember discussing with your friends in the last week or so?

(11)

B. Were there other things? For example, did you talk about any dangers facing people in the United States?

8. Here is a list of topics which have been discussed in the papers recently. (Hand respondent White Card)

A. Which ones do you remember talking about with your friends in the last week or so?

A. Have talked about (12)		B. Most Important	C. Next Most Important
1 ☐	Atom or hydrogen bombs _____	☐	☐
2 ☐	Communists in the United States_____	☐	☐
3 ☐	Crime and juvenile delinquency _____	☐	☐
4 ☐	Danger of World War III __ _____	☐	☐
5 ☐	Farm prices _____	☐	☐
6 ☐	High prices of things you buy _____	☐	☐
7 ☐	High taxes _____	☐	☐
8 ☐	Negro-white problems _____	☐	☐
9 ☐	Possibility of another depression _____	☐	☐
X ☐	Threats to freedom in the United States ☐	☐	☐
Y ☐	None of these, don't know _____	☐	☐

(13)

B. Which one on that whole list seems most important to you? —whether you talked about it or not. (Check answer in appropriate box above)

(14)

C. Which one seems next most important? (Check answer in appropriate box above)

250

9. In your opinion, how likely is it that World War III will break out <u>in the next two years?</u>

(15)

Very likely .... ☐ 1
Rather likely .... ☐ 2
Rather unlikely ...... ☐ 3
Not likely at all ...... ☐ 4
Don't know .... ☐ 0

10. <u>In the long run,</u> how likely is it that Communists can be stopped from taking over the rest of Europe without a World War?

(16)

Very likely .... ☐ 1
Rather likely .... ☐ 2
Rather unlikely ...... ☐ 3
Not likely at all ...... ☐ 4
Don't know .... ☐ 0

11. Suppose it turned out that the only way to stop the Communists from taking over the rest of Europe was for the United States to fight Russia. Should we let the Communists take over the rest of Europe or fight Russia?

(17)

Let Communists take over ...... ☐ 1
Fight Russia .... ☐ 2
Qualified (specify) .... ☐
Don't know .... ☐ 0

12. <u>In the long run,</u> how likely is it that Communists can be stopped from taking over the rest of Asia without a World War?

(18)

Very likely .... ☐ 1
Rather likely .... ☐ 2
Rather unlikely ...... ☐ 3
Not likely at all ...... ☐ 4
Don't know .... ☐ 0

13. Suppose it turned out that the only way to stop the Communists from taking over the rest of Asia was for the United States to fight Russia. Should we let the Communists take over the rest of Asia, or fight Russia?

(19)

Let Communists take over ...... ☐ 1
Fight Russia .... ☐ 2
Qualified (specify) .... ☐
Don't know .... ☐ 0

14. Of these three ways of dealing with Russia, which do you think is best for America <u>now?</u> (Hand respondent reverse side of White Card)

(20)

Talk over problems with Russia ... ☐ 1
Have nothing to do with Russia ... ☐ 2
Fight Russia .... ☐ 3
Qualified (specify) .... ☐
Don't know .... ☐ 0

15. A. Would you favor cutting down our aid to our Allies now?

(21)

Yes .... ☐ 1*
Qualified (specify) ... ☐ 2
No .... ☐ 3*
Don't know .... ☐ 0

*B. IF YES OR NO: Why?

16. A. To reduce taxes, would you favor cutting down the size of our Air Force now?

(22)

Yes .... ☐ 1
No .... ☐ 2
Don't know .... ☐ 0

B. To reduce taxes, would you favor cutting down our Atom Bomb production now?

(23)

Yes .... ☐ 1
No .... ☐ 2
Don't know .... ☐ 0

Now some questions on a different topic.

17. A. Which of these three views is closest to your own? (Hand respondent Blue Card)

(24)

All people in this country feel as free to say what they think as they used to .... ☐ 1
Some people do not feel as free to say what they think as they used to .... ☐ 2*
Hardly anybody feels as free to say what he thinks as he used to .... ☐ 3*
Don't know .... ☐ 0

*IF SOME OR HARDLY ANYBODY ASK B AND C:

B. Which groups or kinds of people may feel less free now to speak their minds? (Why do they feel less free?)

(25)

C. If people do not feel as free to speak their minds, is it a good thing or a bad thing for the country?

(26)

Good .... ☐ 1
Bad .... ☐ 2
Qualified (specify) ... ☐
Don't know .... ☐ 0

251

18. Is this something you have thought about lately a great deal, some, a little, or hardly at all?

(27)

A great deal ....☐ 1
Some ....☐ 2
A little ....☐ 3
Hardly at all ....☐ 4
Don't know ....☐ 0

19. A. What about you personally? Do you or don't you feel as free to speak your mind as you used to?

(28)

Yes, as free ....☐ 1
No, less free ....☐ 2*
Don't know ....☐ 0

* IF NO, ASK B AND C:

B. In what ways? Why?

C. How do you feel about this? Does it bother you, or not?

(29)

Bothers me much ....☐ 1
Bothers me some ....☐ 2
Does not bother me.......☐ 3
Don't know ....☐ 0

20. There are always some people whose ideas are considered bad or dangerous by other people. For instance, somebody who is against all churches and religion.

A. If such a person wanted to make a speech in your city (town, community) against churches and religion, should he be allowed to speak, or not?

(30)

Yes ....☐ 1
No ....☐ 2
Don't know ....☐ 0

B. Should such a person be allowed to teach in a college or university, or not?

(31)

Yes ....☐ 1
No ....☐ 2
Don't know ....☐ 0

C. If some people in your community suggested that a book he wrote against churches and religion should be taken out of your public library, would you favor removing this book or not?

(32)

Yes ....☐ 1
No ....☐ 2
Don't know ....☐ 0

21. Or consider a person who favored government ownership of all the railroads and all big industries.

A. If this person wanted to make a speech in your community favoring government ownership of all the railroads and big industries, should he be allowed to speak, or not?

(33)

Yes ....☐ 1
No ....☐ 2
Don't know ....☐ 0

B. Should such a person be allowed to teach in a college or university, or not?

(34)

Yes ....☐ 1
No ....☐ 2
Don't know ....☐ 0

C. If some people in your community suggested that a book he wrote favoring government ownership should be taken out of your public library, would you favor removing the book, or not?

(35)

Yes ....☐ 1
No ....☐ 2
Don't know ....☐ 0

22. A. Some people say that Americans are getting more distrustful or suspicious of each other than they used to be. Have you thought about this recently, one way or another?

(36)

Yes ....☐ 1*
No ....☐ 2
Don't know ....☐ 0

*B. IF YES: Have you talked with anybody about this subject, one way or another?

(37)

Yes ....☐ 1
No ....☐ 2
Don't know ....☐ 0

23. A. What is your own opinion? Do you think Americans are getting more suspicious of others, or less suspicious?

(38)

More ....☐ 1*
Same ....☐ 2
Less ....☐ 3
Never suspicious ....☐ 4
Don't know ....☐ 0

*B. IF MORE: Why do you say this? In what ways?

(39)

24. A. How great a danger do you feel that American Communists are to this country at the present time—a very great danger, a great danger, some danger, hardly any danger or no danger?

(40)

A very great danger	☐ 1*
A great danger	☐ 2*
Some danger	☐ 3*
Hardly any danger	☐ 4*
No danger	☐ 5*
Don't know	☐ 0

*B. UNLESS DON'T KNOW: Why do you think this?

(41)

25. Do you think a man can believe in Communism and still be a loyal American, or not?

(42)

Yes	☐ 1
Qualified (specify)	☐ 2
No	☐ 3
Don't know	☐ 0

26. What kind of people in America are most likely to be Communists?

(43)

Probe 1, Unless Volunteered: What racial or religious groups are they most likely to be in?

Probe 2, Unless Volunteered: What kind of jobs are they most likely to be in?

27. What kinds of things do Communists believe in? **Probe:** Anything else?

(44)

28. A. Have you ever known a person who you thought might be a Communist?

(45)

Yes	☐ 1*
No	☐ 2

*B. IF YES: How could you tell? What made you think this?

29. In some communities, people have been asked to report to the F. B. I. any neighbors or acquaintances who they suspect might be Communists.

A. As far as you know, has this idea been suggested in your city (town, community)?

(46)

Yes	☐ 1**
No	☐ 2*
Don't know	☐ 0*

*B. IF NO OR DON'T KNOW: Have you read or heard about this idea?

(47)

Yes	☐ 1**
No	☐ 2
Don't know	☐ 0

**C. IF YES TO EITHER A OR B: Have you discussed this idea, one way or another, in conversations with anybody?

(48)

Yes	☐ 1
No	☐ 2
Don't know	☐ 0

253

30. A. <u>On the whole</u>, do you think it is a good idea or a bad idea for people to report to the F.B.I. any neighbors or acquaintances whom they suspect of being Communists?

(49)

Good idea	☐	1*
Bad idea	☐	2**
Don't know	☐	0

*IF GOOD IDEA TO A, ASK B, C & D.
**IF BAD IDEA, SKIP TO E AND F.

B. On the whole, you think it is a good idea. Do you think there are any dangers in it, or not?

(50)

Yes	☐	*
No	☐	2
Don't know	☐	0

*C. IF YES TO B: What dangers?

D. Suppose President Eisenhower were to say publicly that it was a bad idea, on the whole, for people to be reporting any acquaintances they suspect to the F.B.I. Do you think you might come to agree with him, or not?

(51)

Yes	☐	1
No	☐	2
Don't know	☐	0

**IF BAD IDEA TO A, ASK E & F.

E. What dangers do you see in it?

(52)

F. Suppose President Eisenhower were to say publicly that it was a <u>good</u> idea, on the whole, for people to be reporting any acquaintances they suspect to the F.B.I. Do you think you might come to agree with him or not?

(53)

Yes	☐	1
No	☐	2
Don't know	☐	0

31. Do you or don't you think the government should have the right to listen in on people's private telephone conversations, in order to get evidence against Communists?

(54)

Yes	☐	1
No	☐	2
Don't know	☐	0

32. A. If an American opposed churches and religion, would this <u>alone</u> make you think he was a Communist?

(55)

Yes	☐	1
No	☐	2
Don't know	☐	0

B. If an American favored government ownership of all the railroads and big industries, would this alone make you think he was a Communist?

(56)

Yes	☐	1
No	☐	2
Don't know	☐	0

C. If an American favored peace at any price, would this alone make you suspect he was a Communist?

(57)

Yes	☐	1
No	☐	2
Don't know	☐	0

D. **IF NO OR DON'T KNOW TO EACH OF A, B, AND C:** If an American took <u>all three</u> stands—opposed churches and religion, favored government ownership, and favored peace at any price—would that make you think he was a Communist?

(58)

Yes	☐	1
No	☐	2
Don't know	☐	0

33. How many Communists do you think there are now in the United States? Just give me your best guess. (Keep probing. Explain, if necessary, "Include all **Communists,** whether they actually belong to the Communist Party or not.")

(59)

34. Do you think the F.B.I. knows who all the American Communists are, or do they know most of them, a good many of them, or only a few of them?

(60)

All	☐	1
Most	☐	2
A good many	☐	3
Only a few	☐	4
Don't know	☐	0

35. If J. Edgar Hoover were to say that the F.B.I. has most of the American Communists under its eye, would you feel pretty sure it was true, or wouldn't you?

(61)

Would feel pretty sure	☐	1
Qualified (specify)	☐	
Would not	☐	2
Don't know	☐	0

254

36. **A.** Do you think there might be any Communists within the American Government now, or not?

B. IF YES: If you had to guess, how many would you think there are—just a few, or hundreds, or thousands?

(62)

Yes, a few ⬚ 1*

Yes, hundreds ⬚ 2*

Yes, thousands ⬚ 3*

Yes, don't know how many ⬚ 4*

No, don't think there are any ⬚ 5

Don't know if there are any ⬚ 0

***C. IF ANY YES ANSWER:** How much danger is there that these Communists within the Government can hurt the country—a great danger, some danger, not much danger, or no danger?

(63)

Great ⬚ 1

Some ⬚ 2

Not much ⬚ 3

None ⬚ 4

Don't know ⬚ 0

37. **A.** If President Eisenhower were to say, some day, that there no longer is any danger from Communists within the Government, would you feel pretty sure he was right, or not?

(64)

Yes, would feel pretty sure ⬚ *

No, would not ⬚ 5

Don't know or qualified ⬚ 0

***B. IF YES:** If later, the chairman of a Congressional Committee investigating Communism said there was still a great danger from Communists within the Government, would you still believe President Eisenhower was right, or not?

Still believe ⬚ 1

Qualified (specify) ⬚ 2

Would not ⬚ 3

Don't know ⬚ 4

(65)
*p

(66)
*p

38. **A.** Do you think there are any Communists working in key defense plants now, or not?

B. IF YES: If you had to guess, how many would you think—just a few, or hundreds, or thousands?

(67)

Yes, a few ⬚ 1*

Yes, hundreds ⬚ 2*

Yes, thousands ⬚ 3*

Yes, don't know how many ⬚ 4*

No, don't think there are any ⬚ 5

Don't know if there are any ⬚ 0

***C. IF ANY YES ANSWER:** How much danger is there that these Communists in defense plants can hurt the country—a great danger, some danger, not much danger, or no danger?

(68)

Great ⬚ 1

Some ⬚ 2

Not much ⬚ 3

None ⬚ 4

Don't know ⬚ 0

39. If both the management and labor union officials in a large defense plant were to say, some day, that Communists in that plant were no longer a danger, would you feel pretty sure that it was true, or not?

(69)

Would feel it was true ⬚ 1

Would not ⬚ 2

Don't know ⬚ 0

40. **A.** Do you think there are any Communists teaching in American colleges and universities now, or not?

B. IF YES: If you had to guess, how many would you think—just a few, or hundreds, or thousands?

(70)

Yes, a few ⬚ 1*

Yes, hundreds ⬚ 2*

Yes, thousands ⬚ 3*

Yes, don't know how many ⬚ 4*

No, don't think there are any ⬚ 5

Don't know if there are any ⬚ 0

***C. IF ANY YES ANSWER:** How much danger is there that the Communists in colleges and universities can hurt the country—a great danger, some danger, not much danger, or no danger?

(71)

Great ⬚ 1

Some ⬚ 2

Not much ⬚ 3

None ⬚ 4

Don't know ⬚ 0

41. If the head of a college were to say, some day, that there were no Communists teaching in that college, would you feel pretty sure it was true, or not?

(72)

Would feel it was true ⬚ 1

Would not ⬚ 2

Don't know ⬚ 0

42. **A.** Do you think there are any Communists teaching in American public schools, or not?

B. IF YES: If you had to guess, how many would you think—just a few, or hundreds, or thousands?

(73)

Yes, a few ⬚ 1*

Yes, hundreds ⬚ 2*

Yes, thousands ⬚ 3*

Yes, don't know how many ⬚ 4*

No, don't think there are any ⬚ 5

Don't know if there are any ⬚ 0

***C. IF ANY YES ANSWER:** How much danger is there that these Communists in public schools can hurt the country—a great danger, some danger, not much danger, or no danger?

(74)

Great ⬚ 1

Some ⬚ 2

Not much ⬚ 3

None ⬚ 4

Don't know ⬚ 0

43. If the school board in your community were to say, some day, that there were no Communists teaching in your schools, would you feel pretty sure it was true, or not?

(75)

Would feel it was true ____ ☐ 1
Would not ____ ☐ 2
Don't know ____ ☐ 0

44. There is a good deal of discussion these days about Congressional committees investigating <u>Communism.</u> Do you happen to know the names of any of the Senators and Congressmen who have been taking a leading part in these investigations of Communism? Who are they?

(76)

45. In general, what is your opinion of these committees investigating Communism—very favorable, favorable, unfavorable or very unfavorable?

(77)

Very favorable ____ ☐ 1
Favorable ____ ☐ 2
Unfavorable ____ ☐ 3
Very unfavorable ____ ☐ 4
Don't know ____ ☐ 0

46. What are some of the good things (if any) that you feel these committees have done?

(78)

47. A. Do you happen to remember how Alger Hiss was caught? How?

(79)

B. UNLESS CONGRESSIONAL COMMITTEE MENTIONED:
As far as you know, did a Congressional committee investigating Communism help catch him or not?

Yes ____ ☐ 1
No ____ ☐ 2
Don't know ____ ☐ 0

48. A. Do you happen to remember how the Rosenbergs were caught? How?

(5)

B. UNLESS CONGRESSIONAL COMMITTEE MENTIONED:
As far as you know, did a Congressional committee investigating Communism help catch them or not?

Yes ____ ☐ 6
No ____ ☐ 7
Don't know ____ ☐ Y

49. A. Consider the Congressional committees investigating Communism <u>today.</u> Some people think that these committees are actually making it harder for the F.B.I. to catch Communists. Others think that these committees are a real help to the F.B.I. today. What do you think?

(6)

Help the F.B.I. ____ ☐ 6*
Make it harder for the F.B.I. ____ ☐ 7*
Don't know ____ ☐ Y

***B. UNLESS DON'T KNOW:** In what way?

256

50. A. What are some of the bad things (if any) that you feel these committees have done?

(7)

B. IF ALREADY ANSWERED IN A, CHECK APPROPRIATE BOX AND SKIP TO C: Some people say these Congressional committees are as much interested in getting publicity and votes as in protecting the country from the Communist threat. Others have a different view. What is your opinion?

(8)

Selfish interest _____ ☐ 6

Disagree _____ ☐ 7

Don't know _____ ☐ Y

C. IF ALREADY ANSWERED, CHECK APPROPRIATE BOX AND SKIP TO D: It has been said that these Congressional committees investigating Communism are hurting the reputations of some people who really aren't Communists at all. Do you think these committees are or are not hurting the reputations of some people who really aren't Communists?

(9)

Are _____ ☐ 6*

Are not _____ ☐ 7

Don't know _____ ☐ Y*

*D. IF ARE OR DON'T KNOW TO C: Do you think the committees could go after Communists without hurting innocent people, or not?

(10)

Could _____ ☐ 6

Could not _____ ☐ 7

Don't know _____ ☐ Y

51. In your opinion, which one of these two is more important? **(Hand Respondent Reverse Side of Blue Card)**

(11)

To find out all the Communists even if some innocent people should be hurt _____ ☐ 6

To protect the rights of innocent people even if some Communists are not found out _____ ☐ 7

Don't know _____ ☐ Y

(12)
sp

52. A. When a man refuses to tell a Congressional committee whether he ever was a Communist, do you think he probably was a Communist, or not?

B. IF PROBABLY WAS: Would you be almost sure he was a Communist, or would you have some doubt?

(13)

Almost sure _____ ☐ 6

Have some doubt _____ ☐ 7

Probably not _____ ☐ 8

Don't know _____ ☐ Y

53. A. Can you think of any reason why a person would refuse to tell a committee whether he'd ever been a Communist, if he really never had been?

(14)

Yes _____ ☐ *

No _____ ☐ X

*B. IF YES: What sort of reasons might he have for refusing to answer?

54. Sometimes a man says he refuses to answer certain questions about Communism because he does not want to be forced to testify against his former friends. Should he be punished very severely, severely, not too severely, or not at all?

(15)

Very severely _____ ☐ 6

Severely _____ ☐ 7

Not too severely _____ ☐ 8

Not at all _____ ☐ 9

Don't know _____ ☐ Y

55. It has been said that some loyal Americans won't take Government jobs today for fear of unjust attacks on their reputations. Have you ever heard this, or read of it?

(16)

Yes _____ ☐ 6

No _____ ☐ 7

Don't know _____ ☐ Y

56. A. Do you think it is true, or not, that some loyal Americans won't take Government jobs today for fear of unjust attacks on their reputations?

(17)

Yes, true _____ ☐ 6*

Qualified (specify) _____ ☐ 7*

No, untrue _____ ☐ 8

Don't know _____ ☐ Y

*B. IF YES OR QUALIFIED: Do you think this will hurt the country a great deal, some, only a little, or not at all.

(18)

Great deal _____ ☐ 6

Some _____ ☐ 7

A little _____ ☐ 8

Not at all _____ ☐ 9

Don't know _____ ☐ Y

257

57. Now, I should like to ask you some questions about a man who admits he is a Communist.

A. Suppose he is working in a defense plant. Should he be fired, or not?

(19)

Yes ————☐ 6
No ————☐ 7
Don't know ——☐ Y

B. Suppose he is a clerk in a store. Should he be fired, or not?

(20)

Yes ————☐ 6
No ————☐ 7
Don't know ——☐ Y

C. Suppose he is teaching in a college. Should he be fired, or not?

(21)

Yes ————☐ 6
No ————☐ 7
Don't know ——☐ Y

D. Suppose this admitted Communist wants to make a speech in your community. Should he be allowed to speak, or not?

(22)

Yes ————☐ 6
No ————☐ 7
Don't know ——☐ Y

E. Suppose he wrote a book which is in your public library. Somebody in your community suggests the book should be removed from the library. Would you favor removing it, or not?

(23)

Favor ————☐ 6
Not favor ——☐ 7
Don't know ——☐ Y

F. Suppose this admitted Communist is a radio singer. Should he be fired, or not?

(24)

Should be fired ☐ 6
Not be fired —☐ 7
Don't know —☐ Y

G. Now, suppose the radio program he is on advertises a brand of soap. Somebody in your community suggests that you stop buying that soap. Would you stop, or not?

(25)

Would stop ——☐ 6
Would not stop ☐ 7
Don't know — ☐ Y

H. Suppose he is a high school teacher. Should he be fired, or not?

(26)

Yes ————☐ 6
No ————☐ 7
Don't know ——☐ Y

I. Should an admitted Communist be put in jail, or not?

(27)

Yes ————☐ 6
No ————☐ 7
Don't know ——☐ Y

J. Should he have his American citizenship taken away from him, or not?

(28)

Yes ————☐ 6
No ————☐ 7
Don't know ——☐ Y

58. Now I would like you to think of another person. (Hand Respondent Pink Card.) A man whose loyalty has been questioned before a Congressional committee, but who swears under oath he has never been a Communist.

A. Suppose he has been working in a defense plant. Should he be fired, or not?

(29)

Yes ————☐ 6
No ————☐ 7
Don't know.——☐ Y

B. Suppose he is a clerk in a store. Should he be fired, or not?

(30)

Yes ————☐ 6
No ————☐ 7
Don't know ——☐ Y

C. Suppose he is teaching in a college or university. Should he be fired, or not?

(31)

Yes ————☐ 6
No ————☐ 7
Don't know —☐ Y

D. Should he be allowed to make a speech in your community, or not?

(32)

Yes ————☐ 6
No ————☐ 7
Don't know —☐ Y

E. Suppose he wrote a book which is in your public library. Somebody in your community suggests the book should be removed from the library. Would you favor removing it, or not?

(33)

Favor ————☐ 6
Not favor ——☐ 7
Don't know ——☐ Y

F. Suppose this man who swears he has never been a Communist, but who has been criticized by a Congressional committee is a radio singer. Should he be fired, or not?

(34)

Yes ————☐ 6
No ————☐ 7
Don't know ——☐ Y

G. Now suppose the radio program he is on advertises a brand of soap. Somebody in your community suggests you stop buying that soap. Would you stop, or not?

(35)

Would ————☐ 6
Would not ——☐ 7
Don't know ——☐ Y

H. Suppose this man is a high school teacher. Should he be fired, or not?

(36)

Yes ————☐ 6
No ————☐ 7
Don't know ——☐ Y

59. A. Suppose you discovered that one of your friends today had been a Communist ten years ago, although you are sure he is not now. Would you break your friendship with him, or not?

(37)

Yes ——————□ 6
No ——————□ 7
Don't know ——□ Y

B. Suppose you discovered that one of your good friends today had been a Communist until recently, although he says he is not now. Would you break your friendship with him, or not?

(38)

Yes ——————□ 6
No ——————□ 7
Don't know ——□ Y

60. A. Now, please think of some of the important people or leaders in our country today. Among them would you pick out for me one, in particular, whose opinions on how to handle United States Communists you would especially respect?

(39)

Name: _____

B. UNLESS NO ONE MENTIONED: Which of these two statements is closer to the fact? **Hand Respondent Yellow Card.**

(40)

Know his opinions ——————□ 6
Kind of person he is ——————□ 7
Don't know ——————————□ Y

(41)
sp

61. A. IF EISENHOWER MENTIONED IN 60, SKIP TO 62: If President Eisenhower were to say something about how United States Communists should be handled, would you have a good deal of confidence in what he said, or not?

(42)

Yes ——————□ *
No ——————□ **
Don't know ——□ Y

*B. IF YES TO A: Which of the two statements on the card is closer to the fact?

Know his opinions ——————□ 5
Kind of person he is ——————□ 6
Don't know ——————————□ 7

**C. IF NO TO A: Which of the two statements on the reverse side of that card is closer to the fact?

I know pretty well what his opinions about how to handle Communists are ——————□ 8

I doubt whether I would accept his opinions about how to handle Communists—but I don't know too well just what his opinions are ——————□ 9

Don't know ————————————————□ X

(43)
sp
(44)
sp

62. A. Do you suppose that an American can be a Communist without belonging to the Communist Party, or not?

(45)

Yes ——————□ *
No ——————□ 9
Don't know ——□ Y

*B. IF YES: Do you suppose that most American Communists do belong to the Communist Party, or not?

Yes ——————□ 6
No ——————□ 7
Don't know ——□ 8

63. Do you read a daily newspaper every day, almost every day, or only occasionally?

(46)

Every day ——————□ 6
Almost every day——□ 7
Occasionally ——————□ 8
Almost never ——————□ 9

64. A. Do you have a television set in the house?

B. IF YES: Do you listen to news programs on television every day, almost every day, or only occasionally?

(47)

Every day ——————□ 6
Almost every day——□ 7
Occasionally ——————□ 8
Almost never ——————□ 9
No TV ——————————□ X

65. Do you listen to news programs on the radio every day, almost every day, or only occasionally?

(48)

Every day ——————□ 6
Almost every day——□ 7
Occasionally ——————□ 8
Almost never ——————□ 9
No radio ——————————□ X

66. Frequently there is something in the news about Communists in the United States and what is being done about them. On the whole, would you say you follow this news very closely, fairly closely, or hardly at all?

(49)

Very closely ——————□ 6
Fairly closely ——————□ 7
Hardly at all ——————□ 8
Don't know ——————————□ Y

67. Even if people follow the news closely they are likely to form many of their opinions as a result of listening and talking with relatives, friends, and acquaintances. For example, take your own ideas about Communists in the United States and what is being done about them. On the whole, would you say you get your information mostly from what you read or hear on the air, or mostly from what you hear in conversations with other people?

(50)

Read or hear on the air ——□ 6
Conversations with people ——□ 7
Don't know ————————————□ Y

259

68. Now, take a different topic which is on some people's minds: the question of whether we're heading toward more unemployment and harder times. On this subject, would you say you get your information mostly from what you read or hear on the air, or mostly from what you hear in conversations with other people?

(51)

Read or hear on the air ———□ 6
Conversations with people ——□ 7
Don't know ————————□ Y

69. And now please tell me whether you agree strongly, agree, disagree, or disagree strongly with these statements. **Hand Respondent Reverse Side of Pink Card.**

A. Any leader should be strict with people under him in order to gain their respect.

(52)

Agree strongly ————————□ 6
Agree ————————————□ 7
Disagree ————————————□ 8
Disagree strongly ————————□ 9
Don't know ————————————□ Y

B. People can be divided into two classes—the weak and the strong.

(53)

Agree strongly ————————□ 6
Agree ————————————□ 7
Disagree ————————————□ 8
Disagree strongly ————————□ 9
Don't know ————————————□ Y

C. If a child is unusual in any way, his parents should get him to be more like other children.

(54)

Agree strongly ————————□ 6
Agree ————————————□ 7
Disagree ————————————□ 8
Disagree strongly ————————□ 9
Don't know ————————————□ Y

D. A child should never be allowed to talk back to his parents, or else he will lose respect for them.

(55)

Agree strongly ————————□ 6
Agree ————————————□ 7
Disagree ————————————□ 8
Disagree strongly ————————□ 9
Don't know ————————————□ Y

E. No sane, normal, or decent person would ever think of hurting a close friend or relative.

(56)

Agree strongly ————————□ 6
Agree ————————————□ 7
Disagree ————————————□ 8
Disagree strongly ————————□ 9
Don't know ————————————□ Y

70. Whom did you favor for President in 1952—Eisenhower or Stevenson?

(57)

Eisenhower ————————□ 6
Stevenson ————————□ 7
Other ————————————□ 8
Don't remember————————□ Y

71. A. Many people were unable to vote in the 1952 election for President because of illness or for other reasons. Did you vote?

(58)

Yes ————————————□ 6*
No ————————————□ 7
Don't remember————————□ Y

*B. IF YES: Did you vote for the Republican or Democratic candidate for Congressman in your district in 1952?

(59)

Democratic ————————□ 6
Republican ————————□ 7
Other ————————————□ 8
Don't remember————————□ Y

72. A. In 1948, Truman ran for President against Dewey, Wallace, and Thurmond. Do you recall whether you voted in that election?

B. IF VOTED: For whom did you vote—Truman, Dewey, Wallace, or Thurmond?

(60)

Truman ————————————□ 5
Dewey ————————————□ 6
Wallace ————————————□ 7
Thurmond ————————————□ 8
Other ————————————□ 9
Don't remember who ————————□ 9
Didn't vote ————————————□ X
Don't remember if voted————————□ Y

73. In politics today, do you consider yourself a Democrat, Republican, or Independent?

(61)

Democrat ——□ 6
Republican ——□ 7
Independent ——□ 8
Don't know ——□ 9

74. A. What is your religious preference—Protestant, Catholic or Jewish?

(62)

Protestant ————————□ 6
Catholic ————————————□ 7
Jewish ————————————□ 8
Other ————————————□ 9
None ————————————□ X

B. Have you attended church or religious services in the last month?

(63)

Yes ————————————□ 6
No ————————————□ 7
Can't remember ————□ Y

260

75. What is the last grade you finished in school?

(64)

None	☐ 6
Grammar School (1-6)	☐ 6
Grammar School (7-8)	☐ 6
High School (9-11)	☐ 7
High School (12)	☐ 8
College, not graduate	☐ 9
College graduate	☐ X

(65)

76. A. In what country were you born?

....

B. In what country was your father born?

....

C. In what country was your mother born?

....

(66)

77. A. What is your job or occupation?

B. What is the job or occupation of the head of your immediate family?

C. **IF FAMILY HEAD RETIRED, UNEMPLOYED OR DECEASED:** What did he (she) (you) do? ....

78. Are you married, single, widowed, or divorced?

(67)

Married	☐ 6
Single	☐ 7
Widowed	☐ 8
Divorced	☐ 9

79. A. Have you (your husband) ever served in any branch of the armed forces?

(68)

Yes	☐ *
No	☐ X

IF NO SKIP TO 80

*B. Have you (your husband) ever belonged to the American Legion, Veterans of Foreign Wars, or any other veterans' organization?

Yes	☐ 6**
No	☐ 7

**C. If Yes, check below to indicate organization, and whether person currently belongs.

(69)

	Belongs Now	Formerly Belonged
American Legion	☐	☐
V. F. W.	☐	☐
Other (specify)	☐	☐

80. A. Are you (your husband) a member of a labor union?

(70)

Yes	☐ *
No	☐ 9

*B. IF YES: Is that A.F.L., C.I.O. or independent?

A.F.L.	☐ 6
C.I.O.	☐ 7
Independent (specify)	☐ 8
Don't know	☐ X

81. And what is your age?

(71)

21-29	☐ 6
30-39	☐ 7
40-49	☐ 8
50-59	☐ 9
60 or over	☐ X

82. SEX:

(72)

Man	☐ 6
Woman	☐ 7

83. RACE:

(73)

White	☐ 6
Colored	☐ 7

84. Respondent lives in:

(74)

City of over 100,000 or suburbs	☐ 6
City of 2,500 up to 100,000	☐ 7
Town under 2,500 or country (non-farm)	☐ 8
Farm	☐ 9

85. DATE:

(75)

....

(76)

86. Respondent's home address:

....

....

(Place)   *(State)*

87. Serial No. of Interview: ....

88. Sampling Unit or Area No.: ....

Time Interview Ended: ....

I hereby attest that this is a true and honest interview:

....

(Interviewer's Signature)

(77)   (78)   (79)

261

HOW THE SCALES USED IN THIS BOOK WERE CONSTRUCTED

Two scales, each based on answers to *groups* of questions, appear in this volume. They were constructed by a modification of what is known as the Guttman scaling procedure. The basic idea of the Guttman procedure can be illustrated very simply by imagining a spelling test consisting of three words:

> Catastrophe
> Cattle
> Cat

This "test" has a very special kind of built-in internal consistency. If a person can spell the hardest word, he also is very likely to be able to spell the easier words. If he can spell only two words, we know *which* two words they are. If he can spell only one, we know *which* one that is. This is called a cumulative property of a test. When we have only a few items, we need some such built-in property in order to know whether we are measuring a single dimension.

Unless our scale contains one dimension only, we cannot sensibly rank people in it. Consider a scale of "bigness" which mixes up both height and weight. Is a tall thin man who weighs 180 pounds bigger than a short fat man who weighs 220 pounds? One can rank people in terms of one or the other measure but not both on a single scale.

The scales developed for this book will now be described.

WILLINGNESS TO TOLERATE NONCONFORMISTS

This scale is based on 15 items from the questionnaire. There are five sets of three items each. Each set of three items may be thought of as a sub-test. The questions are so chosen that a person who is "tolerant" on a sub-test in which *few* other people would be tolerant is also very likely to be so in a sub-test on which many other people would be "tolerant."

From our five groups of three questions each we can rank people in six groups. Those in Group 5 tend to be tolerant on all five sub-tests, those in Group 4 in all except the hardest to be tolerant on, etc. The last group, Group 0, would be tolerant on none.

To accomplish this, we dichotomized the answer to each item. This was not done arbitrarily, but on the basis of analysis of how each answer category related to a provisional total score. The rank groups are defined as follows:

GROUP 5. The most tolerant of all. Make + answers to at least two out of three of these items:

Now, I should like to ask you some questions about a man who admits he is a Communist.

Suppose this admitted Communist wants to make a speech in your community. Should he be allowed to speak, or not?

> \+ Yes
> — No
> — Don't know

Suppose he wrote a book which is in your public library. Somebody in your community suggests the book should be removed from the library. Would you favor removing it, or not?

> — Favor
> \+ Not favor
> — Don't know

Suppose this admitted Communist is a radio singer. Should he be fired, or not?

> — Should be fired
> \+ Not be fired
> — Don't know

GROUP 4. The next most tolerant. Fail to qualify in Group 5 but make + answers to at least two out of three of the following:

Should an admitted Communist be put in jail, or not?

> — Yes
> \+ No
> — Don't know

263

There are always some people whose ideas are considered bad or dangerous by other people. For instance, somebody who is against all churches and religion.

If such a person wanted to make a speech in your city (town, community) against churches and religion, should he be allowed to speak, or not?

+ Yes
− No
− Don't know

If some people in your community suggested that a book he wrote against churches and religion should be taken out of your public library, would you favor removing this book or not?

− Yes
+ No
− Don't know

GROUP 3. Fail to qualify in Groups 5 or 4, but make + answers to at least two out of three of the following:

Now suppose the radio program he [an admitted Communist] is on advertises a brand of soap. Somebody in your community suggests you stop buying that soap. Would you stop, or not?

− Would stop
+ Would not stop
− Don't know

Or consider a person who favored government ownership of all the railroads and all big industries.

If this person wanted to make a speech in your community favoring government ownership of all the railroads and big industries, should he be allowed to speak, or not?

+ Yes
− No
− Don't know

If some people in your community suggested that a book he wrote favoring government ownership should be taken out of your public library, would you favor removing the book, or not?

− Yes
+ No
− Don't know

264

GROUP 2. Fail to qualify in Groups 5, 4, or 3, but make + answers to at least two out of three of the following:

Now I would like you to think of another person. A man whose loyalty has been questioned before a Congressional committee, but who swears under oath he has never been a Communist.

Suppose he is teaching in a college or university. Should he be fired, or not?

- — Yes
- + No
- — Don't know

Should he be allowed to make a speech in your community, or not?

- + Yes
- — No
- — Don't know

Suppose this man is a high school teacher. Should he be fired, or not?

- — Yes
- + No
- — Don't know

GROUP 1. The next to least tolerant group. Fail to qualify in Groups 5, 4, 3, 2, but make + answers to two out of three of the following (with respect to a man whose loyalty has been questioned but who swears he is not a Communist).

Suppose he has been working in a defense plant. Should he be fired, or not?

- — Yes
- + No
- + Don't know

Suppose he is a clerk in a store. Should he be fired, or not?

- — Yes
- + No
- + Don't know

Suppose he wrote a book which is in your public library. Somebody in your community suggests the book should be removed from the library. Would you favor removing it, or not?

- — Favor
- + Not favor
- + Don't know

265

GROUP 0. The least tolerant group. Fail to qualify in any of the groups above.

A further test of consistency is involved; namely, that anybody who qualifies for Group 5 must also be plus on two out of three of the items in *each and every* set below. Anybody who qualifies for Group 4 must also be + on two out of three of the items in all sets below, etc.

Not everybody, of course, will be wholly consistent. The degree of consistency is measured by a coefficient of reproducibility, which, by convention, must be at least .90. The coefficient for this scale is a very satisfactory .96 and is exactly the same when the scale is constructed separately from the data from each of the two survey agencies. Moreover, separate tabulations by education showed that the reproducibility was approximately the same at all educational levels.

The method used in constructing the scale of willingness to tolerate nonconformists is called the H-technique. It is a new procedure, still not widely used, and is described in Stouffer, Borgatta, Hays, and Henry, "A Technique for Improving Cumulative Scales," *Public Opinion Quarterly,* Vol. 16, pp. 273–91.

We thus are able to order our population into six rank groups. For simplicity in presentation in this volume, these groups have arbitrarily been condensed into three, as follows:

"Relatively more tolerant"—Groups 5 and 4.

"In-Between"—Groups 3 and 2.

"Relatively less tolerant"—Groups 1 and 0.

SCALE OF PERCEPTION ON THE INTERNAL COMMUNIST DANGER

This scale yields the same number of rank groups as the scale of tolerance and is based on the same cumulative principle to provide a test of internal consistency.

The way individual items are cross-tabulated to provide each of the rank groups is somewhat different, however:

GROUP 5. Those in the group seeing greatest danger are scored + on the following questions:

Do you think there are any Communists teaching in American public schools, or not?

IF ANY YES ANSWER: How much danger is there that these Communists in public schools can hurt the country—a great danger, some danger, not much danger, or no danger?

+ Great
— Some
— Not much
— None
— Don't know

GROUP 4. Do not qualify for Group 5, but answer is scored + on the following questions:

Do you think there might be any Communists within the American Government now, or not?

IF ANY YES ANSWER: How much danger is there that these Communists within the Government can hurt the country—a great danger, some danger, not much danger, or no danger?

+ Great
— Some
— Not much
— None
— Don't know

GROUP 3. Do not qualify for Groups 5 and 4, but answer is scored + on the following question:

How great a danger do you feel that American Communists are to this country at the present time—a very great danger, a great danger, some danger, hardly any danger, or no danger?

+ A very great danger
+ A great danger
— Some danger
— Hardly any danger
— No danger
— Don't know

GROUP 2. Do not qualify for Groups 5, 4, and 3, but answer is scored + on the following questions:

Do you think there are any Communists teaching in American colleges and universities now, or not?

IF YES: If you had to guess, how many would you think—just a few, or hundreds, or thousands?

 Yes, a few
 Yes, hundreds
 Yes, thousands
 Yes, don't know how many
— No, don't think there are any
+ Don't know if there are any

OR, IF ANY YES ANSWER: How much danger is there that the Communists in colleges and universities can hurt the country—a great danger, some danger, not much danger, or no danger?

+ Great
+ Some
— Not much
— None
+ Don't know

GROUP 1. Do not qualify for Groups 5, 4, 3, and 2, but answer is scored + on the following questions:

Do you think there are any Communists working in key defense plants now, or not?

IF YES: If you had to guess, how many would you think—just a few, or hundreds, or thousands?

 Yes, a few
 Yes, hundreds
 Yes, thousands
 Yes, don't know how many
— No, don't think there are any
+ Don't know if there are any

OR, IF ANY YES ANSWER: How much danger is there that these Communists in defense plants can hurt the country—a great danger, some danger, not much danger, or no danger?

+ Great
+ Some
— Not much
— None
+ Don't know

268

GROUP 0. Do not give answer scored + in any of the groups above.

An additional requirement is that those in Group 5 be scored + on all items below Group 5; that those in Group 4 be scored + on all items below Group 4, etc.

The coefficient of reproducibility is .94 and is approximately the same for the results from each survey agency and for each educational level of respondents.

With this scale we can order our population into six rank groups. For simplicity in presentation in this volume, these groups have arbitrarily been condensed into three, as follows:

See relatively great internal Communist threat . Groups 5 and 4
In-between .... Groups 2 and 3
See relatively little internal Communist threat .. Groups 1 and 0

Appendix D

HOW TO MAKE AN ALLOWANCE FOR SAMPLING ERROR IN LOOKING AT DIFFERENCES BETWEEN PERCENTAGES[1]

This appendix is written to help the non-technical reader who wants some guidance as to when he should consider a difference between any two percentages significant and when he should not.

In some cases a difference of only 5% may be significant because the samples are large. In other cases a difference of 15% may not be significant because the samples are small. And in all instances we must keep in mind the possibility that questions which might seem to have the same content but which are worded differently can yield different results.

Throughout this report the emphasis has been put on the *pattern* of the percentages, not the actual amounts. If the questions had been phrased somewhat differently, most individual percentages would be shifted in the same direction by such a change, and if that is so, then the *patterns* would remain pretty much the same in spite of the shift produced by varying the precise meaning of the questions.

When we talk about any one percentage we must make some allowance for the effect of choosing a particular form of the question and we must not think of the reported percentage as being very accurate. An equally dependable survey made by similar methods at about the same time might well report percentages that are sometimes the same and sometimes as much as five, ten, or more points different from those that are reported here.

This is not true to the same extent of the *pattern* of percentages— that is, to the differences that are shown between the various percentages that are reported for groupings of people according to region, age, education, interest, tolerance scores, and other individual facts.

[1]The author is indebted to Professor Frederick F. Stephan of Princeton University for preparing most of the substance of this appendix.

Yet some allowance must be made for variations of the patterns too. Many minor things can happen to make the pattern shown by one survey a bit different from the patterns of other surveys of like kind and equal reliability. It is not easy to search for them and determine just how much allowance to make for each of these influences, but nevertheless it is possible to set up some simple recommendations that will help us to avoid two dangers of misinterpreting the information reported here:

(1) taking seriously small differences that are mostly the result of chance in the sampling and minor variations of the survey work;

(2) ignoring differences which may be indicative of important contrasts between two or more kinds of people.

We cannot escape these dangers altogether. Also, one of these dangers may be more serious than the other. Nevertheless, the following recommendations should strengthen the common sense we use in thinking about the patterns and at times correct our common sense when it errs:

(1) When two or more percentages are identical, this is not evidence of almost perfect accuracy. Their agreement will usually be a combination of the effects of chance and rounding the figures to the nearest unit.

(2) When two or more percentages differ, part of the difference may well be due again to chance and rounding as well as to various minor differences in the survey work for each group of people. The effects of chance in the sampling are less when the size of the groupings of people from which the percentages were calculated is larger. Hence our allowance for these effects must take into account the size of the groups, usually shown in tables as the "number of cases." We can find out how much to allow—that is, how much of the difference we would do well to ignore—by looking up the appropriate figure in the following short table:

Comparison	Approximate Size (number of cases)	Recommended Allowance (percentage points)
(A) Average of community leaders	1500	4 to 6
with cross-section of their cities	897	
(B) AIPO sample with NORC sample:		
National cross-section	2483, 2450	3 to 5
Cross-section of same cities		
as leaders	409, 488	6 to 10
Average of community leaders	742, 758	5 to 8
One type of community leader	50, 50	20 to 30
(C) Any grouping of people with another, in which the smaller group has a size approximately equal to:	100	14 to 21
	150	12 to 18
	200	10 to 15
	400	7 to 10
	600	6 to 9
	800	5 to 8
	1000	4 to 6
	2000	3 to 5

The first and smaller allowance should be used when one is interested in several specific comparisons and then looks at the differences of percentages for these pre-selected comparisons. If the difference is not larger than the allowance, then it may be interesting and still worth considering as a weak clue, but it should not be taken seriously as pointing to an established fact. For example, in Chart III. Chapter Two, the AIPO and NORC samples differ for the national cross-section by 1 point on the percentage answering "Yes." This has little if any meaning, since it is smaller than the allowance of 3. On the other hand, the leaders and the people in their cities differ by 16 percentage points in the proportions that answered "Yes," and this is much greater than the allowance of 4. Hence it is to be taken as substantial evidence of a difference between leaders and other people in their cities. How much difference? If we subtract the allowance from the difference, we find that it is very probably greater than 12 points. It may also be greater than 16 percentage points but not likely more than 20 percentage points.

The second and larger allowance is for use when one searches through the tables looking not at specific comparisons but at the larger differences which appear. In picking only these larger differences, one may be capitalizing on chance. If one looks at all possible comparisons, he is more likely to encounter these chance differences than if he looks at some limited set of comparisons. Thus, looking only for the larger differences may mislead us. It may lead us to take seriously patterns that will not reappear when another survey is taken or some other check is made on the validity of the patterns we select. Hence we must make a larger allowance to protect ourselves from this danger of misinterpretation of the reported percentages.

Again let us emphasize the fact that, even when no individual pair of percentages is significantly different, a pattern of such differences, most of them in the same direction, may be highly significant. A good example is seen in Tables 2, 3, and 4 of Chapter Six. Few individual pairs of percentages in these tables differ by enough to be significant in themselves. But when we have, say, 14 out of 17 matched comparisons showing differences *in the same direction,* we get a result which would happen by chance less than once in a hundred times, however small the individual differences.

If it is important to make allowances on a different or more detailed basis than is illustrated in this appendix, one should consult a statistician or refer to a good statistical text. In all important instances, the author has shown the number of cases on which percentages have been calculated. With this information, more nearly exact tests of significance can be readily calculated for any special purpose.

Appendix E

NOTES ON MATERIALS FROM OTHER SURVEYS AS RELATED TO THE FINDINGS IN THIS VOLUME[1]

As stated in Chapter One, this book is not a systematic treatise which organizes and reviews critically all the important essays and research studies in the field. It is a report of the findings of a single study.

While this study has many unique features, it does not stand alone. In Chapters Two through Eight, just before the final summaries, the findings of this study are placed in the context of previously reported data.

The most recent critical bibliography of relevant data from public opinion polls is that by Hyman and Sheatsley, "Trends in Public Opinion on Civil Liberties," *The Journal of Social Issues,* Vol. 9, 1953, No. 3, pp. 6–16. The most recent bibliography of academic studies concerning the entire field of tolerance and intolerance is in G. W. Allport, *The Nature of Prejudice,* Beacon Press, 1954. These authors read the manuscript of the present volume and were of indispensable aid in supplying information about relevant studies, some of which have not been published but are available in the files of a research agency.

In each chapter key numbers in parentheses serve as a reference to citations in this appendix which are preceded by the same numbers.

Sources on Public Opinion Surveys

Elmo Roper and the American Institute of Public Opinion (the Gallup poll) have been publishing national public opinion survey re-

[1]The author is indebted to Paul B. Sheatsley and Herbert H. Hyman for bringing together the major references to public opinion polls, and to Gordon W. Allport for performing the same service with respect to other studies as they relate to the social psychology of prejudice.

274

sults since 1935; the National Opinion Research Center since 1941. The files of these three agencies account for the vast bulk of what we know about American public opinion toward current events and issues since that time. Other agencies differ from these three in that their surveys are usually made among special or local groups of the population rather than on a national cross-section basis; or their questions deal chiefly with subjects of interest to commercial clients, with only occasional items bearing on broader political or social issues.

Roper, AIPO, and NORC survey results, through the year 1946, have been indexed and published in the compendium entitled *Public Opinion, 1935–1946*. This 1200-page volume, prepared by Mildred Strunk under the editorial direction of Hadley Cantril, summarizes the data collected by 23 survey organizations in 16 different countries during the period in question and is the most valuable single source of information on public attitudes during those years.

For the 1945–48 period, a bi-weekly publication issued by the NORC under the title *Opinion News* is perhaps the best all-around source of survey data. Each of the 26 annual issues of *Opinion News* was devoted to a roundup of all the relevant poll data concerning one or two particular topics, and the results cited include not only the three national U.S. agencies but also many state, local, foreign, and special studies.

The *Public Opinion Quarterly* (Princeton University Press), until the year 1951, carried a department called "The Quarter's Polls," which regularly summarized Gallup, NORC, and Roper findings. The *International Journal of Opinion and Attitude Research* (The Social Sciences, Mexico City), until its suspension early in 1952, also included a regular section called "World Opinion," which reported poll results from many different countries, including the United States.

During the last three or more years there has been no systematic attempt to collect or publish summaries of American public opinion survey findings. There are a number of published and unpublished manuscripts by individual scholars which present some of the data on particular subjects, but, by and large, anyone interested in a serious study of American attitudes on current issues in recent years must acquire access to the Roper, AIPO, and NORC files. Usually, too, it is only in these office files that the curious student of opinion can find any detailed information, such as analyses in terms of age, education, political preference, etc. Fortunately, all three agencies maintain indexes of their materials and welcome inquiries from interested and responsible groups and individuals.

The following references may be somewhat helpful as a guide to readers who would pursue further the study of American public opinion in the area of Communism, tolerance, and civil liberties:

1. American Institute of Public Opinion. Gallup poll newspaper releases, generally published four times a week in representative newspapers across the United States. Individual copies often available at the AIPO offices, Princeton, N.J. Relevant releases cited, which are not available from other sources such as *Opinion News*, include those of March 15, April 5, May 24, June 9 and 23, July 19 and 21, August 23, and November 23—all in 1954.

2. American Institute of Public Opinion files, unpublished tabulations.

3. Bernard Berelson, Paul F. Lazarsfeld, and William McFee, *Voting*. Chicago: University of Chicago Press, 1954.

4. Angus Campbell, et al., *The Voter Decides*. Chicago: Row, Peterson & Co., 1954.

5. *Fortune* Surveys, conducted by Elmo Roper, published monthly until 1949. The June 1940 survey is particularly relevant for pre-war attitudes toward Communism.

6. Ben Gaffin and Associates, 141 W. Jackson Boulevard, Chicago, unpublished data on religious attitudes from nation-wide survey.

7. Louis Harris, *Is There a Republican Majority?* New York: Harper & Bros., 1954.

8. Herbert H. Hyman and Paul B. Sheatsley, "Trends in Public Opinion on Civil Liberties," *The Journal of Social Issues,* Vol. 9, 1953, No. 3, pp. 6–16.

9. ————, "American Public Opinion and Civil Liberties," unpublished manuscript, 1954.

10. ————, "Sex Differences in Public Opinion Surveys," unpublished memorandum, 1946.

11. ————, "The Current Status of American Public Opinion," John C. Payne, ed., *21st Yearbook of the National Council for the Social Studies,* 1950, pp. 11–34. Reprinted in Society for the Study of Social Issues, ed., *Public Opinion and Propaganda,* New York: Dryden Press, 1954.

12. Marie Jahoda and Stuart Cook, "Security Measures and Freedom of Thought," *Yale Law Journal,* Vol. 61, 1952, No. 3, pp. 295–333.

13. M. Janowitz and D. Marvick, "Authoritarianism and Political Behavior," *Public Opinion Quarterly,* Vol. 17, 1953, pp. 195–201.

14. Paul F. Lazarsfeld and Henry Field, *The People Look at Radio*. Chapel Hill: The University of North Carolina Press, 1946.

15. Paul F. Lazarsfeld, Bernard Berelson, and Helen Gaudet, *The People's Choice*. New York: Columbia University Press, 1948.

16. National Opinion Research Center, unpublished national surveys dated September 1950, May 1953, June 1953, September 1953, and January 1954.

17. *Opinion News,* published by National Opinion Research Center, University of Chicago. Relevant issues cited here include August 6, 1946; June 10 and November 15, 1947; February 15, March 1, May 1, July 15, and August 1, 1948.

18. *Public Opinion Quarterly,* department called "The Quarter's Polls" (up to 1951).

19. Elmo Roper, 30 Rockefeller Plaza, New York, unpublished tabulations in files.

20. Shirley A. Star, Clyde W. Hart, Herbert H. Hyman, and Paul B. Sheatsley, "Public Opinion and Civil Liberties," unpublished paper read before American Association for the Advancement of Science, Boston, 1953.

21. Mildred Strunk, under editorial direction of Hadley Cantril, *Public Opinion, 1935–1946*. Princeton: Princeton University Press, 1951.

22. Gerhart D. Wiebe, "Responses to the Televised Kefauver Hearings: Some Social Psychological Implications," *Public Opinion Quarterly,* Vol. 16, 1952, pp. 179–200.

Other Research Studies Cited on Tolerance or Intolerance

23. T. W. Adorno, et al., *The Authoritarian Personality*. New York, Harper & Bros., 1950.

24. G. W. Allport, *The Nature of Prejudice*. Boston: Beacon Press, 1954.

25. ———, and B. M. Kramer, "Some Roots of Prejudice," *Journal of Psychology,* Vol. 22, 1946, pp. 9–39.

26. B. Bettelheim and M. Janowitz, *Dynamics of Prejudice. A Psychological and Sociological Study of Veterans*. New York: Harper & Bros., 1950.

27. R. Christie and M. Jahoda, eds., *The Authoritarian Personality—A Methodological Critique*. Glencoe, Ill.: The Free Press, 1954.

28. Else Frenkel-Brunswik, "A Study of Prejudice in Children," *Human Relations,* Vol. 1, 1948, pp. 295–306.

29. J. M. Gillespie and G. W. Allport, *Youth's Outlook on the Future*, Doubleday Papers, 1955.

30. D. B. Harris, H. G. Gough, and W. E. Martin, "Children's Ethnic Attitudes: II, Relationship to Parental Beliefs Concerning Child Training," *Child Development,* Vol. 21, 1950, pp. 169–81.

31. L. Lowenthal and N. Gutterman, *Prophets of Deceit*. New York: Harper & Bros., 1949.

32. R. H. Luthin, *American Demagogues*. Boston: Beacon Press, 1954.

33. F. C. Malherbe, *Race Attitudes and Education*. Johannesburg: Institute of Race Relations, 1946.

34. N. E. Miller and R. Bugelski, "Minor Studies of Aggression: II, The Influence of Frustrations Imposed by the In-Group on Attitudes Expressed toward Out-Groups," *Journal of Psychology*, Vol. 34, 1952, 197–233.

35. Nancy C. Morse and F. H. Allport, "The Causation of Anti-Semitism: An Investigation of Seven Hypotheses," *Journal of Psychology*, Vol. 34, 1952, 197–233.

36. M. Brewster Smith, "Functional and Descriptive Analysis of Public Opinion," Ph.D. dissertation, Harvard University, 1948.

37. B. Zawadski, "Limitations of the Scapegoat Theory of Prejudice," *Journal of Abnormal and Social Psychology*, Vol. 43, 1948, 127–41.